CHAMPIONS OF

The Ludwig von Mises Lecture Series

CHAMPIONS OF FREEDOM
Volume 26

THE AGE OF ECONOMISTS
FROM ADAM SMITH TO MILTON FRIEDMAN

Richard M. Ebeling, Executive Editor

Lissa Roche, General Editor

Hillsdale College Press
Hillsdale, Michigan

Hillsdale College Press

Books by the Hillsdale College Press include The Christian Vision series; Champions of Freedom series; and other works.

The views expressed in this volume are not necessarily the views of Hillsdale College.

The Champions of Freedom series
THE AGE OF ECONOMISTS:
FROM ADAM SMITH TO MILTON FRIEDMAN
©1999 Hillsdale College Press, Hillsdale, Michigan 49242

Printed in the United States of America

Cover illustrations
Adam Smith. Courtesy the Corbis Hulton-Deutsch Collection, Bellevue, WA
Milton Friedman. Courtesy Milton Friedman, Stanford, CA

First printing 1999

Library of Congress Catalog Card Number 98-075798
ISBN 0-916308-61-8

Contents

Contributors vii

Foreword ix

Introduction 1

Adam Smith and *The Wealth of Nations* 7
    Edwin G. West

The Popularizers: Henry Hazlitt, Warren Brookes,
and Thomas Sowell 21
    Walter E. Williams

Economics on the Left: From Marxism to Keynesianism ... 31
    Robert A. Sirico

Frederic Bastiat and the Free Market Ideal 43
    George Roche

F. A. Hayek and the Many Roads to Serfdom 51
    Kurt R. Leube

A Rational Economist in an Irrational Age:
Ludwig von Mises...   69
  Richard M. Ebeling

The Nobel Laureates: Milton Friedman, George J. Stigler,
James M. Buchanan, Ronald H. Coase, and
Gary S. Becker   121
  Charles K. Rowley

The Limits of Economic Policy: The Austrian Economists
and the German ORDO Liberals   145
  Richard M. Ebeling

The Economic Self   167
  Larry D. Baker

Economic Theory and Public Policy   179
  Edward L. Hudgins

Booms, Busts, and the Business Cycle   197
  James Grant

Observations about Economic Ignorance   209
  John A. Sparks

RECOMMENDED READINGS

Why Read Adam Smith Today?   215
  Ludwig von Mises

Carl Menger and the Austrian School of Economics   219
  Ludwig von Mises

Contributors

LARRY D. BAKER had been working as a laboratory technician when he was struck by a rare illness that left him blind at age twenty-five. This became the turning point in his life. He entered school and graduated fifth in a class of nearly eight hundred business majors at Indiana University. In 1972, he earned his doctorate in business administration from the same institution. For the next decade, he taught at the University of Missouri–St. Louis.

Today, Dr. Baker is the president and owner of the Dr. Larry Baker Management Center in St. Louis, one of the nation's most highly respected management and professional development firms. He has won numerous awards, and is the author of several books, as well over one hundred journal articles.

RICHARD M. EBELING is the Ludwig von Mises Professor of Economics at Hillsdale College. A former professor at the University of Dallas, he joined the Hillsdale faculty in 1988. In addition, he serves on the editorial board of the *Review of Austrian Economics* and as vice president of the Future of Freedom Foundation, which regularly publishes his essays on political and economic issues. He has edited *Money, Method, and the Market Process: Essays by Ludwig von Mises* and *The Dangers of Socialized Medicine,* as well as a number of volumes in the Hillsdale College Press book series, Champions of Freedom.

Professor Ebeling has also lectured extensively on privatization and monetary reform throughout the United States, Latin America, and the former Soviet Union, where he has consulted with the Lithuanian government, the city of Moscow, and the Russian parliament. Currently, he is writing a biography of Ludwig von Mises and editing a series of volumes that will feature Mises' recently unearthed pre-World War II papers.

JAMES GRANT, a Navy veteran, earned his master's degree from the Columbia University School of International Affairs. He subsequently worked as a financial reporter for the *Baltimore Sun* and as capital markets editor of *Barron's*. Currently, he is the editor of *Grant's Interest Rate Observer* as well as the editorial director of *Grant's Municipal Bond Observer* and *Grant's Asia Observer*.

Mr. Grant is also the author of four books, the most recent of which is *The Trouble with Prosperity: The Loss of Fear, The Rise of Speculation, and the Risk to American Savings*. His many articles have appeared in such publications as *Barron's, American Banker,* the *Wall Street Journal,* the *New York Times,* the *New Republic,* and *Forbes,* and he frequently appears on such television programs as *Wall Street Week* and *Nightline* and the network news.

EDWARD L. HUDGINS is the Cato Institute's director of regulatory studies and editor of *Regulation* magazine. He is a widely recognized expert on agriculture, the Food and Drug Administration, labor, space, transportation, regulatory costs, and international regulatory comparisons. Prior to joining Cato, he served as a senior economist for the Joint Economic Committee of the U.S. Congress and as deputy director for economic policy studies and director of the Center for International Economic Growth at the Heritage Foundation.

Dr. Hudgins, a past speaker for Hillsdale College's off-campus seminar series, holds a Ph.D. in political philosophy from Catholic University of America. He has taught at several universities in this country and in Germany, and he has edited and contributed to such books as *The Last Monopoly: Privatizing the Postal Service for the Information Age* and *Freedom to Trade: Refuting the New Protectionism*.

KURT R. LEUBE studied and worked with the late Nobel laureate F. A. Hayek and has come to be known, in Hayek's own words, as one of his "closest disciples and a leading authority in the tradition of the Austrian School of economics." Previously a senior economist with the Association of Austrian Entrepreneurs in Vienna, he has been a research fellow at Stanford University's Hoover Institution on War, Revolution, and Peace and a professor of economics at California State University for more than a decade.

Dr. Leube is also the author of numerous books and scholarly publications, including *The Political Economy of Freedom* and a series of primers on F. A. Hayek, Joseph Schumpeter, George Stigler, and Milton Friedman. He was on the Hillsdale campus as a Distinguished Mises Lecturer in 1984 and 1990.

GEORGE ROCHE has served as president of Hillsdale College since 1971. Formerly the presidentially appointed chairman of the National Council on Education Research, the director of seminars at the Foundation for Economic Education, a professor of history at the Colorado School of Mines, and a U.S. Marine, he is the author of thirteen books, including six Conservative Book Club selections.

In 1994, he wrote *The Fall of the Ivory Tower: Government Funding, Corruption, and the Bankrupting of American Higher Education*. Reviews and/or excerpts of this volume have appeared in many sources, including *Forbes*, the *Wall Street Journal*, and *Reader's Digest*. It was also the subject of a cover story in a spring 1994 issue of *Insight* magazine; the editors named it the "Book of the Year." In February 1998, Regnery Publishing released his thirteenth book, *Heroes: Great Men and Women in American History*, the first volume in a historical biographical series intended for students and interested laymen.

CHARLES K. ROWLEY received his doctorate from the University of Nottingham in England and has taught at the University of Newcastle upon Tyne and the University of Kent at Canterbury. He also has held various positions at the Center for the Study of Public Choice and George Mason University. Notably he has served as dean of GMU's graduate school, director of university research, and director of graduate studies in economics. Presently, he is a professor of economics at the university and general director of the Locke Institute. He is also joint editor of the journal *Public Choice* and an editorial board member of the *Review of Austrian Economics*.

Dr. Rowley has written nearly two hundred articles and reviews, and his books and monographs include: *Readings in Industrial Economics*; *Welfare Economics*; *The Political Economy of Rent-Seeking*; *The Next Twenty Years of Public Choice*; and *Classical Liberalism and Civil Society*.

ROBERT A. SIRICO is co-founder and president of the Acton Institute for the Study of Religion and Liberty in Grand Rapids, which seeks to educate religious leaders about basic principles of free market economics. A Catholic priest, he has served as a parish leader and as a chaplain to AIDS patients at the National Institute of Health. For four years, he was also a member of the Michigan Civil Rights Commission. Currently, he is a member of the American Academy of Religion and a frequent lecturer at educational and business institutions in the U.S. and abroad.

Father Sirico has published articles in *National Review*, the *Wall Street Journal*, *Commonweal*, *Crisis*, *Reason*, and the *Catholic World*, and is a regular contributor to *Forbes*. In addition, he has edited such books as *Will It Liberate? Questions About Liberation Theology*. In 1994, his essay, "The Church and Economics," appeared in Hillsdale College's Christian Vision series volume, *Morality and the Marketplace*. This occasion marked his third appearance in a Hillsdale College program.

JOHN A. SPARKS joined the Hillsdale faculty upon receiving his doctorate from the University of Michigan Law School in 1969 and taught economics until 1976. He was honored by the 1973 senior class as "Professor of the Year." From 1977 to 1995, he was president of the Public Policy Education Fund, a nonprofit research corporation. A winner of the George Washington Medal of Honor from the prestigious Freedoms Foundation, he currently chairs the department of business administration, economics and international management at Grove City College in Pennsylvania, where he has taught since 1990.

Dr. Sparks is also a member and principal in the law firm of Bogaty, McEwen, and Sparks. He specializes in the areas of commercial, nonprofit, and educational law. He has published articles in such journals as the *Freeman*, *Private Practice*, *University Bookman*, and the *St. Croix Review*, and he has contributed book chapters to a number of volumes on topics ranging from biblical principles in business to property rights in the Third World.

EDWIN G. WEST received his Ph.D. from England's London University and has held posts (as a professor, research scholar, or fellow) at the Oxford College of Technology, the University of Western Australia, the University of Chicago, Emory University, Virginia Polytechnic, the University of Kentucky, and the University of California–Berkeley. However, his career has largely been dedicated to Carleton University in Ottawa, Canada, where he served on the economics faculty for twenty-eight years.

He has written or edited more than a dozen books, including: *Education and the State: A Study in Political Economy*; *Economics Today: The Micro View* (with Roger LeRoy Miller); *Adam Smith and Modern Economics: From Market Behavior to Public Choice*; and, most recently, *Adam Smith into the Twenty-First Century*. In addition, Dr. West has published numerous articles and book chapters on economic policy and the history of economic thought.

WALTER E. WILLIAMS received his doctorate from the University of California–Los Angeles in 1972 and has been the John M. Olin Distinguished Professor of Economics at George Mason University since 1980. He has been chairman of the economics department since 1995. For his work as one of the nation's best-known and most outspoken free market economists, he has received numerous honors, including the George Washington Medal of Honor from the Freedoms Foundation, the Adam Smith Award from the Association of Private Enterprise Education, and the Heartland Institute Award for Outstanding Journalism.

Despite the fact that he has volunteered much of his free time to serve on the advisory boards of numerous nonprofit organizations, including the National Foundation for Teaching Entrepreneurship to Handicapped and Disadvantaged Youth, Dr. Williams has found time to write nearly one hundred journal articles and five books: *The State Against Blacks*; *America: A Minority Viewpoint*; *All It Takes Is Guts*; *South Africa's War Against Capitalism*; and *Do the Right Thing: The People's Economist Speaks*. This CCA marked his fourth appearance in a Hillsdale College program since 1980.

Foreword

For twenty-six years, America's most distinguished scholars and active decisionmakers have met on the Hillsdale College campus to pay homage to one of the world's greatest champions of freedom, Austrian School economist Ludwig von Mises (1881–1973). Perhaps the College's proudest possession is Mises' personal library. Upon bequeathing his library to us, Professor Mises said he had done so because "Hillsdale, more than any other educational institution, most strongly represents the free market ideas to which I have given my life."

When the history of the twentieth century is written, the Mises name will surely be remembered as that of the foremost economist of our age. Certainly the history of one period during this century ought to include his name writ large: the one in which we are now living, the one that will be forever remembered as the time when the Berlin Wall finally came crashing down. The man who took out the first brick was Ludwig von Mises. He did it with books such as *The Theory of Money and Credit*, *The Free and Prosperous Commonwealth*, *Omnipotent Government*, *Bureaucracy*, and *Human Action*.

Mises based his theory of economics on the supremacy of the individual. The rational, purposeful, day-to-day decisions of ordinary men and women are what constitute the market and are the basis of all human action. It was his understanding of the market as a process, against the background of continually changing conditions and limited individual knowledge, that set his theory so clearly apart from the rigid, mathematical attempts of other economists bent on devising "models" of equilibrium.

Few economists perceived so clearly the consequences of the ideas set in motion by the statist and collectivist mentality. He warned that the greatest danger to Western society would come with the increasing concentration of political and economic power in the hands of the state. He used the example of communism in the Soviet Union and Eastern Europe to point out that the peril was real indeed.

It was Mises who wrote so eloquently and forcefully that the state could never successfully control the marketplace any more than it could control the lives of men. In fact, Mises' testimony finally convinced prominent Marxist–Leninist intellectuals to admit in the 1980s, "The world is run by human action, not by human design."

This twenty-sixth volume of the Champions of Freedom series is based on the same premise, and it explores the history of economics in the context of Mises' important and enduring intellectual legacy.

GEORGE ROCHE
President
Hillsdale College

Introduction

The main achievement of economics is that it has provided
a theory of peaceful human cooperation.

—Ludwig von Mises[1]

Before the eighteenth-century contributions of the French physiocrats and Scottish moral philosophers, social theory and economic policy was dominated by the idea that it was both necessary
and desirable for governments to regulate and control the economic affairs of the people. It was presumed that, when left to
their own devices, individuals would act in ways that would result
in "socially undesirable" outcomes threatening the prosperity and
security of nations. The most powerful governments in Europe
thus followed a set of rigid economic policies that have since become known as "mercantilism." Prices and wages were controlled,
commerce and industry were regulated, and foreign trade was
manipulated and restricted by numerous laws and decrees.

Mercantilism was the eighteenth century's version of the planned economy. Only the successful smuggler operated outside the
watchful eye of the state. But the French physiocrats (led by François
Quesnay) and the Scottish moral philosophers (led by David Hume
and Adam Smith) courageously challenged the foundations of mercantilist thinking. They argued that, just as there is a natural order in
the physical world, there is a similar natural order in the social world.
Men are guided by self-interest. Men attempt to improve their circumstances and the circumstances of their families. These are facts
of nature, just as true as the law of gravity.

1

They also argued that pursuit of men's individual self-interests need not lead to social chaos when left unchecked and unsupervised by political power. Why? Because men need their neighbors. Their own labor and resources are often insufficient to attain all the goals they would like to achieve. Two manifestations of this need for cooperation are seen in the widespread reliance upon the division of labor and the "propensity" (to use Adam Smith's term) for men to enter into mutually beneficial arrangements of trade and exchange. The division of labor increases men's productive capabilities. Trade and exchange creates opportunities for traders to acquire desired goods that they would not otherwise be able to obtain or could only obtain at a greater cost if produced through their own labor.

These simple truths, made famous in Adam Smith's *The Wealth of Nations* (1776), became the basis of the modern theory of markets and competition. Smith argued that individuals know their own interest far better than any government regulator can know it. Individuals know their own local circumstances and opportunities far better than any government regulator can know them. And individuals have greater incentives to take advantage of those opportunities in their local circumstances than any government regulator who tries to direct them in their activities.

In a system of natural liberty, in which government is primarily limited to the protection of life, liberty, and property, men see that their own self-interest is best served when they successfully devote their efforts to the manufacture and sale of those things others might like to buy. The more successful they are in this, the more they will be able to obtain from their trading partners those things they wish to acquire and consume. Thus, as if guided by an "invisible hand," each man, in pursuing his own self-interest, serves the general interest of society as well. No fundamental conflict exists between the interests of individuals and the good of the society as a whole. Nor does any exist between nations, since each tries to improve the economic well-being of its citizens. In fact, the same principles of division of labor and mutually beneficial exchange demonstrate why nations are better off when they participate in peaceful relationships of trade and commerce.

Of course, these insights were not unknown before the eighteenth century. More than two thousand years ago, the ancient

Chinese historian Ssu-ma Ch'ien (145 B.C.–90 B.C.) testified to their universality:

> Society obviously must have farmers before it can eat; foresters, fishermen, miners, etc., before it can make use of natural resources; craftsmen before it can have manufactured goods; and merchants before they can be distributed. But once these exist, what need is there for government directives, mobilizations of labor, or periodic assemblies? Each man has only to be left to utilize his own abilities and exert his strength to obtain what he wishes. Thus, when a commodity is very cheap, it invites a rise in price; when it is very expensive, it invites a reduction. When each person works away at his own occupation and delights in his own business then, like water flowing downward, goods will naturally flow forth ceaselessly day and night without having been summoned, and the people will produce commodities without having been asked. Does this not tally with reason? Is it not a natural result?[2]

In the nineteenth century, these ideas were championed by the "classical economists," including Thomas Malthus, David Ricardo, Jean-Baptiste Say, and John Stuart Mill. But what was even more significant than the theoretical development of these ideas was their impact on economic policy. By the middle of the century, free trade had become the ideal toward which an increasing number of nations were moving. In all the major nations of the Western world, domestic regulations and controls were abolished or significantly reduced. Taxes of all kinds were lowered and made less discriminatory. The gold standard became the basis of all major currencies by the 1890s. International trade and commerce grew dramatically.

Unfortunately, as the nineteenth century drew to a close and the twentieth century began, a different set of ideas gained hold of men's minds. "Socialism," "neo-mercantilism," and the "interventionist–welfare state" captured the imagination of the intellectual elite, including most economists, who seemed to forget the fundamental and simple truths of Adam Smith. Belief in central planning, industrial regulation, managed trade, and political redistribution of wealth became the hallmarks of government policy around the world. It was reinforced in the 1930s by the theories of British economist John Maynard Keynes, who claimed to have discovered a "new economics" through which government could use various monetary and fiscal tools to manipulate employment, investment, and determine output for purposes of macroeconomic stability.

But "by their fruits you shall know them." Socialism led to tyranny and poverty. Neo-mercantilism repoliticized international commerce, creating actual or potential trade wars among nations. The interventionist–welfare state strangled private enterprise with controls and taxes, while redistributive policies divided society into classes of taxpayers and tax recipients and created an underclass of paupers perpetually dependent upon government for their existence.

During the last half-century, the simple truths of Adam Smith have finally been rediscovered. A new generation of economists has arisen. It has been inspired by such long-time "keepers of the flame" as Austrian School economists Ludwig von Mises and Friedrich A. Hayek, German economist Wilhelm Röpke, and American economists Milton Friedman and James Buchanan, and by such persuasive and articulate popularizers of free market ideas as Henry Hazlitt and Warren Brookes. These men have not only developed cogent refutations of the arguments of the socialists, the neo-mercantilists, and the interventionists, but they also refined and improved on the ideas of their eighteenth- and nineteenth-century predecessors. In their hands, a new and vibrant positive vision has been created in defense of the market economy and the free society.

The 1998 Ludwig von Mises Lecture Series (co-sponsored by the Center for Constructive Alternatives) was devoted to an appreciation and better understanding of their important work. The title of the series, "The Age of Economists: From Adam Smith to Milton Friedman," refers to a remark made by British statesman Edmund Burke in the late eighteenth century, when the economics profession was emerging: "The age of chivalry has gone. That of sophisters, economists, and calculators has succeeded, and the glory of Europe is extinguished."[3]

Burke was anticipating the modern notion that "economics is the dismal science." But nothing could be further from the truth, as even he, a great supporter of Adam Smith, was forced to admit in his more serious moments. Economics is about more than compiling and analyzing statistics. It is the science of the logic of choice. Why do people behave the way they do? What choices and trade-offs do they make? In other words, economics is the science of human nature. As such, it requires a deep understanding of history, psychology, sociology, politics, education, culture, religion—and perhaps most important of all—philosophy. It is no coincidence that Adam Smith, one of the first and greatest economists, was trained as a moral philosopher. His interest in men's moral choices inevitably led to his interest in their economic choices.

In this twenty-sixth volume in the Champions of Freedom series from the Hillsdale College Press, some of the great free market economists—from Adam Smith to Nobel laureate Milton Friedman—are profiled. And it is clear that they agree: Human nature is inescapable; one way or another it becomes the focal point of every economic theory. As I noted in an earlier volume in this series, "Marxism was imposed on the Russian people as the result of a 'grand vision' that claimed that man's nature was only a product of social and economic forces." Capitalism, which in various forms has spread to nations around the globe, is based on a very different view of human nature. This view presupposes that man is a sentient and moral creature guided by principle as well as by a combination of motives Adam Smith described as "sympathy," "fellow feeling," and "self-interest."

RICHARD M. EBELING
Ludwig von Mises Professor
of Economics
Hillsdale College

Notes

[1] Ludwig von Mises, "Economics as a Bridge for Interhuman Understanding," [1945] in Bettina Bien Greaves, ed., *Economic Freedom and Interventionism: An Anthology of Articles and Essays* (Irvington-on-Hudson, NY: Foundation for Economic Education, 1990), 235.

[2] Ssu-ma Ch'ien, *Records of the Historian, Chapters from the Shih Chi* (New York: Columbia University Press, 1969), 334.

[3] Edmund Burke, *Reflections on the Revolution in France* [1790] (Buffalo: Prometheus Books, 1987), 80.

EDWIN G. WEST

Adam Smith and
The Wealth of Nations

My primary task here is to acquaint you with the *economics* of Adam
Smith, a writer who is sometimes called the founding father of
that discipline. To the average person who has seen or heard the
name Adam Smith, I suspect it conjures the vision of some smart
but elderly professor who lived a long time ago in Scotland. Smith
is vaguely known, in other words, as some kind of historical celebrity. Since history is no longer taught extensively in U.S. public
schools mention of it often turns off one's audience. So let me start
with the simplest and briefest of questions: Who wrote the Declaration of American Independence? In what year did it appear?
Most readers will correctly cite Thomas Jefferson as the author
and 1776 as the year. Well, it just so happens that it was in this
same year that the spotlight fell on another historical celebrity of
equal stature: Adam Smith. The occasion was the publication of
his book, *An Inquiry into the Nature and Causes of the Wealth of Nations*, later known by the shorter title, *The Wealth of Nations*.[1] I prom-
ise to return from 1776 to the present as soon as possible, especially
because, as I shall argue, Smith was in advance of his time, and on
some aspects the world has not yet caught up with him. But we
cannot fully understand Smith's economics without some minimal knowledge of the eighteenth-century world from which he
was trying to escape.

When writing his classic work, Smith was confronted with an
extensive growth of pamphlet literature written by a wide assort-
ment of self-appointed European experts all recommending the
"proper" course of government economic policy. Describing its

7

authors generally as proponents of what he called the "mercantile system," now known as "mercantilism," Smith criticized this literature partly as propaganda originating with special interests, and partly as flawed analysis. The feature of mercantilist doctrine that he condemned most was its simplistic identification of a country's wealth with its accumulation of precious metals (especially gold). And since the aim of typical mercantilists was to enlarge a nation's holdings of precious metals, a series of auxiliary policy recommendations followed. These nearly always included national plans for increasing exports and restricting imports. In addition, the mercantilists recommended the boosting of domestic employment at the expense of foreign employment, the expansion of population, the direction of labor, the calculated depression of wages, the administration of the colonies (with the prime object of "feeding" the mother country with raw materials), and the suppression of potentially competitive colonial manufactures. Smith rejected each and every one of these policies in Book IV of *The Wealth of Nations*. Newcomers may indeed find it more exciting to begin with Book IV, or at least to glance first at its opening chapter where Smith presented his summary "charge for the prosecution."

The second set of eighteenth-century background circumstances relate to Smith's profound admiration of the scientific principles and achievements of the English mathematician and physicist Sir Isaac Newton. Accordingly, *The Wealth of Nations* endeavored throughout to formulate a "system" in the grand scientific manner of Newton, a system that was based on one simple basic axiom. Whereas Newton's simple axiom system was the universal phenomenon of gravity, Smith's was that of individual self-interest set in a world of what he called "natural liberty." Indeed, upon this axiom Smith built his whole economic system. It was one that was clear, consistent, and insightful. Moreover it stood in stark contrast to the ad hoc proposals of the mercantilists, which included particularly the suggestion that they alone should set investment priorities because ordinary individuals with capital lacked relevant information.

The Invisible Hand Theorem

Analogous with Newton's joining together the movement of the planets by the familiar principle of gravitation and its causes and effects was Smith's quest for a coordinated and mutually interdependent system of *economic* causes and effects. The key idea is suggested by the most famous quotation from Book IV of *The Wealth of Nations*, which refers to what is now described as the "Invisible Hand Theorem":

> But it is only for the sake of profit that any man employs [his] capital. . . . [H]e will always, therefore, endeavour to employ it in the support of that industry of which the produce is likely to be of the greatest value, or to exchange for the greatest quantity either of money or of other goods. . . . [H]e is in this, as in many other cases, led by an invisible hand to promote an end which was no part of his intention. Nor is it always the worse for the society that it was no part of it. By pursuing his own interest he frequently promotes that of the society more effectually than when he really intends to promote it.[2]

In modern terms we might say that a person will be led by self-interest to put his resources to use wherever they earn the most. But to earn, you must produce something that people want to buy. Consequently, seeking your own advantage automatically leads you to produce goods or services that suit the needs of others.

In Smith's time, many people believed that the only way to help others was by benevolent assistance—by "doing good." It is now widely believed that you often help others more by trade than by direct aid. Nevertheless, it is not so easy to understand just why an economic system of untrammeled self-interest does not lead to mutual harm, or even to total chaos. How is it that Britain's City of London, for instance, can be regularly fed by converging food shipments from all corners of the earth, and without any governing plan to make sure that the Canadian farmer, the Scottish fisherman, and the South African orange grower actually deliver to the hungry city? Yet the city is fed, although none of its suppliers need to be motivated by any particular love and concern for Londoners. Canadian farmers simply find it more profitable to ship to London than to eat all their own wheat.

To quote *The Wealth of Nations* once more: "In civilized society [man] stands at all times in need of the cooperation and assistance of great multitudes, while his whole life is scarce sufficient to gain the friendship of a few persons."[3] The "invisible hand" is what leads an individual to work for the good of other persons, practically all unknown to him, in an orderly economy and world market that has arisen without anyone having planned it that way.

Moreover, when government personnel ignore the invisible hand and themselves attempt to control the allocation of resources, they will inevitably fail. And this was Smith's basic answer to the mercantilists, most of whom were aspiring central planners of domestic and foreign trade.

Macroanalysis

Assuming that the first-time reader of Smith is familiar with elementary economics, he will naturally look for key connections between *The Wealth of Nations* and current textbooks. These, of course, quickly draw a distinction between "macro-" and "micro-" analysis, and the former is usually introduced with the aid of a simple "circular flow model" showing how individual components of the economy are integrated through mutual adjustment. Start with the component called "firms." They produce goods for sale at a price that covers their costs. The latter include the costs of hiring factors of production such as labor and capital. These payments to factors are next viewed as incomes, but since the incomes are then spent on the commodities, the (state) circular flow model is completed.

Smith's treatment was novel in that he pioneered the idea of separate categories of costs/incomes, describing them in terms of wages, rent, and profit. Expenditures out of these incomes over a given period, say one year, give rise to a series of *flows* of money that purchase consumption goods from previously accumulated stocks (the "wages fund"). But the acts of consumption make possible acts of production over the same period, including the maintenance or replacement of physical capital.

Smith, however, was not primarily occupied with what is now called "macro-static equilibrium" or "the stationary state," wherein every year "everything exactly replaces itself" so that growth does not occur. Smith recognized that capital supplies may fall short of or go beyond replacing themselves. In addition, there could be improvements in quality. It was with the latter case— positive growth of the wealth of nations—that Smith was mainly concerned. And how could such growth occur? Smith's reply in Book II was unambiguous:

> The annual produce of the land and labour of any nation can be increased in its value by no other means, but by increasing either the number of its productive labourers, *or the productive power of those labourers who had before been employed.*[4]

His words (emphasis mine) contain one of the key points of departure from the mercantilists. Whereas the mercantilists favored encouragement to increase the size of population as a policy measure designed to strengthen a country vis-à-vis its neighbors, Smith saw population expansion as an inevitable *consequence* of growth. It was not, therefore, the growth in the numbers of productive laborers so much as the increase in their productive power that counted. There were two major keys to such productivity improvement: One was the division of labor and the other was capital accumulation (which was a necessary condition for the division of labor). By neglecting these two variables, Smith implied, the mercantilists had been looking in the wrong places.

Another central issue in the macroeconomic reasoning in Smith's time pertains to the mercantilist objective of obtaining a favorable balance of trade that was realized in the form of accumulated gold and other precious metals. Smith's reasoning was an early example of what in modern economics has come to be called the "monetary approach to the balance of payments." Smith's argument was: Suppose mercantilist policy had, in the short run, succeeded in producing an unusual accumulation of gold at home. Adjustment would take place through the balance of international payments as citizens exported the excess money and import goods. And an excess supply of money would simply be resolved in the long run because people would buy things with it. From whom? From the very same foreigners that the mercantilists wanted to impoverish.

Microanalysis

Today's economics textbooks emphasize that the two variables supply and demand determine price or economic value. In Book I of *The Wealth of Nations*, Smith was one of the first to employ such language, although he did not express it exactly as we do today.

The natural price, he told us, is the central price, toward which the prices of all commodities are continually gravitating.

Price fluctuations around the natural price are the consequences of competition, and competition emerges whenever "natural liberty" prevails. Smith's concept of competition was a kind of rivalry between known or previously unknown persons. Knowledge is certainly not perfect, but some knowledge is required. And it will come forth in sufficient quantities if the freedom of competition is allowed. The real problem is how to construct an environment where the available knowledge is used as much as possible. The real question in political economy—the question that Smith was considering—is: What institutional arrangements are necessary to attract the *unknown* persons, who have useful knowledge, to a particular task? The core of Smith's work was his theory of economic development, in which competition, the division of labor, technical change, and capital accumulation play key roles in an unfolding and dynamic interplay of forces. And in this steady march forward, the ordinary workman's wages will begin to rise as the division of labor progresses still further.

Smith first posed the central question: If maximizing a nation's wealth is agreed to be the main objective, how can it best be done? While most mercantilists were obsessed with this or that favorite regulation, the opening sentences of *The Wealth of Nations* drew attention to something that most of them had completely missed: the importance of improving technology and productivity.

> The greatest improvement in the productive powers of labour, and the greater part of the skill, dexterity, and judgment with which it is anywhere directed, or applied, seem to have been the effects of the division of labour.[5]

After making this apparently sweeping proposition, Smith was anxious to follow up with a dramatic example. He chose what he described as a very "trifling" manufacture, the making of pins. Other manufactures were of more importance, Smith conceded, but they were more difficult to illustrate because usually all their subdivisions of labor were not clearly visible under one roof. A workman who did not specialize, but worked on his own with no assistance in his own workshop, "could scarce perhaps, with his utmost industry, make one pin in a day, and certainly could not make twenty." Smith spoke with authority and gave evidence that he had personally checked the facts that he reported. He had seen a small manufacturer where ten men only were employed making pins. Implicitly, he compared the situation of this factory with another, wherein the ten men go their separate ways doing all of the processes of pin making in their own isolated workshops.

He explained that, in the factory environment, the work is divided into a number of branches, of which the greater part are likewise separate trades. "One man draws out the wire, another straightens it, a third cuts it, a fourth points it, a fifth grinds it at the top for receiving the head; to make the head requires two or three distinct operations; to put it on is a peculiar business, to whiten the pins is another; it is even a trade by itself to put them into the paper; and the important business of making a pin is, in this manner, divided into about eighteen distinct operations, in others the same man will sometimes perform two or three of them."[6]

Smith's dramatic conclusion was that each of the ten workers who specialized made on average four thousand, eight hundred pins in a day, whereas "if they had all wrought separately and independently, and without any of them having been educated to this peculiar business, they certainly could not each of them have made twenty, perhaps not one pin in a day."[7]

Smith said, in effect, if the workmen were willing to come out of ten different workshops and organize under one roof, they each would produce two hundred and forty times more per work period than before! Dramatic and spontaneous productivity changes like this, Smith insisted, are what one should concentrate on, and to secure them government need confine itself simply to identifying and removing legal and other impediments to the effective working of the free market economy. Smith was not the first to recognize the importance of the division of labor. Writers before him, such as Martyn, Mandeville, Harris, and Tucker,[8] had noted its useful effects. But most people who read their descriptions and then turn to Smith's will surely agree that his treatment is more sustained and penetrating in the sense of both economic analysis and policy implications.

Probing the deeper economic reasons for unprecedented surges in output via the division of labor, Smith concluded that they were due to three different circumstances:

> . . . first, to the increase of dexterity in every particular workman, secondly, to the saving of the time which is commonly lost in passing from one species of work to another; and lastly, to the invention of a great number of machines which facilitate and abridge labour, and enable one man to do the work of many.[9]

The first circumstance, the increase in dexterity, is today called "learning by doing" and is fairly obvious. The second circumstance, the saving of time, needs further reflection, perhaps. The worker who performs all the processes loses time when he moves from one operation to another. He has to readjust to, or get warmed up to, the new process that is required.

> . . . a man commonly saunters a little in turning his hand from one sort of employment to another. When he first begins the new work he is seldom very keen and hearty; his mind, as they say, does not go to it, and for some time he rather trifles than applies to good purpose.[10]

With the third circumstance, Smith tells us that exclusive attention to one or two tasks can so concentrate the mind that it fosters inventiveness. But it was not just concentration that encouraged invention. Invention also occurs because of the self-interest of every worker to find means to reduce his own effort.

Subsequent argument and observation in *The Wealth of Nations* informs us that the division of labor is everywhere around us, within and without factories, and operates territorially across industries and geographic distances. To reiterate, its development occurs voluntarily, and the assistance of government should be confined to ensuring that natural liberty was being allowed to operate. And Smith insisted once again that in the subsequent rising tide of prosperity everybody benefits: all boats rise.

> It is the great multiplication of the productions of *all* the different arts, in consequence of the division of labor, which occasions, in a well governed society, that universal opulence which extends itself to the lowest ranks of the people.[11]

Here, incidentally, we see Smith's objectives in even more striking contrast to those of the mercantilists. The latter were not interested in extending opulence to the workers, since they feared that this would reduce their effort. But Smith was obviously interested in the well-being of everyone. Smith, in fact, redefined economic ends at the same time as he urged changes in economic means through the invisible hand of the marketplace.

Smith's Microanalysis in New Perspective

We have yet to come to the most profound and "revolutionary" part of Smith's microanalysis. Chapter three of Book I of *The Wealth of Nations* is titled "That the Division of Labour Is Limited by the Extent of the Market." It took over a century and a half before the full implications of this chapter were realized. If the division of labor depends on the size of the market, we can ask just what constitutes a large market? It is not just population or geographic area alone. The key factor is buying power. The capacity to buy, meanwhile, depends on the capacity to produce. We should not be impressed solely with the dramatic increase in numbers of pins produced in Smith's famous pin factory illustration. We should take one more step and realize that the large output of pins means that they are the source of increased demand for other things offered in exchange. The division of labor in pins, therefore, extends the market elsewhere, and this second area of economic activity can, consequently, undertake its own further divisions of labor.

A situation where output more than doubles when inputs double is called by economists a "state of increasing returns." So when the division of labor starts in one area and spreads to another we speak of *generalized* increasing returns. It was this vision that led Smith to challenge the mercantilists' argument for the necessity of import tariffs. If these are abolished, the economic position of foreigners certainly will be strengthened because they will enjoy increased returns as their markets are extended. But the foreigners' new wealth will cause them to demand products from the home country and so enable selected domestic industries to obtain further increasing returns at home. In the words of Nobel

Prize winning economist James Buchanan, "There exist increasing returns to the scale of the inclusive economic nexus."[12] It is on this basic reasoning that the central Smithian and classical economic policy stance was erected. It condemned "artificial, politicized restrictions on or limits to trade and exchange, whether these be within or without the boundaries of an organized polity.[13]

Policy

Primarily, Smith had one grand policy recommendation and that was to abolish almost all of the mercantilists' policies. I haven't space to discuss all of them here, so I shall focus on one policy based on the mercantilists' argument that certain "infant industries" existed in the nation and they needed crucial protection by government in order to grow to their full size. This, of course, is an argument that confidently assumes that governments can, indeed, be relied upon to "pick winners." The idea is that after the protected manufacture eventually takes root at home, it can stand on its own and the protective tariff can be withdrawn.

Smith concedes that it is possible to set up an industry sooner than it could have been otherwise and that, indeed, eventually its products will be as cheap or cheaper than in the foreign country. It does not follow, however, that the total national income will increase by such an arrangement. The increase of national income, says Smith, depends upon the accumulation of capital, which in turn results from savings. The higher the national income, the higher the possible savings, and the faster the introduction of more divisions of labor. But the immediate effect of infant industry regulation is that consumers are obliged to purchase products at a higher price domestically (because in the interim the infant has higher costs). This being so, their ability to save will be diminished and so will the spread of the division of labor. This total cost must be considered in any comprehensive reckoning. Conversely if no such regulation is made, society will have had a greater immediate national income and a greater potential for savings. In that case, there will be more immediate capital accumulation, and growth via expanded division of labor will occur with a different pattern of output. The case for regulation is therefore substantially challenged, Smith insists. Specifically, he says:

Though for want of such regulations the society should never acquire the proposed manufacture, it would not, upon that account, necessarily be the poorer. [I]ts whole capital and industry might still have been employed, although upon different objects, in the manner that was most advantageous at the time. In every period its revenue might have been the greatest which its capital could afford, and both capital and revenue might have been augmented with the greatest possible rapidity.[14]

The next question is: Who decides which manufactures are to be chosen as "infants"? Clearly some are to be chosen and others rejected. From where would the mercantilist planners obtain the relevant information on such decisions? This matter calls for business ingenuity and imagination, rather than political skills. But business acumen is widely dispersed, and such decentralized wisdom Smith believed to be far superior to that possessed centrally by government administrators. Furthermore, a government administrator stands to lose less from his mistakes than does a businessman venturing his own capital. This, Smith concludes, leads to the presumption of more error in government than in private decisionmaking:

> What is the species of domestic industry which his capital can employ, and of which the produce is likely to be of the greatest value, every individual, it is evident, can, in his local situation, judge much better than any statesman or lawgiver can do for him. The statesman, who should attempt to direct private people in what manner they ought to employ their capitals, would not only load himself with a most unnecessary attention, but assume an authority which could safely be trusted, not only to no single person, but to no council or senate whatever, and which would nowhere be so dangerous as in the hands of a man who had folly and presumption enough to fancy himself fit to exercise it.[15]

It is this kind of thinking that leads to Smith's presumption in favor of general decentralized free trade. The presumption is based on the argument, once more, that there are gains to be made from division of labor and specialization.

I must stress once more that Smith's necessary condition for economic progress was "natural liberty," upheld and protected by respect for property rights and the rule of law. Given this, Smith claimed, people will draw individually on their natural instincts to specialize and then trade with each other. This will encourage competition which, in turn, will lead to cost cutting and price reductions to the benefit of all classes in society.

Has all this happened since Smith's time?

The answer is certainly yes, although significant limitations on trade still persist. As we approach the millennium, we are bringing with us a large baggage of trade restrictions and trade retaliation policies that Smith would have abhorred. Consider trade retaliation alone. This is being practiced today throughout the world on an increasing scale. Now described by some as the "crowbar theory," the reasoning holds simply that foreign markets can be forced to reopen if only we are willing to close our markets to foreigners, or at least to threaten such action. The primary target of many countries is Japan, which is commonly believed to have virtually closed most of its markets to foreigners by unnecessary bureaucratic regulations. At the same time substantial retaliatory 'trade wars' are being conducted between the U.S. and Europe, and everywhere offensive and counter-offensive action is occurring in the form of the imposition of anti-dumping duties. The best known crowbar activity, meanwhile, is probably that which features worldwide attempts to limit agricultural subsidies and so reduce the world's food surpluses, a problem that the General Agreement on Tariffs and Trade (GATT) and its successor, the World Trade Organization (WTO), have so far failed to resolve. The cost of such trade restrictions, following our preceding discussion, is largely in terms of a self-inflicted failure to enjoy the full benefits of increasing returns to scale of the inclusive "economic nexus" (to use Buchanan's phrase). This cost is substantial, and we obviously need Adam Smith's reasoning more than ever before.

At the same time, Smith's proposition that prosperity is a function of natural liberty has received weighty endorsement recently. To test formally Smith's proposition, one needs data for as many countries and as many dimensions of economic liberty as possible. In their recent *Public Choice* article, economists G. W. Scully and D. Slottje selected a total of fifteen attributes of economic freedom.[16] These included freedoms of property, international financial transactions, movement, information, peaceful assembly, and communication through the print media. A special feature of the analysis was the weighting of the attributes in their construction of an index of economic liberty. All the rankings indicated that economic growth and real domestic product per capita are positively correlated with economic liberty. This empirical work, completed almost exactly two centuries after Smith's demise, appears then to demonstrate that the central proposition in *The Wealth of Nations* not only lends itself to empirical refutation (and can therefore be classified as scientific), but has so far withstood the test.

Let me conclude with an emphasis on the prior importance of liberty, as expressed in Smith's own words:

> All systems either of preference or of restraint, therefore, being thus completely taken away, the obvious and simple system of natural liberty establishes itself of its own accord. Every man, as long as he does not violate the laws of justice, is left perfectly free to pursue his own interest in his own way, and to bring both his industry and capital into competition with those of any other man, or order of men. The sovereign is completely discharged from a duty, in the attempting to perform which he must always be exposed to innumerable delusions and for the proper performance of which no human wisdom or knowledge could ever be sufficient; the duty of superintending the industry of private people, and of directing it towards the employments most suitable to the interest of the society.[17]

Notes

[1] Because our two celebrities occupied the stage over two centuries ago does not mean we should regard them as old! In 1776, Adam Smith was only fifty-six, while Jefferson was a young man of thirty-three.

[2] Adam Smith, *An Inquiry into the Nature and Causes of the Wealth of Nations*, R. H. Campbell, A. S. Skinner, and W. B. Todd, eds., 2 vols., Book IV (Oxford: Clarendon Press, 1976), 456.

[3] Ibid., Book I, 26.

[4] Ibid., Book II, 343.

[5] Ibid., Book I, 13.

[6] Ibid., 15.

[7] Ibid.

[8] See Edwin G. West, *Adam Smith and Modern Economics* (Cheltenham: Elgar, 1990), 34.

⁹*Wealth of Nations*, Book I, 17.

¹⁰Ibid., 19.

¹¹Ibid., 22.

¹²James M. Buchanan and Yong J. Yoon, *The Return to Increasing Returns* (Ann Arbor: University of Michigan Press, 1994), 11.

¹³Ibid.

¹⁴*Wealth of Nations*, Book IV, 458.

¹⁵Ibid, 456.

¹⁶G. W. Scully and D. Slottje, "Ranking Economic Liberty across Countries," *Public Choice* (1991), 69.

¹⁷*Wealth of Nations*, Book IV, 687.

WALTER E. WILLIAMS

The Popularizers:
Henry Hazlitt, Warren Brookes,
and Thomas Sowell

In the two centuries after the publication of Adam Smith's *An Inquiry into the Nature and Causes of the Wealth of Nations* (1776), economists made significant progress in expanding our knowledge of economic behavior. But much, if not most, of this knowledge was limited to professional journals, college texts, and specialized publications that were not readily accessible to the layperson. Even when economists occasionally appeared in more popular forums—in newspapers and magazines, on radio and television, and before congressional hearings—they tended to lack the communication skills needed to reach a large audience.

In the late twentieth century, however, the situation is quite different. Perhaps it is because more and more economists are heeding the admonition that was given to me when I was a UCLA graduate student. A very wise professor, Armen Alchian, once told me, "Williams, the true test of whether one understands his subject is whether he can explain it to someone who doesn't know a darn thing about it." At the time, I did not give Professor Alchian's statement much thought, but as I matured I did. It is an economist's task to explore the frontiers of knowledge within his field, but it is also his task to make his discoveries widely known. There are a number of contemporary economists who have succeeded in accomplishing both tasks, and I want to discuss a few of them here.

Henry Hazlitt

Henry Hazlitt (1894–1993) was the most prolific popularizer of the modern age. During his lifetime, which fell one year short of a century, he wrote over ten thousand articles, essays, and reviews in such well-known publications as the *Wall Street Journal*, the *New York Times*, and *Newsweek*. Through the mass media, he managed to reach millions of readers, and he introduced them to the pioneering work of such scholars as Austrian School economists Ludwig von Mises and Friedrich A. Hayek. He also helped launch the influential New York-based Foundation for Economic Education (FEE), which to this day provides free market seminars and publications for students, businessmen, and community activists.

Hazlitt's greatest single contribution was his book, *Economics in One Lesson*. Originally published in 1946, this slim volume with the ambitious title has gone through numerous paperback editions and at least eight translations. It offers no equations, no graphs, no economic jargon—just simple, common-sense lessons that make the marketplace understandable. One of these lessons is presented in a chapter on the "Broken Window Fallacy," and it introduces ideas that can be used to counter all manner of political and economic nonsense-speak.

In the chapter, Hazlitt tells of a hoodlum who tosses a brick through a baker's window and flees. The baker is furious, but a person in the crowd that gathers reminds him that his misfortune has a bright side. The $250 it takes to replace his plate glass window will create employment for the glazier. After all, if windows were never broken, what would happen to the glass business? And then there are the "multiplier effects" to consider: The glazier will have $250 to spend with other merchants. Once they receive his money, the merchants will spend it with others, and so on, and so on.

Given the multiplier effects, Hazlitt writes, one might conclude that the brick-throwing hoodlum, far from being a public menace, is actually a public benefactor! In truth, however, only the first conclusion made by the man in the crowd is correct: The hoodlum has created more business for the glazier. The glazier will be no more unhappy to learn about the act of vandalism than an undertaker is to learn of a death. The baker, however, will be out the $250 that he planned to pay the tailor to make him a new suit. Instead of having a window *and* a suit, he has to make due with a window that he hadn't even needed before his property was wantonly destroyed.

The glazier's gain in employment is the tailor's loss of employment. From the point of view of the community, it is poorer by one suit. However, is easy for community members to see the hoodlum's act as stimulating employment because the glazier's work is visible and the tailor's unemployment is invisible—no one can see the suit that he did not make. How many times have we heard mayors, labor union leaders, and city officials argue that publicly financed construction projects such as convention centers and new sports arenas produce the added benefit of job creation? They are merely repeating Hazlitt's Broken Window Fallacy. The money to finance these projects must be confiscated from taxpayers. If taxpayers are able keep their money, it will be spent on something else—cars, home remodeling, vacations, investments, education, etc. Certainly, if publicly financed projects are undertaken some goods and services will be created, but others will be reduced or won't come into being in the first place.

Politicians who call for taxation as a means of job creation have a great advantage because the public-spending projects they propose are very high profile—everyone can see them. And politicians love visible beneficiaries who know whom to vote for at the next election. Politicians also love invisible victims who have no idea of the source of their plight and hence do not threaten retaliation at the polls. It is not hard to visualize the average politician as the hoodlum in Hazlitt's story. If he is not a hoodlum, at least he thinks like one. For example, you will recall that during the devastating 1992 Midwest floods Vice President Al Gore made speeches about all the jobs that would be created by flood repair activities.

Warren Brookes

Warren Brookes was born in 1929. He died an untimely death during the last week of 1991 after succumbing to pneumonia. He wrote for the Boston *Herald-American*, and his columns were also syndicated in approximately forty cities through both the Hearst and Heritage Features syndicates. In Boston, his columns played a key role in the success of Massachusetts' "Proposition 2½," a measure that drastically reduced property taxes. More important, his columns exposed the Governor Dukakis fraud often referred to as the "Massachusetts Miracle."

Brookes' major contribution to economic thinking was to starkly contrast the socialistic vision of the world with the free market vision. He did this by focusing on the true sources of wealth. His major thesis, presented in a thought-provoking book, *The Economy in Mind* (1982), is that wealth is not physical but metaphysical. It is not the direct result of the availability of raw materials but of human imagination and creativity. It is not the sum total of the hoards of property-owning elites and governments but of individual efforts.

Brookes' logic is simple: If wealth, which produces economic growth and a higher standard of living, is determined solely by natural resources, why were the cavemen so poor? They had access to abundant natural resources, but it didn't raise them beyond their primitive state. Brookes concludes that the mind must be brought to bear on the wise use of natural resources and to create value where there was seemingly none before. He, like a few other perceptive observers of the historical record, points out that before the invention of the engine, oil was nothing but a nuisance that ruined farmers' fields. Sand was worthless until someone figured out how to turn it into silicon, thus making possible the computer chip revolution. In the future, he predicts that fusion energy will make energy nearly costless, and biogenetics will end starvation. He sees many other new technologies creating new wealth.

Brookes (who was writing at a time when the Soviet empire was very much alive and when socialism in one form or another was the preferred "ism" of most economists around the globe) reminds us that Marxists and socialists have a very different vision. They believe that the world economy is a zero-sum game. Wealth, therefore, is physical and finite. Marxists and socialists worry less about the health of the goose that lays the golden egg than they do about how to divide up the egg. According to them, the masses are benefited by a "proper redistribution of wealth"—a redistribution carried out by the state through such devices as taxes and regulations. Collective security, not individual liberty, is the ultimate goal, and the government's main job is to manage, direct, and artificially stimulate the economy.

Brookes warns that this vision not only harms the productive sector but also breeds the "politics of envy." Through objective analysis, he makes it clear that wealth is the result of human imagination and creativity. We must inevitably conclude that liberty is the essential condition for prosperity, economic growth, and a rising standard of living for all. We must also encourage the proper institutional conditions for liberty to flourish—conditions based on limited government and inviolable private property rights.

I should also mention that Warren Brookes was widely regarded as the Sherlock Holmes of economic reporting—perceptive, meticulous, and logical. When he went after a story, he thoroughly investigated every lead. His specialty was uncovering contradictions in government policies. One example is his exposé about the federal government's rulings on the fire retardant "TRIS." Consumer safety advocates persuaded bureaucrats in Washington, D.C., that certain kinds of polyester children's sleepwear were highly flammable and hence hazardous. The bureaucrats ordered the nation's garment manufacturers to treat all children's sleepwear with TRIS. It turned out that while TRIS was a good flame retardant, it was also carcinogenic. So the same bureaucrats then ordered retailers to remove all TRIS-treated garments from their shelves. The cost ran into the hundreds of millions of dollars. Many small companies went bankrupt.

Brookes also told his readers about the curious case of the Food and Drug Administration (FDA), which demanded the recall of all salt tablets used for cleaning and storing contact lenses. Why? There was a vague and unsubstantiated charge floating around the agency that some contact lens wearers might not use the tablets correctly. Of course, the FDA's action created a whole new market for manufacturers of preserved saline solutions. Brookes noted that it may not have been coincidental that the FDA official who had stewarded the edict through the FDA had been wined and dined by the Burton-Parsons Company, which stood to make a fortune from increased sales of such solutions.

Thomas Sowell

Thomas Sowell (1930—) is the Rose and Milton Friedman Senior Fellow in Public Policy at Stanford University's Hoover Institution on War, Revolution, and Peace. He also writes a monthly magazine column for *Forbes* and a weekly newspaper column for the Creators Syndicate. He is best known for his scholarship on race and culture, but he has also made significant contributions in the area of economic thought. Among his over twenty books are: *Classical Economics Reconsidered, Knowledge and Decisions, A Conflict of Visions, Say's Law,* and *The Vision of the Anointed* (with the wonderful subtitle, *Self-Congratulation as a Basis for Social Policy*).

Sowell is a brilliant student of human behavior. Over many years, he has provided much insight into the fallacies, misunderstandings, and outright deceptions that plague America's social, political, and economic policies. And through a multitude of popular books, articles, and columns, he has made valuable information available to ordinary people. Let me give you an example: "affirmative action" (a code name for racial preferences) in college admissions is a hot topic today, which has important economic as well as social consequences. When Sowell looks at affirmative action, he asks the question he asks about all such programs: Does it actually benefit its ostensible beneficiaries? Aside from the issues of morality and fairness associated with racial preferences in college admissions, he argues that racial preferences have had a downside for blacks individually and as a group and that preferences have limited their opportunities for economic and social advancement.

Blacks who have been admitted to University of California–Berkeley have average SAT scores of around 952, which is slightly higher than the national average for all students. However, up to 70 percent of all black students admitted to Berkeley under its Affirmative Action program fail to graduate. What is the problem? It turns out that the average SAT score for Berkeley's white and Asian students approaches 1300. Black students are "in over their heads," competing with students who have a primary and secondary education far superior to theirs.

Not too far from Berkeley is the University of California–San Jose. This institution is a respectable university, but it is not nearly as academically challenging as Berkeley. Roughly 70 percent of all black students at this school also fail to graduate. Again, their SAT scores are below those of average students. The tragedy is that black students who would have been successful at San Jose have, in the name of affirmative action, been recruited to Berkelcy, and they have become failures. The same thing has happened at San Jose. Sowell makes the point that these students are not qualified or unqualified for college in any absolute sense; there are some three thousand colleges in the United States that make a college available for every ability level. The problem is not racism but mismatching students and colleges. Students have been encouraged to attend the wrong colleges in the name of a well-intentioned but ultimately destructive social agenda.

Sowell also debunks the idea that statistical disparities between races are evidence of racial discrimination. He does this by citing some notoriously misleading examples of statistical disparities: American men are struck by lightning six times as often as American women. During the heyday of the Soviet empire, per capita consumption of cognac in Estonia was seven times the consumption in Uzbekistan. During the 1960s, the Chinese minority in Malaysia received more university degrees (including four hundred engineering degrees) than the politically dominant Malay majority (which only received four engineering degrees). Politically powerful Afrikaners earned less than half the income of the British in South Africa. A 1985 study showed that the proportion of Asian American students scoring over seven hundred on the math portion of the SAT was more than double that of whites. In the Brazilian state of Sao Paulo, more than two-thirds of all potatoes and 90 percent of all tomatoes are grown by farmers of Japanese ancestry. Nearly one-third of all Americans who have won the Nobel Prize are of Jewish ancestry.

Sowell does not deny that discrimination might explain some statistical disparities, but he points out that one cannot make unambiguous inferences from numbers. And he shows that while many lawyers, social scientists, and economists make the argument that, but for the fact of discrimination, races would be proportionately represented across the board in every area of life, proportional representation cannot actually be found anywhere.

Sowell also answers a question that befuddles many people: Why are honest and intelligent people who have no hidden agenda consistently lined up on one side or the other of many social issues? Sometimes these sides are called "liberal" and "conservative." Rehabilitation advocates are likely to be minimum wage law supporters. People who are in favor of lengthy prison sentences and the death penalty are more likely to be Strategic Defense Initiative (SDI) supporters. Sowell explains that there are two conflicting visions—an unconstrained vision of human behavior and a constrained vision—and each consistently leads people to prefer certain policies.

The eighteenth-century Scottish moral philosopher and economist Adam Smith had a constrained vision of the world. In his view, the job of the state was to create a system of moral incentives for freely acting people. Human nature was not something that could be changed by external means such as social engineering or economic regulation. Moreover, Smith believed that economic benefits to society were largely a consequence of unintended actions by individuals—in other words, they emerged from the unpredictable interactions of buyers and sellers in the marketplace, under the pressures of competition and the incentives for personal gain.

The British social reformer William Godwin had an unconstrained vision of the world. *In Inquiry Concerning Social Justice* (1793), he portrayed human nature as perfectible through the enlightened leadership and direction of elites such as himself. The deliberate intention to benefit others was the essence of virtue, and virtue was the main route to human happiness. Unintentional social benefits were treated by Godwin as scarcely worthy of notice.

Sowell then shows us through countless real-life examples, of how the constrained vision (which sees the world as a set of trade-offs) and the unconstrained vision (which sees the world as a place where total solutions are possible) affect the politics, economics, and culture of modern America.

Keeping It Simple

Most of what is important about economics is not complex at all. There is always a cost to something. People do less of something when its cost (price) rises. People respond to changes in scarcity. But these concepts are often made incomprehensible by economists who prefer economic jargon and mathematical equations to plain speaking and writing. In the works of Hazlitt, Brookes, and Sowell, one is hard put to find any esoteric language or fancy formulas, but at the same time one finds that their work is rich and powerful, and it contributes mightily to a better understanding of human behavior.

ROBERT A. SIRICO

Economics on the Left:
From Marxism to Keynesianism

At century's end, there are many contenders for the title, "Major Intellectual Error of Our Epoch." We must ask, therefore, which among them led to the greatest misery for the greatest number. Perhaps it was the declaration that "God is dead"—that we need no longer be restrained by the limits imposed on us by natural law. Perhaps it was the idea that we should replace traditional institutions like the family and the community with an individualistic–egalitarian commonwealth. Perhaps it was the theory that power should be vested in an all-knowing state. Perhaps it was economic planning, that great error which has crippled economies all over the world. Or perhaps it was the pursuit of empire and the resort to total war as a means of settling disputes among nations.

The Vision of Socialism

All were disastrous errors, resulting in unprecedented levels of social collapse, economic deprivation, human suffering, death, and even genocide. All deserve to be addressed on their own terms. But each is symptomatic of a more dangerous and sweeping vision —a vision that has been reinvented in many countries and in many guises over the course of this century—commonly referred to as "socialism."

It may sound shocking to attribute so much evil to such an innocent-sounding doctrine, but it is an accurate charge. It is also one that we should be deeply concerned about, since socialism—

31

after a brief period of unpopularity in the late 1980s and early 1990s
—is in vogue again on many university campuses and in the highest reaches of many governments. I am sad to report that it is also
favored by many clergymen, and its principles are faithfully taught
in many seminaries.

Nowadays, calling someone a "socialist" suggests not great evil
but, at worst, quirkiness, and at best, an isolated brilliance born of
concern for the poor and the underprivileged. In any case, we are
not inclined to think of the ideas of the socialist as any kind of
threat.

This is a genuine puzzle. It seems that the lessons of our century have yet to be fully absorbed into the public consciousness.
We have not heeded the practical failures of socialism: the communist variety of socialism, stemming from the Bolshevik Revolution in Russia; the nationalist variety that came to fruition with
Hitler's rise to power; the Fabian and Keynesian varieties, which,
in the name of the "War on Poverty," made war on the family.

The Conceit of Socialism

Amazingly, socialism still retains its fundamental intellectual
respectability. The annual Socialist Scholars Conference, held in
Massachusetts, still attracts thousands of attendees. In 1998, organizations and scholars around the world celebrated the one hundred and fiftieth anniversary of the publication of *The Communist
Manifesto.* How can we account for this enduring attraction? Nobel
Prize winning economist Friedrich A. Hayek once theorized that
it stemmed from the desire of men to believe that rational planning undertaken by great minds can remake the world. Hayek
further explained that intellectuals are notoriously unwilling to
accede to the wisdom and experience of common people who
understand better than anyone that human nature cannot be re-
made and society cannot be made to conform to a single will.

Hayek's colleague, Austrian School economist Ludwig von
Mises, offered an even more unsympathetic interpretation. He
asserted that intellectuals' attraction to socialism stemmed from
their very own sense of personal failure, which amounted to a kind
of chronic intellectual insecurity. They wondered how they, who

were so valuable to society, could be making a mere pittance in salary each year while, at the same time, uneducated entertainers and sports stars were pulling down a hundred times more for merely providing the masses with entertainment. Under socialism, these intellectuals believed their true worth would shine forth, and they would surely be paid huge sums to enlighten the masses and redesign the social order.

Mises, who lived from 1881 to 1973, certainly knew something about socialist intellectuals. He was surrounded by them, in Europe and in America. The question of what attracts the clergy is a bit more complicated, however, and neither Hayek not Mises provided a full explanation. Among the clergy, there was a gravely flawed view of justice and the role of the gospel—that is to say, of how the gospel was to be applied to social circumstances. Clergymen generally regarded *any* inequality in wealth as inherently suspect and even as evidence of exploitation and injustice. Lacking understanding of how economies grow and distribute wealth, they believed that only a central authority could "apportion resources" with an eye to helping the poor, the aged, and the underprivileged. Lacking business experience, they could not conceive of the contribution that entrepreneurs and businessmen made to the growth of an economy. They thought only of dividing wealth more fairly, not of generating more wealth.

This is a difficult argument to confront without explaining some technical aspects of economics that most clergy—even today, in the Age of Information—feel that they have no time to read about or have any inclination to understand. At the Michigan-based Acton Institute for the Study of Religion and Liberty, we are dedicated to providing classical economic education for the clergy and the laity. We are making progress, but it is slow. We have found that the first step is to encourage laypersons, clergymen, and seminarians to think more concretely about the socialist alternative and how it would work, or rather, how it would *not* work. It is not enough to complain about the present state of the world if we want to redesign it. We must also think about how that redesign is going to work in reality.

So how has socialism actually worked in this century? I have already mentioned several varieties briefly by name. First among them was the communist variety, as realized in the Soviet Union between 1917 and 1992. Industries were nationalized. Exchange and capital goods were abolished. There was no sound money. There were no real prices. Goods were distributed through a central plan, executed without the benefit of any practical knowledge of consumer preferences, available resources, or producer capacities and abilities. Workers became slaves to the Soviet state with no control over their careers. Producers became pawns of a powerful elite and had no incentives to produce quality goods and services in sufficient supply to meet demand. Central planners became con artists engaged in a vast guessing game that resulted in systemwide corruption and economic deprivation.

In short, the Soviet economy was a disaster. Why? Because socialism in any form is unworkable. We know this from bitter experience. No socialist has ever come up with a satisfactory answer to this ugly little fact. It is the fly in the ointment of the grand theory of socialism. And the harder socialists try to introduce a full-blown version of socialism, the less information (about prices, supply and demand, etc.) is produced by the market. This is information people need to plan their own lives and create their own fortunes. Without it, they are blind, deaf, and dumb.

However, we would do well to remember that, from the beginning, socialism had an agenda that went well beyond economics. It represented an exhaustive view of the whole of life. It was such a "totalist" vision that it even extended to the individual family unit and the church—which Marx and other socialists wanted to abolish. This hostility toward the family and toward religion has characterized every form of socialism in one way or another. In Hitler's Germany and Mao's China, the family was devalued and exploited for state purposes. The new religion of the state came to replace the popular religion of the people.

The idea that the state should be exalted above all extends to all aspects of socialist economic planning, including those that we experienced in the West. Often, respectable intellectuals cry foul when these varieties of socialism are linked to Soviet repression and Nazism. They say that merely because U.S. President Franklin D. Roosevelt had kind words for the economic planning experiment under Soviet dictator Josef Stalin and British economist John Maynard Keynes wrote an introduction to the German edition of his major treatise that came out during Adolf Hitler's rule does not mean that there is any connection. And they add with great conviction, Western-style central planning is, by nature, different from communism and fascism.

I agree with them that there is a fundamental difference in degree. But if we are to be intellectually honest, we also have to ask, is there really a fundamental difference in nature? Perhaps only with the benefit of hindsight can we fully understand what it is about the theoretical and practical core of socialist ideology that is so fundamentally wrong. In this context, I would like to offer here a brief list of what I regard as the six main errors of socialism.

The Errors of Socialism

Error 1: The collective matters. The individual does not.

In this error, which first took root in the ancient world, especially in the writings of the great pre-Christian political philosophers, there is no notion of the inherent dignity or worth of the individual. Plato's theories, for example, were based on the idea of the city as a collective unit that commanded supreme loyalty. Individuals' rights were rigidly determined by the place they occupied in society. Some men at the top of society were likened to gold, others to baser metals.

The West has drawn tremendous wisdom from Plato's writings on politics and on society, but it truly owes its best thinking to the Jewish and Christian traditions. The Old and New Testaments proclaimed that all men should be esteemed equally as divine creations with individual souls. However, the idea that the collective, and not the individual, is what matters has not been vanquished by Judaism or Christianity.

Error 2: There is a collective will.

In the eighteenth century, the French philosopher Jean Jacques Rousseau devised the theory that a single overwhelming "social will" was the relevant unit in society. This theory, which was denounced as "socialism" by its critics as early as 1765, had a profound impact on France, which had a penchant for collectivist schemes.

The first full use of the term "socialist" in the modern sense came from within British socialist reformer Robert Owen's original circle of followers. In 1827, Owen—who had founded a short-lived commune in New Harmony, Indiana, two years earlier—became the first intellectual to use it in print: "The chief question between the modern political economists and the communists or socialists is whether capital should be owned individually or commonly."

Think, for a moment, about that phrase, "common ownership." It is really a political misnomer. It bypasses the central issue in all matters of property: Who owns the title? Who controls it? Who can sell it and keep the profits? None of these actions can take place collectively because there can be no such thing as "collective will." Only individuals have will.

In general practice, common ownership has always meant ownership by the state—ownership by those who have the guns and the privileges of monopoly power. Only that entity acts as a proxy for groups. This was the key to Karl Marx's thinking. He wrote, "Capital should be owned collectively by a group," which he called, "the proletariat," made up of workers, peasants, and anyone else he regarded as exploited by the capitalists. Marx predicted that, in the socialist society, eventually the state would "wither away." But, in fact, the state has always used the proletariat as a cover for despotic rule.

In Germany and elsewhere in Europe during the early to mid-twentieth century, there was also a variety of socialism called "National Socialism," in which nationality, blood, and race, rather than class and economic status, determined the position a person held in the collective society. Once again, the individual was not the focal point. All individuals were expected to submerge their individuality into a collective will, which was embodied in the state. Eventually, National Socialism led to World War II, as its main adherents in the Nazi Party tried to implement it through intimidation, conquest, and extermination.

Tragically, we are seeing a modern version of fascist principles in the Serbian–Croatian conflict of the late twentieth century. No hatred runs deeper than the hatred predicated on bloodlines, and it may be decades until the fighting ends in Eastern Europe. But one thing is sure: Socialism must be rejected before peace is possible.

Error 3: Society is based on conflict, not on cooperation or what facilitates cooperation and ownership.

Marxists expressed this error as "class conflict." They insisted that there is a kind of intrinsic hostility between the lower and upper classes in society. National Socialists referred to it as "racial and national conflict."

In Great Britain, another variety of socialism, "Fabianism," also perpetuated the myth of irreconcilable conflict. The Fabians, nineteenth-century social reformers who would have an enduring impact on the modern Labour movement and who would import their doctrine to the United States during the Progressive era, believed life was an eternal struggle between "the rich and the poor." They inspired the more generic use of the word "poor" to refer to the underprivileged or the marginalized in society. And, according to the Fabians, the poor were to be the main beneficiaries of socialism.

In the United States, Fabianism led to such massive government programs as the "New Deal" and the "Great Society." Publicly funded institutions and agencies were created to "serve the poor," with apparently little concrete regard for their actual impact on the poor themselves. This leads me to conclude that some socialists love the poor so much that they want to see more of them.

Another British import—a mid-twentieth century economic theory known as "Keynesianism" after its creator, John Maynard Keynes—claimed that the real conflict in society was between "consumers versus investors," a ridiculous assertion indeed because the one depends upon the other. This variety had an even greater influence on American economics and politics than Fabianism because it was not generally recognized as socialism. It went instead by the more innocent-sounding name of "central planning." As Keynesianism took the intellectual world by storm, the old idea of the collective took on an economic form with a scientific gloss.

Instead of individual entrepreneurs, owners, and consumers, Keynes posited the existence of huge economic aggregates acting in economic life. They were "capital," "investment," "savings," "national income," and "consumption." The role of the state was to accumulate sufficient data to quantify these huge aggregates and manipulate them so that they fit together according to an overarching design.

The system was enormously complex and intentionally so, but like other complex collectivist ideas, it resulted in the opposite of what it intended to do. Instead of eliminating the ups and downs of the business cycle, it produced more of them. Instead of creating stability, it created volatility. Instead of guaranteeing prosperity, it guaranteed inflation—that invisible thief that creeps into every piggy bank in the country.

Error 4: Only a few can know the truth.

Whether we are discussing Marxism, National Socialism, Fabianism, or Keynesianism, this error traces its roots to an ancient heresy known as "gnosticism." The word is Greek for knowledge— hidden knowledge, possessed by a specific group of men. Marxists believed that the group was comprised of Communist Party intellectuals. National Socialists believed it was the *Führer* and his soldiers. Fabians believed it was social reformers and "enlightened" politicians. Keynesians believed it was scientists, experts, and government agency officials.

The basic notion behind gnosticism was that the group had a privileged insight into the truth by virtue of its status. Of course, this was an absurd notion. When it comes to economics, for example, I would rather trust the insight of someone who has been successful in the market than someone who has failed. Real-life experience and an actual track record are vitally important.

Truth is objective. It doesn't depend on class, bloodlines, intentions, or even on expertise. And something isn't the truth just because those in power declare that it is. Allow me to illustrate. In mid-1998, I visited communist Cuba, which is frequently referred to by its leaders as a "socialist paradise." I found that many buildings were painted with government-sponsored graffiti that urged, "Forward with the revolution!" But there is a problem: There are no real capitalists in Cuba anymore. There haven't been any for decades, thanks to Fidel Castro, who imprisoned them, killed them, or drove them out of business and even out of the country.

So what are the Cubans revolting against? The state tells them that they revolting against capitalism, but, in truth, they are fighting against themselves—the proletariat, on whose behalf the state rules.

Castro has repeatedly boasted to the world press about the strong Cuban economy. But in truth, the preoccupation of the average Cuban is food, which is severely rationed. He subsists mainly on meager portions of bread and rice. He is lucky to get one chicken a month. Poverty is endemic, except among the ranks of the ruling elite. Havana, once one of the world's busiest and most attractive cities is now more like Miss Havisham in Charles Dicken's tragic novel, *Great Expectations*—a half-demented old woman in a tattered bridal gown, sitting in an rotting, vermin-infested house decorated for a wedding that never took place.

Castro says that this is because of the U.S. embargo. Of course, the embargo isn't really to blame, since other countries are free to trade with and invest in Cuba. But they don't; they know that their investments are not safe because of the "Revolution." Castro loves the embargo. One reason is that the embargo is his most potent propaganda tool. He can tell Cubans that all their problems are caused by the evil empire to the North, not by his failed socialist policies. A second reason is that the embargo discourages American tourists from visiting Cuba. Castro knows that every pair of jeans tourists wear, every dollar they spend, is an evangelizing tract against the evils of socialism. They are a threat because they carry messages of truth to the people.

Error 5: *Human nature can be transformed.*

Any janitor scrubbing floors in the lowliest office of the Kremlin knows that human nature just doesn't change. Yet many, if not most, intellectuals persist in thinking that it is possible to shape other people's motivations and actions according to their own designs. As Hoover Institution Senior Fellow Thomas Sowell noted in *A Conflict of Visions* (1987), these intellectuals have an "unconstrained" vision of life that profoundly affects their moral, social, political, and economic views. They do not believe that life consists of making choices and trade-offs, all of which entail certain costs. They believe that, with the power of the state behind them, they can actually attain perfection.

Remember the old phrase, "Every day in every way, we are getting better and better"? Marxists believed that one day all ownership would come to an end. Some, like Castro in his early years as dictator, even wanted to eliminate money to encourage all men to meld into a new Socialist Man. National Socialists desired to use their totalitarian government to create a purebred Superman. And Fabians and Keynesians tried to give birth to Every Man— that is, to make all men equal in wealth and position.

Error 6: God is dead.

In any socialist system, allegiance to God must be replaced by allegiance to the state. The words of Jesus, "Render unto Caesar what is Caesar's, but unto God what is God's," cannot be tolerated. Nothing can be superior to the all-encompassing, all-embracing state. In the Soviet Union, the Marxists' hostility to religion was well-documented. They were determined to destroy the "opiate of the masses." In Germany and Austria, the National Socialists attempted to restore a pre-Christian paganism, with the heads of government basically revered as gods. In Great Britain and America, Fabians and Keynesians felt that religion kept the poor unaware of their plight and that enlightened people shouldn't believe in superstitious dogmas.

Furthermore, socialists of all stripes felt that Christian charity should be replaced by the welfare state. This is one of the historical insights that I think most modern religious leaders have missed. The real threat of the welfare state was to the mission of the church. As the welfare state took over the church's indispensable role of serving the poor, it robbed the church of a rich resource—of its own spiritual nourishment. In effect, religious leaders who became lobbyists for the welfare state rendered their own jobs obsolete.

Keynesians, moreover, claimed that since the state was the "visible hand" designing the economy and holding it together, there was no longer any need for the "invisible hand" of God to work through voluntary exchanges and an ethical code that was meant to guide all his believers. In the 1970s to 1980s, "liberation theologians"—leftist Catholics who found in the gospel a militant call to free Latin Americans from "political, social, and material oppression"—advanced this idea even further by rejecting the very meaning of the term "theology." To them, theology was not the study of God, the Scripture, and the end times. It was "immanetizing of the eschaton." It was bringing the transcendent into this world—bringing God's kingdom to earth, through socialism. The liberation theologians were thus proponents of "practical atheism." They attended church, and they professed their belief in God, but they lived as though God did not exist.

The Power of Ideas

Today, we live in a culture that is dominated by the idea of living in the "here and now." We simply don't want to delay gratification of our needs and wants or to think about the long-term results of our short-term actions. We have become very materialistic, and that means that we have become very socialistic, since socialism is the religion of materialism.

Who is to blame? We are, of course, but we are not alone. James Billington, author of *Fire in the Minds of Men* (1980), noted that all socialist faiths in human history have been conceived in the minds of intellectuals. Socialism did not spring from the "workers" and the "peasants." I have seen this for myself when I have visited socialist nations. The people I have met—selling goods in the marketplace, driving buses and taxis, teaching school, doing the laundry—aren't socialists.

It took the intellectuals and clergymen of the West to introduce the concept of socialism in Russia, Eastern Europe, Asia, and Latin America. The people closest to reality didn't buy it, but they weren't the ones in power. But the ruling classes, which had the supposed benefit of a Western or Western-style education, did.

The socialists had this right: *Ideas determine the course of history.* This is why they dominated the intellectual debate for most of this century. This is also why they made such effective social activists. They knew that they must spread their ideas—through articles, books, conferences, government agencies and programs, and through social activism.

Combating socialism requires the same strategy. Defenders of freedom must ensure that their ideas gain a wide audience.

Socialism may be, practically speaking, dead, but attempts by economists and politicians to manipulate the economy in the name of the poor—via science and aggregates—continue to this day. American Catholic bishops have rightly reminded us that the person does not exist for the economy but that the economy exists for the person. And in this, their wisdom needs to be heard, especially by many of today's economists who have not taken the individual into account. An individual cannot be sidelined by economic theories. He is the central economic actor. Remove the person, and you remove economics.

It is only a system that accounts for human preference and human priority—indeed, for human action—that can account for real and authentic economic science. With regard to the dignity of the person, the Christian apologist C. S. Lewis put it very poetically, "There are no ordinary people. You have never talked to a mere mortal. Nations, cultures, arts, civilizations—these are mortal, and their life is to ours as the life of a gnat. But it is immortals with whom we consort every day." Lewis added, "Your neighbor is the holiest object presented to your senses." He understood the dignity of the individual, which is something that all systems of collectivism seek to ignore and even destroy.

GEORGE ROCHE

Frederic Bastiat and the Free Market Ideal

In the 1990s, many of us have forgotten how hostile the intellectual environment was on college campuses in the 1970s. We have also forgotten that free market economics was a taboo subject. Professors, students, and guest speakers who defended capitalism in the classroom or in public forums were shouted down or even physically harassed. It was in these strongly anticapitalist years that the founder of the Foundation for Economic Education—my old boss Leonard Read—rescued an obscure Frenchman from the ashheap of history. Read was among first to recognize Frederic Bastiat's enormous importance.

Frederic Bastiat (1801–1850) was as consequential a figure as the revolutionary war hero, the Marquis de Lafayette, and the author of *Democracy in America,* Alexis de Tocqueville, but he is seldom mentioned in any contemporary accounts of the nineteenth century. The son of a respectable but undistinguished merchant, he was born in the south of France, in the small provincial town of Bayonne. His mother and father died when he was young, and perhaps this was why he was more comfortable with books than people. He attended college until the age of seventeen. He then tried being a merchant like his father, but it was not in his nature to deal with vendors or customers. He also served as a justice of the peace and town council member for a while, but that was as far as his professional and civic accomplishments went.

Bastiat devoted most of his time to scholarly pursuits. He read prodigiously, and he spent his first forty-five years quietly preparing for a tremendous flash of productivity in the final five years of his life. It was near the end that he began writing seminal articles that were unlike anything else that was being written at the time. These articles were widely read, and his many fans persuaded Bastiat to come out of seclusion to found the French Free Trade Association and to publish the Association's influential weekly journal. In the first issue, which appeared in 1846, Bastiat wrote what has since become the classic argument against protectionism. It took the form of a document addressed to the government called "The Petition of the Candlemakers." It begins with these lines:

> We are suffering from the ruinous competition of a foreign rival who apparently works under conditions so far superior to our own for the production of light that he is flooding the domestic market with it at an incredibly low price; from the moment he appears, our sales cease, all the consumers turn to him. . . . This rival . . . is none other than the sun.

This imaginary petition goes on to encourage the government to pass laws requiring that all windows on French buildings be shuttered so as to block out the sun and give candlemakers special protection.

Bastiat Goes to Paris

Throughout the late 1840s, Bastiat wrote many satirical essays. They caused a firestorm of public comment and earned him the praise of free trade advocates at home and abroad. In 1848, his countrymen elected him to serve in the National Assembly (which was similar to the U.S. House of Representatives). For him to accept this office was truly heroic. He had never been in good health and was slowly dying of tuberculosis. He wanted nothing more than to be left alone to write. But he accepted the duty, and, despite the long hours he devoted to it, he produced a number of masterful books and monographs: *Economic Harmonies*; *Economic Sophisms*; *Individualism and Fraternity*; *Protectionism and Communism*; *What is Seen and What Is Not Seen*; and his most famous treatise, *The Law.*

Bastiat went to Paris to stand up for the principles in which he fervently believed. He knew that he was living at a time when great upheavals were shaking up all of Europe. Indeed, Bastiat was one of those men fated to stand at the crossroads of sweeping historical events and radically conflicting ideologies. Remember the historical context of the 1840s. The impact of the American and French Revolutions was still fresh. Bastiat himself would live through three major revolutions in France[1] and their inevitable traveling companions, anarchy and dictatorship.[2] There were great tensions between the rising middle class and old ruling aristocracy. People were struggling to define the relationship between the state and individuals; for the first time they realized that the state was not the source of all authority. Scholars were beginning to study a whole new subject—economics, which included study of the relationship between the economy, the state, and the rights of the individual. One of the first and best of these scholars was Bastiat. In fact, he was one of the world's first and best economists. He devoted himself to the study of the marketplace and how economics affected the political and cultural life of nations.

Bastiat's Main Observations

It is important to note that Bastiat wrote about economics not as an abstract theorist but as a keen observer of the human condition. Theorists always want to change the nature of man to suit their theories; Bastiat knew that the nature of man was unchanging. He was withering in his condemnation of their arrogance. In brief, here is a summary of his main points:

1. Those who want to study the economy must study human behavior. (He thus anticipated Ludwig von Mises' more detailed study of human action in the twentieth century.)

2. The gradual but steady growth of government not only restricts individual rights but also restricts economic growth.

3. Protectionism (i.e., the restraint of trade) and communism (i.e., the restraint of labor) are simply two sides of the same coin. They are both assaults on the principle of private property.

4. Subsidizing certain industries and groups of people in society actually makes things worse by making them dependent on charity and special protections.

5. Every action has seen and unseen consequences, which is why even well-intended government legislation can be destructive.

6. Free trade is the only basis for peace among nations because it leads people to cooperate with and benefit from others. (Bastiat had ample evidence during his lifetime to testify that "when goods don't cross borders, armies will.")

7. The law is our ultimate refuge—the basic protector of our liberties and the foundation upon which all society is built. But when it is used to serve the interests of bureaucrats, it degenerates into "legalized plunder" and threatens our entire future.

Here, in no particular order, are some quotations from Bastiat's work, which seem as fresh and as topical as if they were quoted from today's issue of the *Wall Street Journal.*

On becoming a deputy in the National Assembly:

Four orators are all trying to be heard in the Assembly. At first they speak all at once, then one after the other. What have they said? Very beautiful things, surely, about the power and grandeur of France, the necessity of sowing in order to reap. . . . The modern socialist factions ceaselessly oppose free association in present-day society. They do not realize that a free society is a true association much superior to any of those they concoct out of their fertile imaginations.

The socialists who have invented these follies, and who in days of distress plant them in the minds of the masses, generously confer on themselves the title of "forward-looking" men, and there is a real danger that usage, that tyrant of language, will ratify both the word and the judgment it implies. "Forward-looking" assumes that these gentlemen can see ahead much further than ordinary people; that their only fault is to be too much in advance of their century; and that, if the time is not yet arrived when certain private services, allegedly parasitical, can be eliminated, the fault is with the public, which is far behind socialism. To *my* mind and knowledge, it is the contrary that is true. . . .

The more one examines these "forward-looking" schools of thought, the more one is convinced that at the bottom they rest on nothing but ignorance proclaiming itself infallible and demanding despotic power. . . ."

On the hypocrisy of leftist politicians:

An atheist was railing against religion, against priests, and against God. "If you keep this up," said one of his listeners, who was not very orthodox himself, "you are going to make a pious man of me."

Similarly, when I hear our callow scribblers, our novelists, our reformers, our perfumed, mincing pamphleteers, gorged with ices and champagne, stuffing their portfolios with gilt-edged securities, or getting richly paid for their tirades against egoism and individualism of our age; when I hear them disclaiming against the harshness of our institutions and bewailing the lot of wage earners and proletarians; when I see them raising to the heavens eyes full of tears at the sight of poverty of the masses—a poverty with which they never have any contact except to paint lucrative pictures of it; I am tempted to tell them: "If you go on like this, you are going to make me indifferent to the fate of the workers."

On taxes:

Do what you will gentlemen; you cannot give money to some without taking it from others. If you absolutely insist on draining the taxpayer dry, well and good; but at least do not treat him like a fool. Do not tell him: "I am taking this money from you to repay you for what I have already taken from you."

On the growth of bureaucracy:

I am a firm believer in the ideas of Malthus [only] when it comes to bureaucrats. For their expansion in numbers and projects is fixed precisely by his principle that the size of the population is determined by the amount of available food. If we vote eight hundred million, we give them two billion; if we give them two billion, they will immediately expand themselves . . . to [devour] the full amount.

On strict constitutional principles as the only proper basis for a legal system:

No society can exist if respect for the law does not . . . prevail; but the surest way to have the laws respected is to make them respectable. When law and morality are in contradiction, the citizen finds himself in the cruel dilemma of either losing his moral sense or losing respect for the law.

On communists:

They do not want a natural society. What they want is an artificial society, which has come forth full-grown from the brain of its inventor. . . . They quarrel over who will mold the human clay, but they agree that there is human clay to mold. Mankind is not in their eyes a living and harmonious being endowed by God Himself with the power to progress and survive but an inert mass that has been waiting for them to give it feeling and life; human nature is not a subject to be studied but a matter on which to perform experiments.

On the state:

Government is the great fiction through which everybody attempts to live at the expense of everybody else.

Bastiat's Enduring Importance

I cannot help but think that it is a great tragedy that so few people read Bastiat today. He has so much to teach us. As House Majority Leader Dick Armey notes,

> [Bastiat] knew that economics is above all about the power of the individual. Although each person has limited knowledge, he has only to do a good job at his specific task to partake in the benefits of others' knowledge and success. He doesn't have to ask the state, "What must I do to prosper?" He decides for himself. Sometimes he fails, of course, but it is an old truth that without failure there can be no success.
>
> Among Bastiat's most important observations was that when "do-everything government" assumes control over things that are properly *our* responsibility, we lose faith in our capacity to make our own decisions.

Nearly two centuries ago, he warned,

> I have seen countries in which the people think that agriculture can make no progress unless the government supports experimental farms; that there will soon be no horses if the government does not provide the studs; that fathers will not have their children educated or will have them taught only immorality, if the government does not decide what is proper for them to learn.

One of Bastiat's greatest fans was Richard Nixon. Now, Nixon wasn't much of a champion of conservatism while he was president, but later in life he had what I believe was a genuine change of heart. He became much more vocal about the need to curb government, and he produced some brilliant books like *Seize the Moment.* In 1993, he even volunteered to provide an endorsement for the revised edition of the biography I had written about Basti-at titled *Free Markets, Free Men.* This is an excerpt from the letter he wrote:

> With the end of the Cold War, democratic and free market principles are triumphing around the world. Yet as the world grows more interdependent, debates over how much exchange—particularly in economics—should be allowed have intensified.
> . . . Bastiat understood two hundred years ago what gives rise to political resistance to free trade. Bastiat had the vision and the courage to stand up for individual liberty, democratic governments, and free markets. . . [his] arguments are as relevant—and correct—today as they were in the nineteenth century.

Vaclav Klaus, until recently the prime minister of the Czech Republic, also contributed an endorsement. He wrote: "This is a book about a great prophet of liberty, the free society, and the free market. History confirms the truth of his brilliant ideas and discloses the fallacies of socialism of all sorts." He closed by reminding the reader, "Still, the struggle between them is never-ending."

Bastiat would have agreed. In fact, in his time he went even further to remind people that those who believe "that the motive force of society is government" are basically admitting that they are sheep and that politicians are the shepherds. In such a world, he concluded, "the responsibility of the government is immense. Good and evil, virtue and vice, equality and inequality, wealth and poverty, all proceed from it. It is entrusted with everything, it undertakes everything, it does everything; hence, it is responsible for everything."

It is a dangerous world Bastiat is describing. Such a world breeds envy, injustice, violence, and revolution, as he was in a position to witness. Near the end of his life, Bastiat predicted, it would be a hard world to escape. "[W]e must wait," he said, "until we have learned by experience—perhaps cruel experience—to trust in the state a little less and in mankind a little more."

I hope that such a day is dawning. I hope that as we are entering a new century, we are entering a new world—one that Bastiat dreamed of and prayed for.

Notes

[1]In the Revolution of 1830, the middle class ousted Charles X, who had sought to reinstitute the "divine right of kings." Soon, they recognized a "Citizen King," Louis Philippe. But this experiment in republican monarchy satisfied no one. Gradually, France slid into socialism. This—combined with bad harvests, epidemics, and political repression—led to the violent Revolutions of 1848 in France, Germany, and Italy. In France at this time, Louis Philippe was overthrown, and the Third Republic was established. In the Third Republic, "The Man on Horseback," Louis Napoleon Bonaparte, came to power. This nephew of the original Bonaparte was named Emperor Napoleon III in 1852; he was deposed in 1871 at end of the Franco-Prussian War.

[2]During the carnage in France in 1848, Bastiat, with no regard for his own health, roamed the streets tending the wounded.

KURT R. LEUBE

F. A. Hayek and the
Many Roads to Serfdom

I

The task to cover "The Essence of Hayek" in a brief space is impossible. Therefore, I can offer you only a sketch of the major stations of Hayek's remarkably long intellectual life, describe his most important works, and summarize a few of his seminal ideas.

Friedrich August von Hayek was born on May 8, 1899, in Vienna into a family that could lay claim to a great academic tradition. His paternal grandfather taught zoology at the University of Vienna, and Franz von Juraschek, his maternal grandfather and a colleague and climbing partner of the famous economist Eugen von Böhm-Bawerk of the Austrian School, was professor of public law at the University of Innsbruck and later became first president of the k.u.k. Statistische Zentralkommission (National Statistical Office of Imperial Austria) in Vienna. His father was a physician and taught plant geography as a *privatdozent* at the University of Vienna. Additionally, the professional careers of his two brothers, as well as his children, reflect the scholarly tradition of the Hayek family. One of his younger brothers became professor of anatomy at the University of Vienna, the other, professor of chemistry at the University of Innsbruck. Hayek's daughter, Christine, became

The material in this essay originally appeared in Kurt R. Leube's biographical introduction to Chiaki Nishiyama and Kurt R. Leube, *The Essence of Hayek* (Stanford: Hoover Institution Press, 1984).

a biologist at the British Museum; his son, Laurence, became a medical doctor specializing in pathology.

In March 1917, Hayek entered the k.u.k army as an artillery officer; in November 1918, he returned to Vienna after being wounded on the Piave front in Italy. In October 1918, while still in service, Hayek was allowed to obtain his gymnasium degree, which enabled him to enroll at the University of Vienna shortly after World War I. Late in November of the same year, he began to study law, preferring to attend the lectures of Friedrich von Riser and Othmar Spann, and courses on psychology and philosophy. Wieser was the other leading economist of the second generation of the Austrian School of economics; Spann was a relatively obscure figure in the fields of economics and sociology. During this time, Hayek took a great deal of interest in the writings of Ernst Mach, the famous physicist and philosopher of science, which had a lasting influence on his philosophical and psychological thinking. After obtaining a law degree in November 1921, Hayek decided to continue studying political science and in March 1923 received a doctorate in political science (*Doctor rerum politicarum*).

During the cold winter of 1919–20, when the University of Vienna had to be closed for lack of heating material, Hayek spent a few intellectually stimulating months in Zurich, where he came across Moritz Schlick's influential *General Theory of Knowledge*.

In those days, long since gone, when Vienna had a lively intellectual climate, Hayek, still a student in 1921, had helped to found a small circle of young social scientists who met regularly and informally to present papers and discuss problems of mutual interest. More than half of the participants later became world-famous, such as the economists Gottfried von Haberler, Fritz Machlup, and Oscar Morgenstern; the sociologist Alfred Schutz; the political philosopher Eric Voegelin; the historian Friedrich Engel-Janosi; the art historians Otto Benesch and Johannes Wilde, the musicologist Emanuel Winternitz; the philosopher Felix Kaufmann; the psychoanalyst Robert Waelder; and the mathematician Carl Menger. A few years later, most of the participants also joined the famous "Mises seminar," which Ludwig von Mises had established in his office at the Vienna Chamber of Commerce. This *privatseminar*, conducted by Mises, was more or less the nucleus of the fourth generation of the Austrian School of economics, the most important representative of which is Friedrich A. Hayek.

In October 1921, Hayek took a job in the *Osterreichische Abrechnungsamt* (a government office for settling prewar debts), one of whose directors was Mises. This was the beginning of a most fruitful intellectual relationship. In March 1923, Hayek undertook at his own risk a visit to New York in order to become a research assistant to Jeremiah W. Jenks of New York University, a leading authority on trusts and a professor of government. While in New York, Hayek attended the lectures at Columbia University of Wesley C. Mitchell on the history of economic thought and the last seminar of John B. Clark, in which Clark read a paper on the value of money.

Greatly stimulated and with an intense interest in the newly developed techniques and the new forms of monetary policy with which the Federal Reserve System was experimenting, Hayek returned to Vienna in May 1924. He then published some articles in this field and began the research in monetary theory that paved the way to his later work.[1]

In the summer of 1926, he married Hella Fritsch in Vienna.

II

Stimulated by the advanced techniques for analyzing time series and forecasting industrial fluctuations that had just been developed in the United States, Hayek, together with Mises, founded the Austrian Institute for Business Cycle Research in 1927. Under Hayek's directorship until 1931, this institute soon became a European center for trade cycle research. As a result of some penetrating work on monetary theory, in February 1929, in one of the institute's periodicals, Hayek published a comment that anticipated ideas that he was later to develop more fully on the monetary aspects of the investment cycle. Hayek thus became the first to predict the coming crisis in the United States.

In 1929, Hayek presented his *habilitation* lecture, "*Geldtheorie und Konjunkturtheorie*," which under this title was later published as his first book.[2] His test lecture, "The Paradox of Savings," led to an invitation from Professor Lionel Robbins to visit the London

School of Economics. Hayek accepted, and in 1931 delivered four lectures on "Prices and Production."[3] That same year, he was offered a professorship at the London School of Economics and became the first foreign professor at this then unique stronghold of theoretical economic research.

From those early days at the London School of Economics, a deep and stimulating friendship with Lord Robbins originated. Hayek was to spend the next eighteen years in England and to become virtually the only influential intellectual opponent of John Maynard Keynes. Their points of disagreement were often to turn into heated debates.

III

"When the definitive history of economic analysis during the 1930s comes to be written, a leading character in the drama (it was quite a drama) will be Professor Hayek. . . . [T]here was a time when the new theories of Hayek were the principal rival of the new theories of Keynes. Who was right, Keynes or Hayek?"[4]

During the course of these heated controversies, Hayek was asked to review Keynes' recently published *Treatise on Money*, and Keynes to evaluate Hayek's *Prices and Production*. Hayek's powerful review was published in two parts; Keynes replied to the first part only, mainly criticizing *Prices and Production*.[5] (Soon afterward Keynes changed his basic ideas.) Hayek reacted with a brilliant rejoinder[6] and also published a reply to Pierro Sraffa's review of his *Prices and Production*.[7] This major intellectual controversy, in a way comparable only to the *methodenstreit* between the Historical School and the Austrian School, involved all eminent economists. In addition to his extensive reviews, replies, and reactions, Hayek in the years 1931–37 published some ten essays on capital theory, investment theory, and the theory of savings, all of them crucial to his later work.[8]

The most striking characteristic of the "Austrian" trade cycle and monetary theory, as represented by Hayek, is the idea that any shortage of capital immediately causes a crisis. Classical economic theory never elucidated what causes such a shortage. Hayek's theory is that overinvestment leads to a capital shortage, which unavoidably leads to a decline in investment and hence to the loss of a part

of the real capital, produced because of the overly high investment rate. The central thesis of Hayek's trade cycle theory, in sharp
contrast to that of Keynes, maintains that the monetary factors are
the original ones and that the cycle arises from real alterations in
the structure of production.

When, in 1935, Gottfried von Haberler drew Hayek's attention to Karl Popper's *The Logic of Scientific Discovery*, Hayek discovered thoughts similar to those he had worked out in the
introduction to his *Collectivist Economic Planning*. But Hayek found
Popper's hypothetical–deductive approach to scientific explanation
much more satisfactory than his own interpretation. This was the
beginning of a mutually stimulating influence and a long-lasting
friendship.

In 1936, Hayek invited Popper to the London School of Economics to read his *Poverty of Historicism* in the seminar Hayek held
together with Lionel Robbins, Ernst Gombrich, G.L.S. Shackle,
and others.

Even as Hayek's interest in technical economics finally cul-
minated in the publication of *The Pure Theory of Capital* (1942),
which the late Fritz Machlup, one of Hayek's world-famous contemporaries and his old friend, rated as "the first full treatise on
capital since Böhm-Bawerk's *Positive Theory*," Hayek devoted himself more and more to the sociophilosophical problems of economics. In a lecture entitled "Economics and Knowledge,"
published in 1937,[9] Hayek first introduced his basic idea of the
"division of knowledge." Here he criticized Mises' a priorism and
argued very convincingly that only the pure logic of choice was an
a priori discipline, whereas the market process itself was an empirical one. This essay, originally presented as a presidential address
to the London Economic Club, clearly shows Hayek's turn toward
the more philosophical concerns of the economic sciences.

The London School of Economics, then in Cambridge because
of the bombing of London, granted Hayek a D.Sc. (econ.) in 1941.

IV

When the second edition of Ludwig von Mises' *Gemeinwirtschaft*
(*Socialism*) initiated the big debate on socialism in the 1930s, with
Mises and Hayek on one side and Oskar Lange and Henry Douglas

Dickinson on the other, Hayek contributed three path-breaking and still extremely relevant essays. These thoughts, later assembled in *Individualism and Economic Order*, demolished the theories of the so-called market socialism.[10] His intensive engagement with the various insoluble problems of socialism, the terror of fascism, and the outbreak of World War II made Hayek write a book that, when first published in 1944, was a revelation for those who desperately wanted freedom. This best-seller of the immediate postwar years, significantly dedicated "to the Socialists of all parties," became a ray of hope, especially in Europe. An excellent condensation appeared in the *Reader's Digest* and made Hayek world-famous overnight. Still in print and of great relevance, as are all of his works, it celebrated its fortieth anniversary in 1984.

The Road to Serfdom,[11] which even Joseph A. Schumpeter called a book written by "one of the most eminent economists of our time,"[12] has been translated into some sixteen languages, including recently Polish and Russian. This stimulating book was Hayek's warning against not only the dangerous totalitarianism then rampant under the mantle of socialism and fascism but also against the risks of welfare statism and welfare dictatorship. In the philosophical parts of this courageous book, Hayek does not hesitate to demonstrate the links between socialisms of all stripes and fascism. Hayek shows that no variety of socialism, no matter what its name or however modified by adjectives, carries with it any adequate provisions for the preservation of political and economic freedom. The popular view of the convergence of economic systems, quite widespread in the German-speaking world and invoked on more than one occasion, is rooted in an economic error, as Hayek impressively illustrates. He also concludes that efforts to establish a so-called "Third Way," often suggested in recent times, are a totally unsatisfactory experiment and an attempt to link principles of economic orders that in reality exclude one another.

In this period, Hayek became increasingly interested in methodological questions concerning the social sciences in general, and he particularly concentrated his efforts on refuting the ideas of a dangerous train of thought—scientism.

To this very important field, he contributed three outstanding essays, which were first published in *Economica* for 1941 and 1942–44, respectively. These essays in intellectual history are crucial for understanding Hayek's work as a whole and are collected in his book *The Counter-Revolution of Science*.[13] They trace the roots of scientism to the *Ecole Polytechnique* and the early socialists influenced by Saint-Simon. Their hubris-filled thoughts lead in a direct line to contemporary late Marxism. Here, we find the origin of the idea of scientism, which claims to be able to "foresee the future progress of the human race, accelerate and direct it. But to establish laws that will enable us to predict the future, history must cease to be a history of individuals and must become a history of the masses."[14] This statement of Hayek's makes the illogic of a mechanistic interpretation of historical evolution and the collectivistic view of history obvious. It is like the man in the well-known German fable who tries to pull himself out of a bog by his own hair. Hayek shows that the pretense of knowledge is an error fatal to individual freedom.

In the second part of *Studies on the Abuse of Reason,* Hayek systematically treats a comprehensive problem that, at first glance, seems to be a somewhat remote subject. To the contrary, however, it is the source of all the methodological confusions of the social sciences. Hayek accuses scientism of being "a very prejudiced approach which, before it has considered its subject, claims to know what is the most appropriate way of investigating it."[15]

In the third part of this book, written later from notes collected at the same time as those for the other parts, Hayek points out with striking clarity that whereas the ideas of Hume and Voltaire, of Adam Smith and Kant, produced the liberalism of the nineteenth century, those of Hegel and Comte, Feuerbach and Marx, produced the totalitarianism of the twentieth century. (Note: throughout this essay, the word "liberalism" is used in the classical sense.)

V

With the publication of his very influential essay "The Use of Knowledge in Society,"[16] Hayek refined an argument previously treated in his "Economics and Knowledge." He once joked that he had made "one discovery and two inventions" and believes this work, in which the leading role of the "division of knowledge" is clearly developed, to be his most important discovery. According to Hayek, what counts in this connection is not scientific knowledge but the unorganized knowledge of the particular circumstances of time and place. The central problem of economics is how the spontaneous interaction of a number of people, each possessing only certain bits of knowledge, creates circumstances that could be brought about only by somebody who possessed the combined knowledge of all these individuals. In our society, in which the knowledge of the relevant facts is dispersed among many people, the price system is the only mechanism that communicates information. The price mechanism is a system of signals that puts us in the situation of adapting to circumstances and experiences of which we know nothing. Our whole modern order and well-being rest on the possibility of adapting to processes that we do not know.

Hayek's "Individualism: True and False," the twelfth Finlay Lecture at the University College, Dublin, is a masterpiece in the history of ideas.[17] Here, he relentlessly exposes the whole confused state of thought regarding the terms of philosophical individualism.

Still in London, Hayek in 1947 organized a conference for like-minded liberal scientists, journalists, and politicians in a hotel on Mont Pelerin near Vevey, Switzerland. From this first important meeting of Hayek's contemporaries, called together to exchange ideas about the nature of a free society and about the ways and means of strengthening its intellectual support, derived the exclusive Mont Pelerin Society. Hayek served for over twelve years as president and, when he resigned from this office in 1960, was elected honorary president; he is still the society's intellectual mentor. This scholarly association boasts hundreds of members, drawn from nearly all the states of the free world.

During his almost twenty years in England, Hayek spent some time in Gibraltar doing field research in order to prepare his "Report of the Changes in the Cost of Living in Gibraltar, 1939–44, and on Wages and Salaries."

VI

Due to the outstanding success of his best-known book, *The Road to Serfdom,* Hayek was invited to the United States to address countless audiences in many locales.

In December 1949, he resigned from the London School of Economics, spent the spring quarter at the University of Arkansas, Fayetteville, and in October 1950, accepted a professorship in social and moral sciences at the University of Chicago. That same year, he married his second wife, Helene Bitterlich, in Vienna.

At the University of Chicago, he associated with such figures as Frank Knight, Milton Friedman, and Aaron Director; somewhat later George Stigler joined this outstanding group of liberal scholars.

In this intellectually stimulating climate—many prominent scholars from different fields attended his seminar as regular members or as visitors—Hayek published a great number of important works. I shall concentrate here on surveying the most important ones only.

In his inaugural lecture, "Comte and Hegel," Hayek returned to the subject of scientism. He published the substance of this lecture as the third part of his *Counter-Revolution of Science: Studies on the Abuse of Reason.*

The Sensory Order (1952) once again shows Hayek's continuing interest in psychology. This book contains some of his most original and important ideas and thoughts[18] and, as such, deserves much more attention than it has received to date. It is a discourse in pure psychology, the preliminary thoughts and notes dating back to the early 1920s, when Hayek spent a few months in Zurich and was still uncertain whether to become a psychologist or an economist. This ambitious book was highly acclaimed by some eminent experts and has recently become the central topic of scholarly conferences.

With the penetrating essay "History and Politics," written as the introduction to *Capitalism and the Historians*, which Hayek edited, he initiated a long-overdue critical approach to economic history and the treatment of capitalism.[19]

His deep concern with social, political, and legal philosophy led to the work that is regarded as his magnum opus. Hayek finished the typescript of his monumental *The Constitution of Liberty* on his sixtieth birthday.[20] In this milestone in the literature of social philosophy, he developed the ethical, anthropological, legal, and economic bases of a liberal economic and social order.

While for most modern social philosophers the chief aim of politics consists in setting up an ideal social order through utopian reforms, Hayek sees its main task as that of finding rules to enable men with different values and convictions to live together. These rules should be so constructed as to permit each individual to fulfill his aims. In this famous book, Hayek further develops his unique idea of spontaneous order, through which things are brought about that no individual can comprehend. In this massive contribution to the persistent question of the limits of state action, Hayek composed one of the great books of our times.

VII

After twelve years of exceptionally successful lecturing at the University of Chicago, Hayek accepted a call to professorship of political economy at the University of Freiburg (Germany) in the spring of 1962. He assumed the chair of his old friend Walter Eucken, who had established the famous ORDO School there shortly after World War II. This typically German-liberal school provided some of the theoretical base for the so-called German Economic Miracle.

In Hayek's first Freiburg period, which lasted seven years, besides translations, he published two books, five brochures, and some thirty articles. Only the most important among these will briefly be described.

With his essay "Competition as a Discovery Procedure,"[21] Hayek contributed some major new insights of lasting significance to the somewhat deadlocked area of the theory of competition. Although the successor of Walter Eucken, who might be considered the head of the Freiburger School, Hayek never changed his characteristically Austrian point of view. To the contrary, he built the basis for the revival of the Austrian School, now so visible, especially in the Anglo-American academic world.

During this time, Hayek repeatedly returned to technical economics and refined, so to speak, as a by-product of his social-philosophical work, some of his arguments on pure economic theory.[22]

In 1964, Rikkyo University in Tokyo awarded him an honorary doctorate. There he delivered his influential lecture "Kinds of Rationalism," which reveals his preoccupation with themes he would much later publish in the three-volume *Law, Legislation, and Liberty*.

Hayek included his inaugural lecture at Freiburg, "The Economy, Science, and Politics," in his famous *Studies in Philosophy, Politics, and Economics*,[23] which he dedicated to his old friend Sir Karl Popper. this volume contains an important selection of his work dating from the early 1950s to the mid-1960s.

Hayek's lecture on Bernard Mandeville,[24] delivered to the British Academy in 1966, again reveals him as a master in the history of ideas.

During his years in Freiburg, he was invited by the Austrian government to discuss the possibility of taking over the presidency of the Austrian National Bank, which he refused in order to complete his monumental *Law, Legislation, and Liberty*. It seems to be typical of Hayek's uncompromising devotion to scholarship that he left a country the moment he was offered a public position. This was the case in the late 1920s in Austria, after almost twenty years in England, after twelve years in the United States, and after seven years in Freiburg.

Some of the preliminary studies to his *Law, Legislation, and Liberty* were collected in a German book titled *Freiburger Studien: Gesammelte Aufsatze* (1969).

Hayek contributed two very important articles to the *International Encyclopedia of the Social Sciences*, one on the Austrian School and one on Carl Menger. Both of these became noted for their detailed treatment of these subjects.

VIII

After becoming professor emeritus at the University of Freiburg in 1969, Hayek accepted a visiting professorship at the recently reestablished University of Salzburg and returned to his native Austria after spending almost forty years abroad. But a number of factors made this temporary move to Salzburg somewhat disappointing. One of them was the fact that at this university economics was taught as a subsidiary to law, and therefore the faculty's and the students' level did not meet his academic expectations. Also the Anglo-American scholarly tradition seemed more distant than in Freiburg.

In spite of his rather poor health and his intellectual isolation, he published a number of significant works. Again, I shall confine myself to mentioning only the most interesting ones.

In his famous essay, "The Errors of Constructivism,"[25] delivered as an inaugural lecture at the University of Salzburg, Hayek developed the idea of constructivism and introduced this term into sociophilosophical discussion, in order to depict the errors of "social engineering" and "welfare statism." This preliminary study points toward Hayek's later fully developed theory of evolution.

Due to the undeniable fact that the liberal aim of a free society runs the risk of collapsing because of a misconstruction and misunderstanding of the democratic ideal, Hayek made a striking proposal for reform and reconstruction of democratic institutions. In the fourth Wincott Memorial Lecture,[26] Hayek for the first time criticized democratic institutions for enforcing mainly egalitarian targets and proposed a quite unorthodox model constitution in order to limit the powers of government. This important idea, which lately has become the subject of a very lively political discussion, is one of Hayek's intellectual inventions. He [later] elaborated on this subject.[27]

In 1973, he published the first of the three volumes of *Law, Legislation, and Liberty*.[28] In this first volume, subtitled *Rules and Order*, Hayek refined his argument that a spontaneous order and an organization are distinct and that their distinctiveness is closely related to the two different kinds of rules that prevail in them. Special attention should be drawn to his treatment of "principles and expediencies" in politics in this major work on political philosophy.[29]

In May 1974, on the occasion of his seventy-fifth birthday, Hayek was awarded an honorary doctorate by the University of Salzburg.

The totally unexpected award of the Nobel Prize in Economics in the late fall of 1974 forced Hayek to write his courageous Nobel lecture, "The Pretense of Knowledge," which was composed in a very short span of time.[30] In this essay, written during a visit to Japan, Hayek again successfully refuted Keynesian economics, basing himself on his concept of the division of knowledge. Ironically enough, he had to share the Nobel Prize with an adversary, Gunnar Myrdal, one of the founders of the Swedish welfare state. Nevertheless, this award to some extent initiated the long-overdue counter-offensive against Keynesianism and strengthened the revival of the Austrian School of economics.

His second important invention originated in Salzburg, where he prepared an address titled "International Money" for the Geneva Gold and Monetary Conference. Hayek's unusual proposal, which he later developed in detail in his *Denationalization of Money*,[31] aroused a fierce discussion in the field of monetary theory and, of course, contributed to the debate over interventionism. He seems to have been developing this idea since its first mention in *The Constitution of Liberty*.[32] Hayek argues that inflation can be avoided only if the monopolistic power of issuing money is taken away from government and state authorities and the task given to private industry in order to promote competition in currencies.

Three years after publication of the first volume of *Law, Legislation, and Liberty*, Hayek published the second volume, subtitled *The Mirage of Social Justice*.[33] In this fundamental analysis, he explains why the misleading term "social justice" has meaning in a strict organization only and not in the spontaneous order of a free society. The dangerous and narcotic term "social or distributive justice" is meaningless in, and totally incompatible with, any free or "open" society.

Hayek regained his old form in the summer of 1974, just prior to his vacation, which he and his wife always spent in a tiny village high in the Tyrolian Alps.

IX

Somewhat disappointed with Salzburg, as mentioned above, Hayek decided to leave his native Austria for Freiburg in early 1977, reluctantly leaving behind his unique library of some seven thousand volumes, which he had sold for financial reasons to the University of Salzburg when he assumed the visiting professorship.

Back in Freiburg, he published a third volume of collected essays as his *New Studies in Philosophy, Politics, Economics, and the History of Ideas*.[34]

Three years after the publication of the second volume of his *Law, Legislation, and Liberty*, he concluded this trilogy with the final volume, *The Political Order of a Free People*.[35] Hayek here refined his proposal for reform and reconstruction of democracy. The predominant tendency of liberal democratic institutions, in which the same representative body sets up "rules of just conduct" and directs government, necessarily creates a gradual transformation of the spontaneous order of a free society, which in the long run unavoidably leads to a totalitarian system dominated by "coalitions of organized interests."

After moving back to Freiburg, Hayek published numerous other works. I mention here only two of the more outstanding examples. In 1977, he presented an enlarged German translation of *Denationalization of Money—The Argument Refined: An analysis of the Theory and Practice of Concurrent Currencies*. And in May 1978, he gave the Hobhouse Lecture at the London School of Economics. Titled "The Three Sources of Human Value," this lecture treated "the destruction of indispensable values by scientific error." It was published as the epilogue to the third volume of *Law, Legislation, and Liberty*.

In the late 1970s, Hayek became attracted to the idea of a public confrontation with socialist thinkers and wanted to organize a conference in Paris that would bring together some of his liberal colleagues with contemporary left-wing intellectuals. In order to structure this "Paris Challenge," as we have called it, he laid down some twelve points of discussion, which have exploded into an unmanageable manuscript of well over 1,200 pages. In order to bring the text into a publishable form it has regretfully been massively edited and was published in 1989 and advertised as the culmination of his work. *The Fatal Conceit* (1989) is his last, but by far not his best, book. This work is in my opinion not the proper start to get acquainted with Hayek's social philosophy.[36]

X

Hayek passed away in 1992. He left behind a rich body of work that arose from a comprehensive approach to various intellectual disciplines that condition and influence one another. We owe to

Hayek's tireless labors not only important contributions to pure economic theory and profound studies in the philosophy of science, the history of ideas, and political philosophy, but also the most penetrating insights into social philosophy and psychology.

His work in pure economic theory was pioneering and is still very influential in the further development of theories of the trade cycle, monetary factors, and capital. Within the history of ideas, his careful studies of Mandeville, Mill, Menger, Ricardo, Wieser, and the Austrian School are intellectual masterpieces.

His achievements in the philosophy of science and in economics are widely acknowledged. His books have become classics of the literature of liberty. The better part of his work has been translated into the major languages of the world. It seems to be almost impossible to count all his memberships in distinguished societies and academies, his honorary doctorates, his honors, awards, and orders. His brilliant writing style with clear arguments and honest scholarship, his command of the field is simply unequaled. As a scholar, a patient, fatherly friend, and mountaineering partner, he came as close to the vanishing ideal of a gentleman as human frailty will ever permit.

Most important, he lived to see his ideas triumph—the Berlin Wall fell in the late 1980s and Soviet-style communism collapsed completely in the early 1990s. The challenges to freedom around the world are still monumental, and socialism is still an attractive fantasy in the minds of many academics and bureaucrats, but, thanks to Hayek, the "road to serfdom" now is plainly marked for all to see.

Notes

[1] Cf. "Das Stabilisierungsproblem in Goldwahrungslandern," *Zeitschrift fur Volkswirtschaft und Sozialpolitik*, Vienna, n.s. 4 (1924); "Die Wahrungspolitik der Vereinigten Staaten seit der Uberwindung der Krise von 1920," in ibid., n.s. 5 (1925); "Das amerikanische Bankwesen seit der Reform von 1914," D*er osterreichische Volkswirt, Vienna*, no. 17 (1926); and "Die Bedeutung der Konjunkturforschung fur das Wirtschaftsleben," in ibid., no. 5 (1926).

[2] *Geldtheorie und Konjunkturtheorie* (Vienna and Leipzig, 1929); 2nd ed. (Munich, 1976); English trans.: *Monetary Theory and the Trade Cycle* (London, 1933; New York, 1933 and 1966).

[3]See Chapter 2 of Chiaki Nishiyama and Kurt R. Leube, *The Essence of Hayek* (Stanford: Hoover Institution Press, 1984).

[4]Sir John Hicks, "The Hayek Story," in *Critical Essays in Monetary Theory* (Oxford, 1967), 203.

[5]"Reflections on the Pure Theory of Money of Mr. J. M. Keynes," Part 1, *Economica* 11, no. 33 (August 1931): 270–95; Part 2, *Economica* 12 (February 1932): 22–44.

[6]"The Pure Theory of Money: A Rejoinder to Mr. Keynes," *Economica* 11, no. 34 (November 1931): 398–413

[7]"Money and Capital: A Reply to Mr. Sraffa," *Economic Journal* 42 (June 1932): 237–49.

[8]See Profits, *Interest and Investment* (London, 1939; Clifton, NJ, 1969 and 1975); *Monetary Nationalism and International Stability* (Geneva, 1937; London, 1937; New York, 1964, 1971, and 1974); "Uber neutrales Geld," *Zeitschrift fur Nationalokonomie*, Vienna, 4 (1933); and "On the Relationship Between Investment and Output," *Economic Journal* 44 (1934).

[9]"Economics and Knowledge," *Economica*, n.s. 4 (1937); reprinted in *Individualism and Economic Order*; see also Chapter 11 of Nishiyama and Leube.

[10]For bibliographical details, see Chapters 4, 7, and 11 of Nishiyama and Leube.

[11]*The Road to Serfdom* (London, 1944, 1945, 1960; Chicago, 1944, 1945, 1969; German trans.: Zurich, 1945 and 1952; 6th ed., Munich, 1976).

[12]*Journal of Political Economy* 54 (1946): 269.

[13]*The Counter-Revolution of Science: Studies on the Abuse of Reason* (Glencoe, IL, 1952 and 1964; Indianapolis, 1979; German trans.: 1959; 2nd enl. ed., Munich, 1979).

[14]Ibid., 192.

[15]Ibid., 24.

[16]See Chapter 11 of Nishiyama and Leube.

[17]See Chapter 7 of Nishiyama and Leube.

[18]For bibliographical details, see Chapter 12 of Nishiyama and Leube.

[19]For bibliographical details, see Chapter 8 of Nishiyama and Leube.

[20]For bibliographical details, see Chapters 15 and 18 of Nishiyama and Leube.

[21]See Chapter 13 of Nishiyama and Leube.

[22]See "Alte Wahrheiten und neue Irrtumer," in *Freiburger Studien* (Tubingen, 1969); and "Three Elucidations of the 'Ricardo Effect,'" *Journal of Political Economy*, 77 (March–April 1969).

[23]See Chapter 8 of Nishiyama and Leube.

[24]See Chapter 9 of Nishiyama and Leube.

[25]See Chapter 9 of Nishiyama and Leube.

[26]*Economic Freedom and Representative Government*, Occasional Papers 39 (London: Institute for Economic Affairs, 1973).

[27]See Chapters 19 and 21 of Nishiyama and Leube.

[28]For bibliographical details, see Chapter 16 of Nishiyama and Leube.

[29]See Chapter 16 of Nishiyama and Leube.

[30]See Chapter 14 of Nishiyama and Leubee.

[31]*Denationalization of Money: An Analysis of the Theory and Practice of Concurrent Currencies,* Hobart Paper Special 70 (London, 1978).

[32]*The Constitution of Liberty* (Chicago: University of Chicago Press, 1952), 520 n2.

[33]For bibliographical details, see Chapter 5 of Nishiyama and Leube.

[34]For bibliographical details, see Chapter 9 of Nishiyama and Leube.

[35]For bibliographical details, see Chapter 21 of Nishiyama and Leube.

[36]Cf. Chapter 17 of Nishiyama and Leube.

RICHARD M. EBELING

A Rational Economist in an
Irrational Age: Ludwig von Mises

Every period of history is indelibly stamped with the impression of the dominant ideas of its time. It is for this reason that students of history sometimes claim that the nineteenth century began in 1815 with the downfall of Napoleon and ended with the advent of the Great War in August 1914. The dominant ideas of this century (ideas that owed their origins to eighteenth-century ideas about the natural order, the rights of man, and representative government) were the ideas of classical liberalism. Moreover, it was due to these ideas that the nineteenth century saw the rise of great political and economic reform movements that liberated man from autocracy and mercantilism and that gave many people in Europe and North America more limited government, more free enterprise, more peace and tranquillity than had ever been known before.

Our century, which had its dawn with the opening shots of the First World War, really ended in 1991 with the collapse of the Soviet Union. It was dominated by ideas of a radically different sort. It can legitimately be claimed that the twentieth century was a counter-revolution against the "classical liberalism" of the previous century. Wherever we looked, the state grew in power. Constitutionally limited government was perverted into a process of interest-group plundering through the mechanisms of seemingly unlimited democracy or totalitarian dictatorships. The free market economy was either strangled in a web of controls and regulations or extinguished under the blows of various forms of socialist central planning. Free trade and international peace were replaced with war, conflict, genocide, and mass terror.

The totalitarian variants of the counter-revolution against classical liberalism symbolically came to an end with the collapse of the Soviet Union in 1991. Thus, the demise of the most radical and extreme form of collectivism can be said to have marked the intellectual end of the twentieth century. What these collectivist demons held in store for mankind was prophesied in 1919, only a year after the end of the First World War, by Austrian School economist Ludwig von Mises. In a much neglected, but profoundly insightful book titled *Nation, State, and Economy*, Mises analyzed the causes and consequences of the First World War. Toward the end of the book, he warned,

> With the World War mankind got into a crisis with which nothing that happened before in history can be compared. There were great wars before; flourishing states were annihilated, whole peoples exterminated. All that can in no way be compared with what is now occurring before our eyes. . . . War has become more fearful and destructive than ever before because it is now waged with all the means of the highly developed technique that the free economy has created. Bourgeois civilization has built railroads and electric power plants, has invented explosives and airplanes, in order to create wealth. [Statism] has placed the tools of peace in the service of destruction. With modern means it would be easy to wipe out humanity at one blow. In horrible madness Caligula wished that the entire Roman people had *one* head so that he could strike it off. The civilization of the twentieth century has made it possible for the raving madness of the modern [statists] to realize similar bloody dreams. By pressing a button one can expose thousands to destruction.[1]

Mises' audience was the German-speaking people of Central Europe who had suffered great losses of life and wealth during the war and who were now facing the burden of the Treaty of Versailles, with its imposition of heavy reparations payments to the victors and its significant transfers of German territory to surrounding countries. He told his German readers that, in facing their future, they had two alternatives. One was to plot revenge, plan for a second world war, and make each individual subservient to the political goals of conquest and domination. If Germany followed this path, Mises said, "A new war that Germany might wage could easily . . . end with the complete annihilation of the German people." The other path was to renounce war, conquest, and collectivism. He reminded them:

> The second course that the German people can take is that of completely turning away from imperialism. To strive for reconstruction only through productive labor, to make possible the development of all powers of the individual and of the nation as a whole by full freedom at home—that is the way that leads back to life. . . . The Germans . . . will better serve their [interests] if they strive for democracy and self-government. . . . Never has the German people sunk so low as today. If it is now to rise again, then it can no longer strive to make the whole great at the expense of individuals but rather must strive for a durable foundation of the well-being of the whole on the basis of the well-being of individuals. It must switch from the collectivistic policy that it has followed so far to an individualistic one.[2]

In the twentieth century, Germany and many other countries around the world chose to follow the collectivist path. Whether in the extreme forms of the Nazi and Soviet regimes or the more moderate forms of the interventionist–welfare state, governments have dominated man and society in our times. They have chosen domestic and foreign plunder as avenues to wealth and power. The consequences have been all around us our entire lives: fascist and communist totalitarianism, the Great Depression, the Second World War, disastrous experiments in socialist planning and control, the growth of the taxing and spending state, the regulated economy, and the welfare state.

Mises' Life and Contributions

From before the First World War until his death in 1973, Ludwig von Mises spoke for reason and rationality in a world that was caught in the grip of irrational dreams—dreams of wealth through the destruction of war, freedom through the mechanisms of oppression and terror, human harmony through group conflicts and mass murder, and greater prosperity through confiscation of property and control over people's lives.

In place of these irrationalities, Mises developed what he called a theory of "human action" and social cooperation through the peaceful relationships of the market economy. He based his theory on the intellectual foundations laid by the economists who had come before him. He placed great emphasis, for example, on the lasting contributions of the classical economists of the eighteenth and nineteenth centuries, especially on their discovery of the workings of a "spontaneous market order," independent of and superior to any system of government design, control, or command. He also believed that several of the classical economists had pointed in the right direction toward an understanding of the epistemological and methodological foundations of economic science.[3]

An equally important influence on Mises were the contributions of the Austrian School economists who preceded him, especially those of Carl Menger, Eugen von Böhm-Bawerk, and Friedrich von Wieser. From these men, Mises adopted and developed the theories of "subjective value and marginal utility," the theory of "production and interest," and the theory of "costs as opportunities forgone."[4]

Born in 1881 in Lemberg, Austria-Hungary,[5] Mises studied at the University of Vienna and graduated in 1906 with a doctorate in jurisprudence. He began working for the Austrian Chamber of Commerce and Industry as an economic analyst in 1909, a full-time position he retained until 1934. Beginning in 1913, he taught at the University of Vienna as a *privatdozent* (an unsalaried lecturer), through which he influenced an entire generation of young Austrian economists. He also formed a *privatseminar* (a private seminar) beginning in 1920, which met twice a month from October to June at his Chamber of Commerce office; the members included economists, sociologists, political scientists, philosophers, and historians, many of whom became leading figures in their respective disciplines.[6]

In 1926, Mises organized the founding of the Austrian Institute for Business Cycle Research. Friedrich A. Hayek served as the first director, and Oskar Morgenstern soon joined the staff as a researcher. The Institute rapidly acquired international recognition for its analytical and statistical studies on Austrian and Central European economic trends, often preparing reports for the

League of Nations. Until 1934, Mises served as Acting (Executive) Vice President of the Institute.

Mises also was a prominent participant in the Austrian Economic Society, the German-based Association for Social Policy, the European Free Trade Association, and the International Rotary Club. He was frequently invited to deliver lectures before various industrial associations and at universities throughout Central and Western Europe. He also often wrote articles for the Austrian press, analyzing the events and trends in economic policy.

In 1934, Mises accepted a position as Professor of International Economic Relations at the Graduate Institute of International Studies in Geneva, Switzerland, a position he held until July 1940, when, as an exile from the hostile environment of Nazi-occupied Europe, he left for the United States. For several years he had difficulty in finding a teaching position at an American university. Finally, in 1945, he was appointed as a visiting professor in the Graduate School of Business Administration at New York University. He retained this "visiting" status at NYU until he retired at the age of 89 in 1969. At NYU, Mises attracted a new generation of students who helped bring about a revival of the Austrian School of economics in the United States beginning in the 1960s and 1970s. He died on October 10, 1973, at the age of 92.

What gained Mises an international reputation was a series of brilliant books that not merely broke new ground in various areas of economic theory and policy, but also challenged the collectivist and interventionist biases of his time. The most important among his many writings are *The Theory of Money and Credit* (1912; 2nd ed., 1924); *Socialism, An Economic and Sociological Analysis* (1922; 2nd ed., 1932); *Liberalism* (1927); *Critique of Interventionism* (1929); *Epistemological Problems of Economics* (1933); *Nationalökonomie* (1940); *Bureaucracy* (1944); *Omnipotent Government* (1944); *Human Action, A Treatise on Economics* (1949; 3rd ed., 1966); *Planning for Freedom* (1952); *The Anti-Capitalistic Mentality* (1956); *Theory and History* (1957); *The Ultimate Foundations of Economic Science* (1962); and *The Historical Setting of the Austrian School of Economics* (1969). There appeared, posthumously, his memoirs written in 1940, *Notes and Recollections* (1978), and most recently another previously unpublished work originally written in 1940, *Interventionism: An Economic Analysis*

(1998). And collections of some of his essays have been published under the titles *Money, Method and the Market Process* (1990) and *Economic Freedom and Interventionism* (1990).

The Rationality and Logic of Human Action

To fully appreciate a writer and his work, it is important to recall the historical and intellectual context in which he developed and argued his ideas. This is especially true for a fair interpretation of Mises' conception of human action and the premises on which it was based. From the perspective of the modern philosophy of science —with its insistence on never assuming anything, except the tentativeness and uncertainty of human knowledge—some of Mises' phrases seem misplaced or anachronistic. Nowadays, methodologists and philosophers of science wince when they read Mises' statements that our knowledge in economics is a priori, or prior to any empirical experience and has the status of "apodictic certainty."[7]

In the 1920s through the 1940s, a strange set of ideas had gained hold of the minds of intellectuals, especially on the European continent. Particularly in the German-speaking world in which Mises lived and worked there had occurred what he referred to as a "revolt against reason."[8] The Nazi-type of philosophy of man and science rejected the existence of a universal reason to guide man's understanding of the physical world and of man himself. It also assumed that German science, and the reasoning upon which it was based, were different from Jewish, Hungarian, Czech, or Polish science, because German reason was guided by the special racial group characteristics unique to the German people. German logic was different from Jewish, Hungarian, Czech, or Polish logic, and, therefore, German thought and reality were distinct from Jewish, Hungarian, Czech, or Polish thought and reality. Logic, reason, and reality were "in the blood" and stored as the racial heritage of the group to which the individual belonged.[9] Only the *Führer*, the embodiment of the spirit and soul of the racial group, through the power of his will, could envision and guide the destiny of the German people.

Marxism offered merely a different version of the same idea. The consciousness, and therefore the reasoning of the individual, was defined by the class to which he belonged. The material methods of production determined the property relationships of the society (the "superstructure" of the society); and the relationships that men had to property ownership defined them as belonging to one class or another. This, in turn, determined the logic appropriate for each individual in the context of the requirements and "interests" of his class. Only the select few who were part of the leadership of the revolutionary cadre had the capacity to understand what the "laws of history" required of each individual, as a member of a class, in that irreconcilable conflict between classes that would eventually generate the inevitable triumph of the socialist future to come.

A third strain of thought during these decades was that of "positivism," which argued that the only reality was that of the physical and quantitatively measurable objects and relationships of the world. This applied to man himself; our understanding of ourselves was to be reduced and confined only to those qualities and characteristics that were open to "objective" measurement and quantification. Mind was to be thought of purely as matter—which responded, in principle, in determinate ways to external stimuli. Through this "scientific method," matter and man would be both predictable and open to manipulation for various social engineering purposes.

Mises' own views about the nature of reason and reality were direct responses to these intellectual currents in the Europe of his time. In reply to alternative conceptions of man and man's place in the world, he argued that reality was the same for all men. The external world and its natural scientific laws and relationships were not different for different racial groups. Regardless of the rhetoric used, German scientists were confronted with the same reality as Jewish, Hungarian, Czech, or Polish scientists. They operated on the basis of the same hypotheses, they performed similar experiments, and they worked with the same laws of physics, chemistry, and biology. And they reasoned about laws, relationships, and hypotheses according to the same logic as that used by scientists of all nationalities.

Mises argued that our experience of interacting with other human beings demonstrates that all men, regardless of their race or class, possess the same logic of thought. They can and do draw the same inferences from the reasoning process. In other words, all men clearly possess a similar logical structure of thought.[10] If this was not the case, then it would be impossible for men of the twentieth century to read the writings that have been passed down to them from the ancient Greeks, Egyptians, and Chinese. They simply could not comprehend what men of an earlier age were saying.[11] Furthermore, it would be both meaningless and a waste of time for men to attempt to persuade, argue with, or reach common conclusions with other human beings. They could not "reason together." The fact that men in all times and in all places *do* reason with each other implies that in all human interactions men work from the assumption that others can understand (and then either concur or disagree with) the logic they have employed in order to get others to see their point of view.

Mises noted that if the National Socialists and the Marxists were correct concerning the existence of different logic among racial groups or classes, then there would be no solution to differences in ideas and opinions among men. Racial wars and class conflicts would be the inevitable result, and would threaten the destruction of civilization.[12] He expressed this at a September 1932 meeting of professional economists and social scientists in Dresden, Germany, only four months before Hitler came to power:

> We must take it for granted that the logical structure of thought is immutable throughout the whole course of time and is the same for all races, nations and classes. We know very well that the majority of the German people—and even most educated Germans—do not share this point of view. . . . A Marxist . . . who condescends to discuss a scientific problem with people who are not comrades of his own class has given up the first and most important principle of his theory. If thought is conditioned by the thinker's social existence, how can he understand me and how can I understand him? If there is a "bourgeois" logic and a "proletarian" logic, how am I, the "bourgeois" to come to an understanding of him, the 'proletarian"? Whoever takes the Marxist point of view seriously must advocate a complete division between "bourgeois" and "proletarian" science; and the same is true, *mutatis mutandis,* of the view of those who regard thought as determined by the race or the nationality of the thinker. . . . In my opinion, the position of dogmatic Marxism is

wrong, but that of the Marxist who engages in discussions with representative of what he calls "bourgeois science" is confused. The consistent Marxist does not seek to refute opponents whom he calls "bourgeois." He seeks to destroy them physically and morally.[13]

If we do not assume that there is a common logic and logical way of thinking that all men share, then there is no way for men to agree about the nature and properties of the physical world around them. Nor can men have any hope of coming to conclusions concerning the most appropriate means to attain their mutual social ends. Applying our reason to the problems of understanding the natural and social world neither assures certainty of results nor provides protection from fallibility nor removes the likelihood that other minds in the future will discover things that will supersede the knowledge of the present. Nonetheless, reason remains man's only distinctive tool to comprehend the world and devise ways for improving his existence.[14]

Obviously, other minds and their workings are not open to direct observation and study; the only mind to which we have any such direct access is our own, through self-reflection and introspection. And thus we can never claim conclusive proof that other minds are logically structured exactly like our own. But it is a "working hypothesis" that has so clearly shown its validity throughout human experience that its certainty cannot reasonably be denied.[15] (Even the "madman" follows a similar logic in his actions that, if we but place ourselves into his world and assume his points of reference, are understandable and even "rational." It doesn't matter if we disagree with the premises upon which he has drawn certain conclusions—it is enough that he presumes they are true.[16]

Let us agree, for the moment, that all men's minds do share a common logical structure and that they do understand and communicate with one another. On what basis can it be assumed that the way their minds work is consistent with an ability to correctly master the workings of the physical laws of the natural world? This is an important question, since comprehension of the world is essential if men are to discover the causalities upon which their survival and improvement are dependent. Mises' answer was delivered in the form of a hypothesis. He suggested that it might have well been the case that, in the long evolution of man, there may have been branches of the human family that did not possess logical structures of thought consistent with, and therefore able to successfully adapt to, the laws through which the natural world operates. As a result, these branches died out. Only the branch that developed the logical structures of thought compatible with physical reality prospered. The human race, as we know it from recorded history, is the branch that had developed those ways of thought most compatible with discovering the laws and causal relationships of the natural world.[17]

While man lives and acts in a world of physical objects and causalities, the laws of human action, Mises argued, reside within himself. Action is none other than *reason applied to purpose*. Therefore everything there is to know about the essence and meaning of human action is discoverable through introspective reflection—through that which allows our own minds to tell us what it means "to act."[18] This is all that Mises meant when he said that *praxeology* (the name he used for what he called the "science of human action") begins with a self-evident and a priori truth, and that all of the logic of economics is then a deductive spinning out of all the implications from the concept of "action." Why is the concept of "action" an axiom rather than a postulate? Well, perhaps in this case it is better to answer a question with another question: Who cannot look within himself, reflect on the nature of his own conscious conduct, and see that all his conscious actions (regardless of their many concrete forms) have a unifying general characteristic, which is the purposeful and intentional pursuit of chosen ends?[19] Mises first clearly expressed his views on this subject in 1933:

> In our view the concept of man is, above all else . . . the concept of the being who acts. Our consciousness is that of an ego which is capable of acting and does act. The fact that our deeds are intentional makes them actions. Our thinking about men and their conduct, and our conduct toward men and toward our surroundings, in general, presuppose the category of action.[20]

You are reading these words I have written; you turn the page to read the next passage in which I am trying to explain more of Mises' ideas and arguments; you stop, perhaps, to think about the reasonableness of what I am trying to argue; you pick up a glass or cup that may be sitting on a table next to the chair in which you are sitting; you notice that it is getting dark, so you reach over and turn on a lamp; you hear the telephone ring, and you put down this book to pick up the receiver; after the call, you decide that there is something else you would rather do than finish reading my essay right now (or ever!). Everything you do in your conscious life is a manifestation of man as an acting being. You cannot deny this self-evident truth, because to deny it would be to deny what you are and what you do every waking moment of your life.

You are the being who acts, and in interacting with others, you assume the same about them. If this is not true, then what is it you are doing right now? If it is not true, then why do you act toward others—your family, your friends, your associates, or even strangers—in a way that is different from the way that you act toward inanimate objects? Even a madman who talks to his pencil does so because he believes (however erroneously) that the pencil has consciousness, that it can understand what he is saying and will therefore behave differently toward him than those other objects in his imaginary world to which he does not assign such humanlike characteristics.

If it is now asked, what does it mean to act and to be able to act, Mises asserted that three prerequisites must be and always are present:

1. *Causality.* The actor must believe that there exists discoverable causal relationships in the world that, if applied in some appropriate way, can bring about a desired effect. In other words, if "B" is a desired goal or change of circumstance, the actor must believe there that there exists a causal factor "A" that can be brought into play to bring "B" into existence. If he does not believe in "A," then any action to try to bring about "B" is pointless and impossible.[21]

2. *Uncertainty.* The actor must believe that he can influence the course of events in such a way as to change his circumstances from what they are or will be if he does not intervene. From his point-of-view, the actor must believe that the future can be made different through his action. From his perspective, there is a range of uncertainty about how the future may develop and which he can try to influence.[22]

3. *Temporality.* The existence of causality incorporates the reality of the presence of time. Every effect is preceded by the

cause. Every action contains within it distinctions between "before," "during," and "after." Every action, therefore, occurs through time and in time. And as a result, every action contains within it a conception of a "period of production" that leads to the desired outcome, regardless of whether that period of time is a matter of a few minutes or many years.[23]

While these three elements—causality, uncertainty, and time —are inseparable from the very notion of the "doing" of action, they remain necessary, but not sufficient, conditions. For an action to be undertaken, that is, for the actor to want and to be able to undertake some action, three other conditions must be present:[24]

1. *Felt Uneasiness.* The actor must be dissatisfied in some way with existing circumstances, or the circumstances that he believes are likely to develop if he does not act in some manner to change them.

2. *Imagined and Preferred State of Affairs.* The actor must be able to imagine a situation that would be more desirable than the present one, or the one that is likely to arise if he does not try to do something to change it. No matter how unsatisfactory the existing or expected state of affairs may be, if he could not imagine one that would be an improvement, then any action on his part would be to substitute a less preferred state of affairs for a more preferred one.

3. *Beliefs or Expectations about the Availability of Means and Methods to Bring a Preferred State of Affairs into Existence.* The actor must believe that he has or can have access to and disposal over appropriate means to bring his preferred state of affairs into existence when and how he expects he will need to do so. If he does not have such beliefs and expectations, then he will regard action as futile.

From these fundamental concepts of and preconditions to all conscious human action, Mises argued, all the core principles and relationships of economics can be derived. To say that man is purposeful is to say that he pursues *ends*; to pursue ends, he must believe that there are *means available* to attain them. The reality of the world in which man finds himself is one in which *useful means are found to be insufficient to simultaneously attain all his desired ends*

(if nothing else were scarce, the time at man's disposal is insufficient to achieve all his desired ends simultaneously). That man
must choose among the ends for which the means at his disposal
shall be applied implies that *the means have degrees of multiple use* so
that a decision has to be made as to whether they should bc used
in one way or another. And *having to choose among the ends for which
the scarce means shall be applied requires man to rank or arrange his ends
in order of importance to him.*

But ranking ends in order of importance also implies that
man weighs the *costs* and *benefits* from making one choice rather
than another. What must be foregone or given up as the *price* for
possibly attaining some other goal ranked as more important is
the *cost* of the individual's decision. And that which he pursues or
possibly achieves by paying that price is the *benefit* he may receive
from the choice he has made. Thus, he chooses that end to pursue which he believes will be more *profitable* (the one that, on net
balance, will make him better off) and he tries to avoid selecting
some alternative that would in comparison generate a *loss* (the
one that, on net balance, would make him worse off). Furthermore, most choices are not categorical (either/or decisions), but
instead *marginal* ones (choices concerning incremental *trade-offs*
of a little more of one desired end at the expense of a little bit less
of some other desired end).[95]

Now, all of these concepts and relationships—ends and
means, costs and benefits, profits and losses, prices to be paid and
trade-offs to be made at the margin of decisionmaking—are the
stock and trade of practically all modern economists. They provide the analytical schema within which economists arrange and
order the human events of the world for theoretical understanding and application. But Mises' point was to emphasize that these
are not merely useful categories and concepts—not just good working hypotheses that economists may adopt or not, depending upon
how they wish to organize the "data" or "facts" of the human world.
Instead, they are the only way the data and facts can be organized
so as to present the general and universal properties necessary for
comprehending and understanding the reality of the human
world. Why? Because these are the concepts, categories, and relationships through which real men act and choose; there are no
others from which to select. They represent the way our minds

actually work and which comprise the *logic of action*. We cannot separate ourselves from them, since they represent the mental framework within which our minds operate.[26]

Human Cooperation and the Rationality of the Market Economy

Since the time of the ancient Greeks, the benefits of human cooperation through a social system of division of labor has been understood in Western thought.[27] But it was in the eighteenth-century writings of the French Physiocrats and the Scottish Moral Philosophers that its significance and importance for social theory was fully appreciated. Through a division of labor, productivity is increased far above what men in isolation can ever hope to attain. It also acts as a stimulus for industry, since now the variety and the quantity of goods that may be obtained through the exchange of specialized productions work as incentives for each to increase his own output of tradable wares as the means of acquiring what others may have for sale. And the more extensive the market becomes on which goods can be sold, the greater now the potential benefits from a more intensive development of the division of labor.[28]

From this insight, these eighteenth-century thinkers were able to undermine much of the mercantilist ideology of their time. They demonstrated that trade among nations is mutually beneficial and in no way harmful to any nation's "interests." Indeed, as other nations become more developed and more prosperous, the market expands for one's own nation's specialized productions.[29] But the advantage from international trade comes not from the ability to export but from the opportunity to import. Exports are only the means through which a nation can acquire from other nations products that it cannot produce at home, or cannot produce at a cost less than the price offered by another country. Trade among nations offers the consumers of each participating country more goods, different goods, and cheaper goods than if the suppliers of desired commodities were limited to the production possibilities of domestic producers.[30]

The final demonstration of the mutual benefit from international trade came with the development of the theory of "comparative advantage" in the early nineteenth century. That trade would be beneficial can be seen clearly enough if each nation can produce some product that its trading partners cannot produce at all, or if each nation can produce some product at a lower cost that none of its trading partners can match. But the English classical economists, especially David Ricardo, showed that trade can still be beneficial for a nation even if it is absolutely more cost-efficient in producing every product in comparison to its potential trading partners.

Suppose that Englishmen could produce one yard of cloth in four hours and harvest a bushel of potatoes in one hour, while Irishmen took twelve hours and two hours, respectively. Clearly, England is a lower cost producer than Ireland in both cloth and potatoes. England is three times more productive at cloth manufacturing and twice as productive in potato harvesting. But equally clear is the fact that England is comparatively more cost-efficient in cloth manufacturing. That is, when England foregoes the manufacture of a yard of cloth, it can harvest four bushels of potatoes. But when Ireland foregoes the manufacture of a yard of cloth, it can harvest six bushels of potatoes. If England and Ireland were to trade cloth for potatoes at the price ratio of, say, one yard of cloth for five bushels of potatoes, both nations could be better off, with England specializing in cloth manufacturing and Ireland in potato harvesting. England would now receive five bushels of potatoes for a yard of its cloth, rather than the four bushels if it harvested at home all the potatoes it consumed. And Ireland would receive a yard of cloth for only giving up five bushels of potatoes, rather than the six bushels if it manufactured at home all of the cloth it used.[31]

In these ideas, Mises saw the basis for a comprehensive theory of society, the social order, and the market economy. Ricardo's theory of comparative advantage, he said, should more rightly be called the "Ricardian Law of Association":[32]

> Ricardo expounded the law of association in order to demonstrate what the consequences of the division of labor are when an individual or a group, more efficient in every regard, cooperates with an individual or a group less efficient in every regard. . . . The law of association makes us comprehend the tendencies which resulted in the progressive intensification of human cooperation. We conceive what incen-

tive induced people not to consider themselves as rivals in a struggle for the appropriation of the limited supply of means of subsistence made available by nature. We realize what has impelled them and permanently impels them to consort with one another for the sake of cooperation. Every step forward on the way to a more developed mode of division of labor serves the interests of all participants. . . . The factor that brought about primitive society and daily works toward progressive intensification is human action that is animated by the insight into the higher productivity of labor achieved under the division of labor.[33]

What are the origins of the advantages from a division of labor? Mises argued that division of labor arose from two conditions found in the human circumstance: the inherent inequality among men to perform various tasks and the unequal distribution of natural resources and raw materials with which men are able to manufacture the goods that service their ends. There is also the frequent situation that the strength necessary to perform various physical tasks is beyond the capacity of one man. While this would create occasional instances in which men would need each other's assistance, this alone would not generate the incentive for permanent human bonds of association and collaborative effort. Only those two inequalities in the human condition create the lasting benefit from mutual assistance through specialization of activities.[34]

Herein lies the origin of society, the mutual and permanent cooperative endeavor of men to improve their circumstances and expand the possibilities before them:

> Society is cooperation; it is community in action. . . . Once labor had been divided, the division itself exercises a differentiating influence. The fact that labor is divided makes possible further cultivation of individual talent and thus cooperation becomes more and more productive. Through cooperation men are able to achieve what would have been beyond them as individuals, and even work which individuals are capable of doing alone is made more productive. . . . The greater productivity of work under the division of labor is a unifying influence. It leads men to regard each other as comrades in the joint struggle for welfare, rather than as competitors in a struggle for existence. It makes friends out of enemies, peace out of war, society out of individuals. . . . Society

exists only where willing becomes co-willing and action co-action. To strive jointly towards aims which lone individuals could not reach at all, or not with equal effectiveness—that is society. Therefore, society is not an end but a means, the means by which each individual member seeks to attain his own end. That society is possible at all is due to the fact that the will of one person and the will of another find themselves linked in a joint endeavor. Community of work springs from community of will. Because I can get what I want only if my fellow citizen gets what he wants, his will and action become the means by which I can attain my own end. . . . The division of labor is what first makes social ties: it is the social element pure and simple.[35]

However, Mises pointed out that there were, in general terms, two forms in which cooperation could be established and maintained in society: *hegemonic* and *contractual* relationships. The hegemonic relationship is based on command and subjugation. One group of individuals imposes its will upon another group through the use or threat of force, making the subjugated group serve and obey the interests and orders of the ruling or commanding group. Cooperation by some is made compulsory. The contractual relationship is based on voluntary agreement and mutual consent of the participants of the association. This distinction between systems of social cooperation, he said, has long been understood in social theory as the distinctions between the society of status or contract, military nations or industrial nations, collectivist economies or market economies. But the advancement of civilization has arisen from the slow replacement of the hegemonic relationship with the society of contract.[36] Individual freedom, voluntary association, and market-based cooperation have served as the basis for the material and cultural advancement of mankind.[37]

But the potential for cooperation through contractual association in a market economy depends upon the emergence and maintenance of certain crucial institutions, Mises explained: [38]

1. *Private Property*, that is, the private ownership of the means of production. Individuals have the right of possession and use of not only goods ready for consumption, but the factors of production out of which goods and services can be manufactured for sale and use.[39]

2. *Freedom,* that is, the liberty of each and every individual to be guided by his own purposes and plans, on the basis of which he voluntarily integrates himself into the social system of division of labor through contract and mutual agreement.[40]

3. *Peace,* that is, the removal and abolition of violence from human relationships, because it is only in a climate of tranquil association that each individual can feel secure to apply his mind and efforts to creative improvements to the human condition.[41]

4. *Equality,* that is, equal personal and political freedom before the law so each individual may have the liberty to integrate himself into the system of division of labor as he thinks more profitable, without legal barrier or restriction.

5. *Inequality of wealth and income,* that is, each individual's material position in society is dependent upon his success in serving others in the system of division of labor, with the relative income and wealth positions of each individual reflecting his inevitably unequal accomplishment in this endeavor.[42]

6. *Limited government,* that is, the political authority is restricted in its powers and responsibilities to those tasks required for the securing of the peace under which each individual's freedom and property is protected from violence and aggression.[43]

Mises stressed that the foundation of society was the first item on the list, the institution of private property. It is the basis on which individuals have had the incentives and the capabilities to apply themselves to improve their own circumstances and that of others, through their participation in the division of labor.[44] And, finally, it is the basis on which a rational use of the resources at people's disposal in society can be most efficiently applied to serve various ends.

In a market economy, Mises explained, it is not necessary for each individual to have possession and direct control over the particular resources, raw materials, land, or labor skills upon which the satisfaction of each of his individual wants and ends are dependent. In a system of division of labor, these means of production are set to work for him, even though they are owned and controlled by others with whom he has no immediate or personal association. The owners of these things can only attain their own particular purposes if they successfully put them to work manu-

facturing and providing what others desire, so they in turn can
obtain in exchange what they desire for the satisfaction of their
own ends.[45]

But how do those owners of the means of production know
what others in the society desire to purchase and how do they know
if they are utilizing in a cost-efficient manner the resources they
either own or can acquire on the market in manufacturing goods
that they can sell to those others? The solution to this dilemma is
provided by economic calculation. The fact that resources are pri-
vately owned and may be bought and sold on the market along
with finished consumer goods enables the emergence of ratios of
exchange, or prices, which reflect the appraised value of the means
of production in alternative uses. These market-generated prices
then serve as the basis for evaluating their use in alternative productive activities in the society. Mises explained the nature of economic calculation in the following manner:

> Money calculation . . . provides a guide amid the bewildering throng
> of economic possibilities. It enables us to extend judgments of value
> which apply directly only to consumption goods—or at best to
> production goods of the lowest order [those closest to the finished
> consumer goods stage]—to all goods of higher order [factors of
> production applied at more indirect stages of production processes].
> Without it, all production by lengthy and roundabout processes
> would be so many steps in the dark. Two things are necessary if
> computations of value in terms of money are to take place. First,
> not only goods ready for consumption but also goods of higher
> orders must be exchangeable. If this were not so, a system of
> exchange relationships could not emerge. . . . No single man, be
> he the greatest genius ever born, has an intellect capable of deciding
> the relative importance of each one of the infinite number of goods
> of higher order. No individual could so discriminate between the
> infinite number of alternative methods of production that he could
> make direct judgments of their relative value without auxiliary
> calculations. In societies based on division of labor, the distribution
> of property rights effects a kind of mental division of labor, without
> which neither economy nor systematic production would be
> possible. In the second place, there must be a general medium of
> exchange, a money, in use. And this must serve as an intermediary
> in the exchange of production goods equally with the rest. If this
> were not so, it would be impossible to reduce all exchange relation-

ships to a common denominator. . . . Without such assistance, in the
bewildering chaos of alternative materials and processes, the human
mind would be at a complete loss. . . .[46]

Mises continued in the same vein,

Capitalist economic calculation, which alone makes rational production possible, is based on monetary calculation. Only because
prices of all goods and services in the market can be expressed in
terms of money is it possible for them, in spite of their heterogeneity,
to enter into a calculation involving homogeneous units of
measurement. . . . In the market, where all goods and services can
be traded, exchange ratios, expressed in money prices, can be
determined for everything bought and sold. In a social order based
on private property, it thus becomes possible to resort to monetary
calculation in checking on the results of all economic activities.
The social productivity of every economic transaction may be tested
by the methods of bookkeeping and cost accounting. . . . This is
the decisive objection that economics raises against the possibility
of a socialist society. It must forgo the intellectual division of labor
that consists in the cooperation of all entrepreneurs, landowners,
and workers as producers and consumers in the formation of market
prices. But without it, rationality, i.e., the possibility of economic
calculation, is unthinkable.[47]

In Mises' view, economic calculation is the mental tool that
enables the development and evolution of the complex system of
division of labor upon which the modern market economy is
dependent. It is what gives rationality to the economic order and
its market processes.[48] Given the scarcity of the means to serve
human ends, we see that men must weigh their competing ends,
rank them in order of importance, and proceed to assign the
means at their disposal in a manner that applies them in way that
reflects the relative significance of the ends they can serve. But
the more intricate and indirect the production processes utilized
to satisfy those numerous ends, the more there is a need for a way
to reduce physically heterogeneous means to some type of common denominator to determine whether or not, in value terms,
they are being employed for the satisfaction of some end less important than some other for which they might be applied. The

prices competitively formed on the market provide this device. Once more, we may refer to Mises' own words:

> We may view the whole market of material factors of production and of labor as a public auction. The bidders are the entrepreneurs. Their highest bids are limited by their expectations of the prices consumers will be ready to pay for the products. The co-bidders competing with them, whom they must outbid if they are not to go away empty-handed, are in the same situation. All these bidders are, as it were, mandatories of the consumers. But each of them represents a different aspect of the consumers' wants, either another commodity or another way of producing the same commodity. The competition among the various entrepreneurs is essentially a competition among the various possibilities open to individuals to remove as far as possible their state of uneasiness by the acquisition of consumer goods. . . . The competition between the entrepreneurs reflects these prices of consumer goods in the formation of the prices of the factors of production. The fact that the various wants of the individual, which conflict because of the inexorable scarcity of the factors of production, are represented on the market by the various competing entrepreneurs results in prices for those factors that make economic calculation not only feasible but imperative. . . . To the entrepreneur of capitalist society a factor of production through its price sends out a warning: Don't touch me, I am earmarked for the satisfaction of another, more important need. . . . An entrepreneur who does not calculate, or disregards the result of calculation, would very soon go bankrupt and be removed from his managerial function.[49]

Economic calculation serves two functions in the market economy, Mises concluded. It enables the entrepreneurial decisionmaker to evaluate after a production process has been undertaken and goods have been sold to consumers whether his economic plans had been successful or not, that is, whether, *ex post*, a profit or a loss has resulted from his activities. It also serves as the anticipatory framework enabling the entrepreneur to make decisions concerning the future. The entrepreneur, on the basis of the prices of the immediate past, forms his judgments, *ex ante*, concerning the direction and intensity of consumer demand for various products in the future. This then serves as the limit for appraising the usefulness and value of bidding for and utilizing various factors of production in different combinations, given the prices those factors of production are found to cost in the markets for resources. The rivalrous bids of competing entrepreneurs assures that the prices that emerge on the market for the factors of production tend to reflect the relative values of the consumer goods they can assist in manufacturing. Market prices and competition assure that the value of the means of production represents the value of the consumer ends that they can serve.[50]

Mises observed that the competition of the market doesn't just enable the formation of the prices that serve as the tool for economic calculation, it also serves as the method by which each participant in the division of labor discovers his most advantageous employment. "Competition is an element of social collaboration, the ruling principle within the social body," he explained.[51] Rather than implying conflict, competition is a method for peaceful cooperation. Each man estimates what his most highly valued use might be in the social system of division of labor, as a source of potential income for himself. Through the process of competition, he discovers whether his judgment has been correct. If someone else can perform a task more successfully and profitably in the competition for a particular consumer business, then the lower than expected income or profits he earns serves as a signal that his contribution to the social process of production should be found elsewhere. Through this process each finds his most socially valuable function—as entrepreneur, landowner, capitalist, or laborer—in the division of labor.[52]

At the same time, the competitive process of social cooperation reduces the capricious element from human relations. Precisely because of the near universal reduction of human relationships in the market economy to an "exchange nexus" of dollars and cents, arbitrary or discourteous behavior toward others carries a price that makes each think twice before he acts thoughtlessly or rudely in the consumer–producer or employer–employee relationships of the market. Explained Mises:

It is customary to complain that, nowadays, personal considerations are banished from business life and that money rules everything. But what really is here complained of is simply that, in that department of activity which we call purely economic, whims and favors are banished and only those considerations are valid which social cooperation demands. . . . There is no place for the arbitrary, where exact money reckoning enables us completely to calculate action. If we allow ourselves to be carried away by the current laments over the stony-heartedness of an age which reckons everything in terms of shillings and pence, we overlook that it is precisely this linking up of action with considerations of money profit which is society's more effective means of limiting arbitrary action. It is precisely arrangements of this kind which make the consumer, on the one hand, the employer, the capitalist, the landowner and the worker on the other—in short, all concerned in producing for demands other than their own—dependent upon social cooperation. . . . The conduct of the employer to the employee is part of a social process. If he does not deal with the employee in a manner appropriate to the social valuation of the employee's service, then there arise consequences which he himself has to bear. He can, indeed, deal badly with the employee, but he himself must pay the costs of his arbitrary behavior [in losing a valuable employee to a rival employer]. . . . This, then is freedom in the external life of man— that is, he is independent of the arbitrary power of his fellows. . . . Capitalism . . . no longer divides society into despotic rulers and rightless serfs. All relations are material and impersonal, calculable and capable of substitution. With capitalistic money calculations freedom descends from the sphere of dreams to reality.[53]

Through the emergence of a social system of division of labor, men learned how to increase their ability to materially and culturally improve their earthly circumstances from primitive subsistence to one of humane comfort and ease.[54] Instead of a struggle for existence not only against the niggardliness of nature but in conflict with their fellow human beings, they devised a civil society for peaceful cooperation and collaboration for mutual improvement and betterment. The institutions of the market economy offered the methods for a rational economic calculation and allocation of the scarce resources of the earth for the satisfaction of their ends. It also offered a reasonable and nonarbitrary way of determining what the relative income and wealth of each man should be as an indicator of his reward for serving others in the pursuit of the fulfillment of his own ends in the system of division of labor. And it enabled even the weak and the less efficient to find a niche for earning the means for life through the logic of comparative advantage.[55]

The insights and analysis of the classical economists had created the basis for the political and legal reforms of the nineteenth century that resulted in the freeing of men and markets from the regulatory and controlling hands of governments. The philosophy of classical liberalism had created the foundation for an appreciation of the importance and value of individual liberty, private property, and free markets. The results were rising standards of living, growing populations, improved quantity and quality of the amenities of life, more leisure time, and more resources for science, art, literature, and all the other signifiers of a great and good society.

Using his reason, Mises argued, men had not only been able to comprehend the nature and laws of the physical world; they had also begun to comprehend the logical character of human action and the potential for a rational social order. Facing an inescapable scarcity of insufficient means to serve their various ends, men must order their affairs to logically go about the satisfaction of the things they consider, in their own minds, as the most important goals to fulfill. But two problems face them in this endeavor: Their own strength and abilities are limited, and they know others are facing the same perennial problem. They can either try to satisfy their desires through self-sufficient efforts while at the same time initiating or warding off the plundering attacks of others, or they can devise ways of drawing others into cooperative activities for improving their circumstances.

Through much of human history, cooperation was imposed by compulsion or hegemonic bonds, as Mises calls them. Slowly, men came to see that cooperation could be extended and made more productive when consent and voluntary agreement served as the basis of collaboration for mutual rather than unilateral benefit. The society of contract began to replace the society of status, caste, and command. The market economy started to supersede the regulated economy. The classical economists had shown that there could be order without design, that market competition could both integrate and coordinate multitudes of people in a great society of "natural liberty," as Adam Smith had called it.

The coordination and rationality in the social system of division of labor was dependent, as Mises made clear, on the institutions of private property and market competition that enabled the formation of money prices on the basis of which economic calculation became possible. All the goods and resources that might enter the orbit of human use and exchange could now be valued and appraised to determine what their most highly valued uses and most cost-effective applications might be in the interdependent and intricate network of production and trade. The nexus of market prices that emerged out of the interactions of all the participants in the marketplace assured a rational allocation of the scarce means of production for the satisfaction of consumers' ends and at the same time determined the relative income share that each participant earned as a reflection of the market's judgment of the value of his contribution to the social process of production. At the same time, competition served as the peaceful means through which each member of this collaborative process found his appropriate niche in the division of labor, through which he served his fellow men and they in turn served him.

But before a completely free market capitalism could be established and achieve even greater heights in improving and civilizing mankind, opposing forces arose in the late nineteenth and twentieth centuries. Socialism and interventionism emerged as the two challengers to and enemies of the rationality of the free market economy.[56]

The Irrationality of Socialist Planning
and Interventionist Regulation

Before Ludwig von Mises published his article on "Economic Calculation in the Socialist Commonwealth" in 1920,[57] most criticisms of socialism and a planned economy focused on the weakening of work incentives with the abolition of private property and the threat to human freedom if the state became the monopoly producer and employer under nationalization of the means of production. Though a few writers before the First World War had criticized the possibility for successful central planning, Mises' analysis was the first thorough challenge to the socialists' claim that central planning could economically outperform private, competitive market capitalism.[58]

The economic problem, Mises argued, concerns the efficient use of the scarce means of production to serve our various ends. If all means of production, regardless of their physical characteristics, were, for production purposes, perfectly interchangeable (or substitutable) for one another there would be little difficulty in deciding how to apportion them among competing production uses. They could, in random fashion, be distributed among chosen production purposes, with the only criterion being that they would be applied for those activities that reflected in descending order the preferred consumer ends for which they could be used until no further production plan could be undertaken because the means had been completely exhausted.

There would also be no difficulty in deciding how to utilize available means of production if each and every such physical factor of production was usable for one and only one production activity. In other words, if there were no substitutability among them at all. Means "X" would be used for production purpose "X" and means "Y" would be used for production purpose "Y," or they could not be used at all. In other words, there would be no problem in having to decide whether some amount of means "X" should be used to for production purpose "Y" instead of production purpose "X."

Now, for some purposes some physical means of production can be almost perfectly substituted for each other, and there may be some physical means of production that are almost uniquely use-specific. But in a wide variety of cases the various physical means of production have degrees of substitutability among themselves for desired production activities. The economic problem, Mises said, is precisely to have some way of determining which use, in value-terms, is the most efficient application for such means of production.[59]

For example, Mises suggested, suppose that it was being decided whether it would be economically advantageous to build a railway line between two cities separated by a mountain. The rail line could be built over, around, or through the mountain. How would it be decided whether or not it would be worth the cost in resources, raw materials, and labor that would have to be expended in its construction by one of these possible routes, in terms of the alternative production uses in the society for which those factors of production could be utilized?

In the market economy, Mises replied, the solution to this problem is fairly simple. The decisionmaker would make an estimate whether or not the prospective revenue to be earned by selling passenger tickets and charging cargo fees to potential users would be greater than the expenditures necessary for the construction and maintenance of the rail line along one of those routes. Suppose that the over-the-mountain route would involve a greater cost than the expected monetary return, but that either the around-the-mountain or through-the-mountain routes would cost less than the expected revenue. Which of these two routes should be chosen? Suppose that the around-the-mountain route could be built and maintained at less cost than the through-the-mountain route, if the tunnel through the mountain were to be constructed with the technologically very durable material, say, of platinum. If the tunnel were to be constructed with concrete rather than platinum it would be less durable and would require more frequent maintenance. On the other hand, the concrete-lined tunnel would then result in the through-the-mountain route coming in at a lower cost (even with the higher maintenance expenses) than the around-the-mountain route. The through-the-mountain route with a concrete-lined tunnel would clearly be the most cost-efficient project for the decisionmaker to undertake.

The economic calculations that enable this decision to be made would, as we have seen, been due to the existence of market-based prices for both the finished good (passenger and cargo transportation) in comparison to the alternative methods for utilizing scarce means of production in providing this service to the consuming public. But how would the socialist central planner be able to make this decision, Mises asked? How would he know which of the technologically feasible methods of production was most economical and most efficient? Having nationalized all the means of production, abolished market competition, and eliminated the ability of people to openly express their valuations and appraisals in the form of market-based prices for both finished goods and the factors of production, how would the central planner know the real opportunity costs—the foregone benefits—from applying and using goods and resources in any number of alternative ways? He would not.[60] Socialist central planning, therefore, meant the end of economic rationality. As Mises wrote,

> In any social order, even under Socialism, it can very easily be decided which kind and what number of consumption goods should be produced. No one has ever denied that. But once this decision has been made, there still remains the problem of ascertaining how the existing means of production can be used most effectively to produce these goods in question. In order to solve this problem it is necessary that there should be economic calculation. And economic calculation can only take place by means of money prices established in the market for production goods in a society resting on private property in the means of production. That is to say, there must exist money prices of land, raw materials, semi-manufactures; that is to say, there must be money wages and interest rates. . . . Where there is no market there is no price system, and where there is no price system there can be no economic calculation.[61]

Mises readily admitted that one could imagine a socialist world in which the preceding capitalist methods of production were taken over with no modifications or changes. One could also imagine that no further changes would ever again affect this socialist society. And one could imagine that this economy was in equilibrium before the "socialist triumph," now remained frozen in time. Then the socialist central planners would not have to worry about the problem of economic calculation. They would merely, year-in and year-out, reproduce the methods of production found when the private owners of the means of production were expropriated.

But this is not, and would never be, the world in which a socialist regime would find itself. If nothing else, income and wealth would be redistributed according to socialist conceptions of "social justice" following the great transformation, and, therefore, the patterns of demand for various goods would be different. This would in itself require a redirection of production and the reallocation of the factors of production, meaning a set of new decisions concerning the most rational use of the resources at the central planners' disposal. And apart from this, in the real world technological possibilities do change, available resources do become greater or smaller due to various causes, and the demands of the public (even the socialist proletarian public) do change over time. All these changes, whether occurring in sequence or simultaneously, would require readjustments in the forms and types of production. But the socialist central planners would lack the ability to know rationally how to respond and adjust to a world of inevitable change. "Thus," judged Mises, "in the socialist commonwealth every economic change becomes an undertaking whose success can be neither appraised in advance nor later retrospectively determined. There is only groping in the dark. Socialism is the abolition of rational economy."[62]

Mises' 1920 challenge to the advocates of socialist central planning created a firestorm of controversy that did not completely come to an end until the final collapse of the Soviet Union in 1991. But it can be said that, by the 1930s, Mises had won the great debate of capitalism versus socialism, because beginning in the late 1920s the more astute advocates of socialism realized that Mises had made a devastating criticism in his analysis of the role of market-based prices for the rational use of resources in any complex economic order. They attempted to construct alternative theories of "market socialism."[63] But Mises and his Austrian colleague Friedrich A. Hayek were able to demonstrate the limits and unworkability even in this strange contortion of attempting to combine markets with central planning.[64]

If socialist central planning represented a reversion to economic irrationality, did this then mean that a free market economy was the only rational system of economic order? Not in the eyes of many in the twentieth century. Instead, the ideal in most Western countries became a "middle way," or "mixed economy" of regulated markets, politically redistributed income, and partially controlled prices and production. Mises argued that this form of state interventionism was, in the long run, no more workable and sustainable than socialism. Indeed, he insisted that the distorting effects of government intervention into the workings of the market economy necessarily leads to a situation in which those introducing such interventions must each reverse themselves and allow a freer market to be reestablished or extend the interventions and controls until a form of socialist-type command economy is imposed through the accumulation of government rules and regulations over the market system.

What is a state intervention in the market economy? Mises defined it in the following way:

> Interventionism is a limited order by a social authority forcing the owners of the means of production and entrepreneurs to employ their means in a different manner than they otherwise would. . . .
>
> The authority interferes with the operation of the market economy, but it does not want to eliminate the market altogether. It wants production and consumption to develop along lines different from those prescribed by an unhampered market, and wants to achieve its aim by injecting into the working of the market orders, commands, and prohibitions for whose enforcement the police power and its apparatus of violent compulsion and coercion stand ready. But these are *isolated* acts of intervention. It is not the aim of the government to combine them into an integrated system which determines all prices, wages, and interest rates and thus places full control of production and consumption into the hands of the authorities. . . . What characterizes it as such is the fact that the government does not limit its activities to the preservation of private ownership of the means of production and its protection against violent or fraudulent encroachments. The government interferes with the operation of business by means of orders and prohibitions. . . . The intervention . . . forces the entrepreneurs and capital-ists to employ some of the factors of production in a way different from what they would have resorted to if they were only obeying the dictates of the market. Such a decree can be either an order to do something or an order not do to something.[66]

Mises also emphasized the nature of such intervention by pointing what stands behind the government's regulations:

> It is important to remember that government interference always means either violent action or the threat of such action. . . . Government is in the last resort the employment of armed men, of policemen, gendarmes, soldiers, prison guards, and hangmen. The essential feature of government is the enforcement of its decrees by beating, killing, and imprisoning. Those who are asking for more

government interference are asking ultimately for more compulsion and less freedom.[67]

Mises did not deny an essential role for government in society. Indeed, if there were not an agency that had the ability to protect life and property, enforce contracts, and guard against fraud, the social order of peaceful cooperation through division of labor would be impossible.[68] But he argued that the task of social and economic theory was to determine the limits beyond which extension of government coercion no longer serves the maintenance of the social order of mutual interdependency through specialization and market exchange and instead threatens to weaken or undermine its operation.

In a free market, the structure of competitively determined prices serve the function of coordinating the actions of multitudes of participants in the division of labor. Every change in supply or demand ultimately represents a change either in the preferences of consumers for various goods or the willingness and ability of producers to provide their services, resources, and abilities in the processes of production. Entrepreneurs function as the actual decisionmakers in the market economy, who determine what shall be produced, employ the factors of production, and direct and coordinate those factors in the production processes. But entrepreneurs are guided in their decisions and activities by their anticipation concerning the goods and services consumers may desire to buy at various points in the future. Failure to correctly anticipate consumer demand means that the entrepreneur will suffer losses rather than earn the profits for which he had hoped.

The prices he offers and pays for employing those factors of production are determined by the prices he believes he will recoup from sales to those consumers in the future. The competition among rival entrepreneurs means that the prices and wages paid for the purchase or hire of the factors of production are tending to equal the market value of the products their employment assists in producing.

In the market, the ability of entrepreneurs to successfully offer consumers the products they want, and to offer them on better terms than their closest rivals, is tested constantly every day in the arena of exchange. Control over production decisionmaking in the market, therefore, is always open to change and modification. Successful entrepreneurs earn profits that enable them to expand their production activities. Less successful entrepreneurs either earn small or no profits, or suffer actual losses; these entrepreneurs lose the financial wherewithal over time to maintain their control over the production processes in the market. Hence, in the market economy decisionmaking and control over the production processes in society are tending to be maintained or transferred to those individuals who demonstrate their continuing ability to perform this specialized and important task better than others in the social system of division of labor.[69]

According to Mises, government interventions disturbed and redirected this market-based process from following the patterns and forms it would have taken if guided solely by the anticipated and actual demands of the general consuming public. State interventions, he said, can be understood under several broad headings: consumption prohibitions, taxation, production restrictions and regulations, and price controls.

Consumption prohibitions attempt to directly prevent individuals from consuming or using particular goods or services. The rationale for such prohibitions has to do with the desire of some members of the society to restrain or prevent other members of the society from satisfying their wants for particular types of commodities. Thus, the government may make illegal the purchase, sale, and consumption of narcotics or alcoholic beverages or the use of tobacco products. The goal is to eliminate the demand for certain goods by banning their acquisition and use under threat of governmental punishment.

Mises admitted that the issue of whether or not to prohibit certain consumer desires goes beyond the purely economic question of the direct and indirect market consequences that may follow such bans. But he pointed out that once the government takes on the responsibility for determining which goods and services individuals may peacefully and voluntarily purchase and use, there is no logical limit to extending such prohibitions:

> But once the principle is admitted that it is the duty of government to protect the individual against his own foolishness, no serious objections can be advanced against further encroachments. A good

case can be made out in favor of the prohibition of alcohol and nicotine. And why limit the government's benevolent providence to the protection of the individual's body only? Is not the harm a man can inflict on his mind and soul even more disastrous than any bodily evil? Why not prevent him from reading bad books and seeing bad plays, from looking at bad paintings and statues and from hearing bad music. . . . These fears are not merely imaginary specters terrifying secluded doctrinaires. It is a fact that no paternal government, whether ancient or modern, ever shrank from regimenting its subjects' minds, beliefs, and opinions. If one abolishes man's freedom to determine his own consumption, one takes all freedoms away.[70]

As Mises also perceived, "A free man must be able to endure it when his fellow men act and live otherwise than he considers proper. He must free himself from the habit, just as soon as something does not please him, of calling for the police."[71]

Taxation may be necessary for the funding of the limited, though essential functions of a government devoted to the protection of individual liberty and property, but Mises said that when it goes beyond the modest levels that would be required in a truly free market society, it threatens to become a vehicle for the distortion or destruction of the market economy. Thus, an excise tax or an import tax may be imposed as a source of government revenue. But the same tax can be utilized as a device to repress or restrict the purchase or sale of a commodity or service. Thus, a tax on tobacco products can be raised to a level sufficiently high that the government's tax revenue is less than if it were set at a lower level. But it can be set at that higher level precisely to serve as a method for inducing a decrease in the quantity demanded by the smoking public, with the tax potentially high enough that it suppresses all legal purchases of tobacco products. In this case, the tax serves as a tool for the government's attempt to prohibit consumption.

Or an import tax or tariff can be raised to a height that it also brings in less government revenue than if it were set at a more modest level. But in this case, it serves as a method to make the importation and sale of a foreign commodity more costly for the consuming public than their purchasing of a domestic alternative to the foreign good. Its purpose is to act as a protectionist device to secure a larger portion of the domestic market to a domestic producer than would have been the situation under a regime of free trade. Protectionist import duties, however, reduce the benefits and potentials from an international division of labor, resulting in goods being more costly and the variety available to the consuming public being reduced. Resources and labor are misdirected into less efficient uses, lowering the standard of living of both the domestic and the foreign community of buyers and sellers.

Taxation can also serve as a method of partial expropriation of wealth and income. Thus, a progressive income tax penalizes success and achievement on the part of some members of the society in better satisfying the consuming public. As such it reduces the incentives for savings, investment, and work. The end result is a slowing down of the rate of capital formation, technological innovation, and entrepreneurial creativity in improving the economic conditions of the society. The society is poorer and is kept poorer than might have been the case if taxation did not discriminate against excellence and ability.

Finally, total confiscatory taxation has as its purpose the actual destruction of the market economy by expropriating wealth and property with the implicit or explicit purpose of transferring the ability to produce from the hands of private individuals to the government.[72]

Production restrictions and regulations are designed to prevent production methods from taking the form they would have if guided purely by entrepreneurs' estimates concerning the types of goods consumers desire and their judgments concerning the most efficient way to produce them. Mises elucidated:

> Each authoritarian interference with business diverts production, of course, from the lines it would take if it were only directed by the demand of the consumers as manifested on the market. The characteristic mark of restrictive interference with production is that the diversion of production is not merely an unavoidable and unintentional secondary effect, but precisely what the authority wants to bring about. . . . Restrictions of production means that the government either forbids or makes more difficult or more expensive the production, transportation, or distribution of definite articles, or the definite modes of production, transportation, or distribution. . . . The effect of the interference is that people are prevented from using their knowledge and abilities, their labor

and their material means of production in the way in which they would earn the highest returns and satisfy their needs as much as possible. Such interference makes people poorer and less satisfied.[73]

Production restrictions can take the form, for example, of licenses to practice various professions or trades, tax benefits that favor certain types of enterprises and industries, labor laws that limit or prohibit employment of women or children, or the requirement of membership in a union to be employed.[74] They can also take the form of regulations on the size of enterprises, the form and type of marketing methods that firms may utilize, the technical methods that can be employed in production processes, or regulations on the ways enterprises in the market are permitted to compete for consumer business.

The price of such production restrictions and regulations, Mises emphasized, included higher costs of production, limitations on innovation and product development, rigidity in the adaptability of firms to market conditions, and barriers preventing various individuals and groups from taking advantage of market opportunities to improve their material and social circumtances. The cumulative result of such restrictions and regulations, he concluded, was a tendency to reduce or retard the development of the productive capacity of people in the society. The evolution of the division of labor is forced to take a less efficient path than the market, left to itself, would have taken. Society, again, is poorer than it would have to be if only the market was left free and unencumbered by state interventionism.[75]

Finally, Mises wrote that price controls undermine the most fundamental functioning of the market economy. Prices, as we have seen, act as the central coordinating device in the market. Through them, production is directed toward the satisfaction of consumer demand, and the costs of the means of production (through entrepreneurial competition for their purchase, hire, and use) tend to reflect the value of the goods that can be manufactured. Every change in prices, either for finished consumer goods or the factors of production, serves as a signal of market change and as the data for revised economic calculations regarding new, more cost-efficient ways in which those factors should be utilized and combined to satisfy consumer demands.

A change in price is precisely meant to act as the information and the inducement for any needed changes concerning what should be produced and how. Government control or manipulation of a market price brings about distortions in market activity that are inconsistent with the actual supply and demand conditions prevailing in the overall economic order. Furthermore, the distortions and imbalances price controls induce create a situation in which such controls may end up being extended throughout more and more segments of the economy until the entire structure of market prices and the direction of production come under government command.

Mises' classic example to demonstrate this process was a government control on the price of some basic product such as milk. Suppose that the government wishes to make milk more readily available at a more reasonable price by setting the price of milk below the free market price. Milk retailers would now find their selling price set by the government was at a level below their cost of buying that milk at the wholesale level. The supply of milk at the retail level would, as a result, decrease—the opposite of what was the intention behind the government price control! The government now finds itself in a dilemma: It can either repeal the price control and let the market determine the price, or it can extend the control to the wholesale milk market by imposing a maximum price at which wholesale dealers may sell milk to retail outlets. If it does extend the control, the government now creates the same type of imbalance, but at one stage further removed from the consumer. The wholesale dealer finds that his selling price is now set below the price he must pay for milk from the dairy farmer. The wholesaler now purchases less milk from his farming sources, once again reducing the amount of milk available at the retail level. The government once again, faces the same dilemma, to either free prices from its controls or extend the controls once more, this time to the price the dairy farmers can charge the wholesale purchasers.

If the government once more extends the range of its price controls, a milk shortage results from production cutbacks at the farming level, since the farmers, too, have costs of manufacturing that are now found to be higher than the maximum price the government lets them charge to the wholesalers. If the government insists upon enforcement of its price controls, they must now be extended to those sectors of the market that provide the resources and equipment upon which the farming industry is dependent.

The dynamics of this government-created series of price and production distortions finally must lead to the controls being extended to wider and wider segments of the economy, until finally the entire structure of market prices come under government command. The necessary and essential connection and interdependency among the entire network of prices means that either they are left free to coordinate the interacting demands and supplies of the market, or the government must replace the market with its own network of administratively imposed price and production controls. If the latter occurs, the market has been replaced with planning. As Mises frequently reminded his readers, the interventionist "middle-of-the road" threatens to lead to socialism, if the interventions are taken to their logical end.[76]

Economic Rationality and Irrational Economic Policy

Mises' conclusion from his investigation into the nature and workings of socialist and interventionist systems was that there was no viable alternative to a functioning free market economy.[77] Socialist central planning meant the end of all economic rationality through the abolition of private property, market competition, and prices. Interventionism, while not so radical in its effects, nonetheless disrupted the functioning of the price system and undermined the activities of market-directed entrepreneurs and enterprise decisionmakers guided by the profit motive to attempt to best serve the consuming public.

Not only could the market economy be shown theoretically to be far superior to any other system of economic organization but the history of the last three hundred years also demonstrated the market's liberating quality in providing a wide range of freedom, unsurpassed economic improvement, and potential for peace and cultural advancement. So why was the market economy opposed, resisted, and condemned by so many in society? Mises offered several reasons for this strange and peculiar phenomenon.

First, he suggested that modern society still carried the cultural residue of the ancient world, with its hostility to work and money. Among the ancients, money-making, commerce and trade, middleman speculation, and money-lending were condemned as beneath and unseemly for a free man of culture and refinement. These were lower aspects of the daily affairs of life, often involving tasks and activities properly belonging to the slave or servant.

In the Middle Ages and the early modern period, the man of letters and the artist lived outside the arena of market transactions for their existence; instead, they had patrons among the nobility or the Church who subsidized and sheltered them from the uncertain winds of earning a living. With the dawn of the market economy, such patronage began to diminish in size and security. Intellectuals were now increasingly thrown upon the market to make their own way, and to do so by serving the tastes and fashions of an emerging middle class and the wider general public. They were unable to pursue a calling for its own sake, for a higher purpose above the cultural vulgarity of the presumably uneducated common man.

Resentment, Mises suggested, often grew into a matching envy and anger when friends, relatives, and those of apparently lesser cultural sensitivity earned far greater incomes than the intellectual and artist, while at the same time these "bourgeois" increasingly held a higher social status in society than this cultural elite. Intellectuals dreamed of better worlds, more cultured social arrangements, different human relationships than those fostered and rewarded in the market. They became social engineers conjuring up visions of planned societies more to their liking and within which they would be appreciated and have positions of power and recognition. The intellectuals became the designers and proselytizers of beautiful socialist futures to come.[78]

Second, Mises said, the market economy has been opposed because it not only ignores privilege and status, it also undermines them. Each individual's social and economic position must be won and retained through one means: success in serving the other members of the society by offering a product or service in the social system of division of labor better than that of rivals. There are no guarantees in the market. As a result, those whose economic and social position is challenged by the competition of others attempt to use the government to restrict free competition. Special interest group politics resists the functioning of the market. And in the process of successfully winning privileges and favors, special interests also succeed in creating conflicts among a growing number of segments of the society as groups vie with each other for the fruits of state intervention.[79]

Third, said Mises, there is a significant lack of understanding on the part of most people about the nature and actual working of the market economy. Understanding the market order requires a certain degree of abstract reasoning in which the individual appreciates how his actions and those of multitudes of others are integrated into a interdependent system of cooperation connected through the incentives and valuation information provided by the price system. As a result, the arguments for socialism or interventionism have often seemed appealing to many.[80] If an individual does not hold the position he would like to have, or does not earn the income that he thinks he deserves, he easily is persuaded that his circumstance is not due to the reality of his ability and worth as estimated in the processes of market exchange. No, it is due to greedy employers, selfish businessmen, and sinister speculators manipulating markets and prices. The "solution" seems to be government mandated minimum wages, government-guaranteed prices, government redistribution of "unearned" wealth to the deserving and needing. "Unfair" competition can be rectified through regulatory policies and business taxes.

Finally, Mises provided another reason for the resistance to the rationality of the market economy: a cultural lag. The market economy and its institutions have developed and incorporated a increasing number of people and generations who find themselves living and working in the capitalist society, but their everyday thinking about man and the social order are still based on older conceptions of man and society more appropriate to precapitalist existence. "One cannot make a social philosophy one's own as easily as a new costume. It must be earned—earned with the effort of thought," Mises said. "More menacing than barbarians storming the walls from without are the seeming citizens within—those who are citizens in gesture but not in thought."[81]

Conclusion

All these reasons for opposition to the market economy have helped create the philosophies and ideologies of socialism and interventionism that have dominated the twentieth century. They have produced that "revolt against reason" that Mises fought to oppose through his analysis of the logic of human action and the rationality of the market economy.

Both supporters and opponents of Ludwig von Mises and his ideas have called him dogmatic, uncompromising, and intransigent. But if one actually reads his work, it is clear that Mises had only one dogma: the importance of using our reason. He had one uncompromising principle: the rule of rational argument. He had one intransigence: the courage and duty to accept and act upon what our logic dictates.

In spite of the trends prevailing during his lifetime, Mises chose to swim against the tide. He was confident that trends could change. They had in the past, and they would again.[82] He devoted his life and work to reasoning and writing both for those in his own time and for others who would follow. He said as much in the preface for the 1932 edition of *Socialism*:

> I know only too well how hopeless it seems to convince impassioned supporters of the Socialist Idea by logical demonstration that their views are preposterous and absurd. I know too well that they do not want to hear, to see, or above all to think, and they are open to no argument. But new generations grow up with clear eyes and open minds. And they will approach things from a disinterested, unprejudiced standpoint, they will weigh and examine, will think and act with forethought. It is for them that this book is written.[83]

Mises believed that no man could stand apart as a passive observer of the great intellectual battles of the time. Each man was called upon to make his contribution:

> Everyone carries a part of society on his shoulders; no one is relieved of his share of responsibility by others. And no one can find a safe way out for himself if society is sweeping towards destruction. Therefore everyone, in his own interest, must thrust himself vigor-

ously into the intellectual battle. None can stand aside with unconcern, the interests of everyone hangs on the result. Whether he chooses or not, every man is drawn into the great historical struggle, the decisive battle into which out epoch has plunged us. . . . Whether society shall continue to evolve or whether it shall decay lies . . . in the hand of man. Whether Society is good or bad may be a matter of individual judgment; but whoever prefers life to death, happiness to suffering, well-being to misery, must accept society. And whoever desires that society should exist and develop must also accept, without limitation or reserve, private ownership in the means of production.[84]

Ludwig von Mises' writings stand as one of the great contributions in this intellectual battle of ideas. And if the twenty-first century turns out to be freer and more prosperous than the twentieth century, it will have been in some part due to his unrelenting defense of human freedom, economic liberty, and the free market order.

Notes

[1]Ludwig von Mises, N*ation, State and Economy: Contributions to the Politics and History of Our Time* [1919] (New York: New York University Press, 1983), 216.

[2]Ibid., 218–19. Twenty years before the Second World War began, Mises warned the Germans that militarism would lead to unprecedented disaster. Given the millions of German lives lost and the near-destruction of German industry, he was proven right. At the same time, he predicted that sticking to production and trade would lead to unprecedented peace and prosperity. In postwar Germany, he was proven right once again.

[3]Ludwig von Mises, *Epistemological Problems of Economics* [1933] (New York: New York University Press, 1981), 17–22; also, Murray N. Rothbard, "Praxeology as the Method of the Social Sciences," [1973] in *The Logic of Action*, Vol. I (Lyme, NH: Edward Elgar, 1997), 40–52.

[4]On the central ideas of the Austrian School of economics, see Ludwig von Mises, "The Historical Setting of the Austrian School of Economics," [1969] in Bettina Bien Greaves, ed., *Austrian Economics: An Anthology* (Irvington-on-Hudson, NY: Foundation for Economic Education, 1996), 53–76; Ludwig M. Lachmann, "The Significance of the Austrian School of Economics in the History of Ideas," [1966] in Richard M. Ebeling, ed., *Austrian Economics: A Reader* (Hillsdale, MI: Hillsdale College Press, 1991),

17–39; and Richard M. Ebeling, "The Significance of Austrian Economics in Twentieth-Century Economic Thought," in Richard M. Ebeling, ed., *Austrian Economics: Perspectives on the Past and Prospects for the Future* (Hillsdale, MI: Hillsdale College Press, 1991), 1–40.

[5]Now known as Lvov, Ukraine.

[6]For recollections of Mises' private seminar by some of its members, see Margit von Mises, *My Years with Ludwig von Mises* (Cedar Falls, IA: Center for Futures Education, 2nd ed., 1984), Appendix I: "Impressions of the Mises Vienna Seminar," 199–211; and Ludwig von Mises, *Notes and Recollections* [1940] (South Holland, IL: Libertarian Press, 1978), 97–100.

[7]Ludwig von Mises, *Epistemological Problems of Economics*, 17: "The theorems of economics are derived not from the observation of facts, but through deduction from the fundamental category of action. . . . They are of aprioristic derivation and therefore lay claim to the apodictic certainty that belongs to basic principles so derived." And *Human Action, A Treatise on Economics* (Irvington-on-Hudson, NY: Foundation for Economic Education, 4th ed., 1996), 39: "The theorems attained by correct praxeological [economic] reasoning are not only perfectly certain and incontestable, like the correct mathematical theorems. They refer, moreover, with the full rigidity of their apodictic certainty and incontestability to the reality of action as its appears in life and history. Praxeology conveys exact and precise knowledge of real things."

[8]Mises, *Human Action*, 72–91.

[9]As an example of this, see Johannes Stark, "National Socialism and Science," [1934] in George L. Mosse, ed., *Nazi Culture* (New York: Grosset & Dunlap, 1966), 205–7: "The slogan has been coined, and has been spread particularly by the Jews, that science is international. . . . From the National Socialist side, in opposition to this view, it must be insisted upon with all possible emphasis that in the National Socialist state, even for the scientist, the duty to the nation stands above any and all other obligations. The scientist, too, must consider himself a member and a servant of the nation. Rather, in his work, he must serve the nation first and foremost. For these reasons, the leading scientific positions in the National Socialist state are to be occupied not by elements alien to the *Volk* but only by nationally conscious German men. But aside from this fundamental National Socialist demand, the slogan of the international character of science is based on an untruth, insofar as it asserts that the type and the success of scientific activity are independent of membership in a national group. . . . The spirit of the German enables him to observe things outside himself exactly as they are, without interpolation of his own ideas and wishes. . . . The German's love of nature and his aptitude for natural science are based on this endowment. Thus it is understandable that natural science is overwhelmingly a creation of the Nordic–Germanic blood component of the

Aryan peoples. . . . The Jewish spirit is wholly different in its orientation: above everything else it is focused on its own ego, its own conception, and its own self-interest. In accordance with this natural orientation the Jewish spirit strives to heed facts only to the extent that they do not hamper his opinions and purposes." See also Bruno Thüring, "German Mathematics" [1936], Ibid., 208–15.

[10]Mises, *Epistemological Problems of Economics*, 12–13; *Human Action*, 25 & 32–41; and *The Ultimate Foundation of Economic Science*, 11–14 & 17–21.

[11]Mises, *Epistemological Problems of Economics*, 27: "If thinking and action were really conditioned by place, time, race, nationality, climate, class, etc., then it would be impossible for a German of the twentieth century to understand anything of the logic and action of the Greek of the age of Pericles." See also Ernst Cassirer, *The Myth of the State* (New Haven: Yale University Press, 1946), 13–15: "Language always shows us a definite and thoroughgoing logical structure, both in its sound system and in its morphological system. We have no evidence whatever for a 'pre-logical' language. . . . What holds for 'primitive' language holds also for primitive thought. Its structure may seem to us to be strange and paradoxical; but it never lacks a definite logical structure. Even the uncivilized man cannot live in the world without a constant effort to understand that world. And for that purpose he had to develop and to use some general forms and categories of thought. The savage is no discursive thinker and dialectician. Nevertheless, the same capability of analysis and synthesis, of discernment and unification, that, according to Plato, constitute and characterize the dialectic art. When studying some very primitive forms of religious and mythical thought—for instance, the religion of totemistic societies—we are surprised to find to what a high degree the primitive mind feels the desire and the need to discern and divide, to order and classify the elements of its environment. There is hardly anything that escapes its constant urge for classification. . . . The results of these first attempts to analyze and systematize the world of sense-experience are far different from ours. But the processes themselves are very similar; they express the same desire of human nature to come to terms with reality, to live in an ordered universe, and to overcome the chaotic state in which things and thoughts have not yet assumed a definite shape and structure."

[12]On Mises' critique of Marxian philosophy and class analysis, see *Theory and History*, [1957] (Auburn, AL: Ludwig von Mises Institute, 1985), 102–58; and *Socialism, An Economic and Sociological Analysis* (Indianapolis: Liberty Classics, 1981), 279–320; also, "The Clash of Group Interests" [1945] in Richard M. Ebeling, ed., *Money, Method and the Market Process: Essays by Ludwig von Mises* (Norwell, MA: Kluwer Academic Press, 1990), 202–14.

[13]Mises, *Epistemological Problems of Economics*, 204–6; and 186–94.

[14]Mises, *Human Action*, 21 & 89.

[15]Ibid., 24. Mises readily conceded, "It may be admitted that it is impossible to provide conclusive evidence for the proposition that my logic is the logic of all other people and by all means absolutely the only human logic and that the categories of my action are the categories of all other people's action and by all means absolutely the categories of all human action. . . . But is beyond doubt that the principle according to which an Ego deals with every human being as if the other were a thinking and acting being like himself has evidenced it usefulness both in mundane life and in scientific research. . . . [T]he positivist must not overlook the fact that in addressing his fellow men he presupposes—tacitly and implicitly—the intersubjective validity of logic and thereby the reality of the realm of the alter Ego's thought and action, of his eminent human character." See also Alfred Schutz, *The Phenomenology of the Social World* [1932] (Evanston, IL: Northwestern University Press, 1967), 21–22.

[16]On Mises' analysis of "rationality" and its meaning, see *Epistemological Problems of Economics*, 31–35; *Human Action*, 19–22; and "The Treatment of the 'Irrational' in the Social Sciences," [1944] in Ebeling, ed., *Money, Method and the Market Process*, 16–36.

[17]Ludwig von Mises, *The Ultimate Foundation of Economic Science* (Princeton: D. Van Nostrand, 1962), 14–17.

[18]Mises, *Epistemological Problems of Economics*, 23–30; *Human Action*, 32–41; *The Ultimate Foundations of Economic Science*, 17-21. Also, Friedrich von Wieser, *Social Economics* [1914] (New York: Augustus M. Kelley, 1967), 8–9: "The theoretical economist need never deplore a lack of the instruments which are employed in the exact natural sciences. Whatever advantages they may otherwise enjoy and great as are their achievements, they are none the less strangers to their object, nature. They may never scan the innermost recesses of nature. . . . The group of practical sciences, of which economic theory is one, can accomplish more. The object of investigation is man in a condition of activity. Hence our mind ratifies every accurate description of the processes of his consciousness by the affirmative declaration that such is the case, and by the compelling feeling that it must be so necessarily. . . . In these cases we, each of us, hear the law pronounced by an unmistakable inner voice. What unequaled advantage to the naturalist, could he, too, appeal to the voices of nature for their confirmation of the laws prevailing in the organic and inorganic world! Where the natural sciences can only offer proof, the theory of economics can persuade; it can enlist the unqualified inner consent of readers." Also, Fritz Machlup, "If Matter Could Talk," [1969] in *Methodology of Economics and Other Social Sciences* (New York: Academic Press, 1978), 309–32.

[19]Mises, *Epistemological Problems of Economics*, 13: "[Praxeology's] goal is the comprehension of the universal, and its procedure is formal and axiomatic. It views action and the conditions under which action takes place not

in their concrete form, as we encounter them in everyday life, nor in their actual setting, as we view them in each of the sciences of nature and history, but as formal constructions that enable us to grasp the patterns of human action in their purity. . . ." Also, *Human Action*, 39: "The starting point of praxeology is not a choice of axioms and a decision about methods of procedure, but reflection about the essence of action." Also, *The Ultimate Foundations of Economic Science*, 5–6: "The starting point of praxeology is a self-evident truth, the cognition of action, that is, cognition of the fact that there is such a thing as consciously aiming at ends." Also, *Theory and History*, 12–15 & 283–84.

[20]Mises, *Epistemological Problems of Economics*, 14.

[21]Mises, *Human Action*, 22: "Man is in a position to act because he has the ability to discover causal relations which determine change and becoming in the universe. Acting requires and presupposes the category of causality. Only a man who sees the world in the light of causality is fitted to act. In this sense we may say that causality is a category of action. The category *means and ends* presupposes the category *cause and effect*."

[22]Mises, *Human Action*, 105: "The uncertainty of the future is already implied in the very notion of action. That man acts and that the future is uncertain are by no means independent matters. They are only two different modes of establishing one thing. . . . If man knew the future, he would not have to choose and would not have to act." Also, *The Ultimate Foundations of Economic Science*, 62–72.

[23]Mises, *Human Action*, 99: "The notion of change implies the notion of temporal sequence. . . . The concepts of change and of time are inseparably linked together. Action aims at change and is therefore in the temporal order. Human reason is even incapable of conceiving the ideas of timeless existence and of timeless action. He who acts distinguishes between the time before the action, the time absorbed by the action, and the time after the action has been finished."

[24]Ibid., 13–14: "Acting man is eager to substitute a more satisfactory state of affairs for a less satisfactory. His mind imagines conditions which suit him better, and his action aims at bringing about this desired state. The incentive that impels a man to act is always some uneasiness. A man perfectly content with the state of his affairs would have no incentive to change things. . . . But to make a man act, uneasiness and the image of a more satisfactory state alone are not sufficient. A third condition is required: the expectation that purposeful behavior has the power to remove or at least to alleviate the felt uneasiness. In the absence of this condition no action is feasible. Man must yield to the inevitable. He must submit to destiny."

[25]Mises, *Epistemological Problems of Economics*, 24: "As thinking and acting men, we grasp the concept of action. In grasping this concept we simultaneous-

ly grasp the closely corresponding concepts of value, wealth, exchange, price, and cost. They are all necessarily implied in the concept of action, and together with them the concepts of valuing scale of value and importance, scarcity and abundance, advantage and disadvantage, success and failure, and profit and loss. The logical unfolding of all these concepts and categories in systematic derivation from the fundamental category of action and the demonstration of the necessary relations among them constitutes the first task of our science." Also, *The Ultimate Foundations of Economic Science*, 8. For a clear exposition of the logical unfolding of these basic and fundamental concepts of economics from the axiom of action, see Murray N. Rothbard, *Man, Economy and State: A Treatise on Economic Principles*, Vol. I [1962] (Los Angeles: Nash Publishing, 1970), 1–66.

[26]Mises, *Human Action*, 198: "Both in acting and in theorizing about acting, man can neither free himself from these categories nor go beyond them. A kind of acting categorically different from that determined by these categories is neither possible nor conceivable for man." Also, Mises, *Epistemological Problems of Economics*, 95–96: "Though the men of the Middle Ages would not have understood the law of marginal utility, they nevertheless did not and could not act otherwise than as the law of marginal utility describes. Even the man of the Middle Ages sought to apportion the means at his disposal in such a way that he attained the same level of satisfaction in every kind of want. . . . Even in the Middle Ages no one voluntarily exchanged a horse for a cow unless he valued the cow more highly than the horse." Also, Eugen von Böhm-Bawerk, *Capital and Interest*, Vol. II [1914] (South Holland, IL: Libertarian Press, 1959), 204: "And for centuries long before science set up the doctrine of marginal utility, the common man was accustomed to seek things and abandon things, not in accordance with the highest utility that they are by nature capable of delivering, but in accordance with the increase or decrease in concrete utility that depends on each given good. In other words, he practiced the doctrine of marginal utility before economic theory discovered it." Also, Eli F. Heckscher, "A Plea for Theory in Economic History," *Economic History* (January 1929), 525–34.

[27]See Albert A. Trever, *A History of Greek Economic Thought* [1916] (Philadelphia: Porcupine Press, 1978), 34–37, 70–71, 96, 146–47.

[28]See Edwin Cannan, *Collected Works of Edwin Cannan*, Vol. VIII: "A Review of Economic Theory" [1929] (London: Routledge/Thoemmes Press, 1997), 93–121; Frank Taussig, *Principles of Economics*, Vol. I (New York: Macmillan Co., 1913), 30–48; John Bates Clark, *Essentials of Economic Theory* [1907] (New York: Augustus M. Kelley, 1968), 59–73.

[29]David Hume, "Of the Jealousy of Trade," in *Essays: Moral, Political and Literary* (Indianapolis: Liberty Classics, 1987), 331: "Were our narrow and malignant policies to meet with success, we should reduce all our neighboring

nations to the same state of sloth and ignorance that prevails in Morocco and the coast of Barbary. But what would be the consequence? They could send us no commodities: They could take none from us: Our domestic commerce itself would languish for want of emulation, example, and instruction: And we ourselves should soon fall into the same abject condition, to which we had reduced them. I shall therefore venture to acknowledge, that, not only as a man, but as a British subject, I pray for the flourishing commerce of Germany, Spain, Italy, and even France itself."

³⁰Adam Smith, *The Wealth of Nations* (New York: Modern Library, 1937), Book I, Chapters I–III and Book IV, Chapter II.

³¹David Ricardo, *The Works and Correspondence of David Ricardo*, Vol. I: "On The Principles of Political Economy and Taxation," (Cambridge: Cambridge University Press, 1962), 128–49; see also Jacob Viner, *Studies in the Theory of International Trade* [1937] (New York: Augustus M. Kelley, 1965), 437–526; Gottfried Haberler, *The Theory of International Trade* (London: William Hodge, 1937), 125–44.

³²Mises, *Human Action*, 159–64; and *Nationalökonomie: Theorie des Handelns und Wirtschaftens* [1940] (Munich: Philosophia Verlag, 1980), 126–33. *Nationalökonomie* was the original German language precursor to *Human Action*, published in Geneva, Switzerland, shortly before Mises' immigration to the United States in the summer of 1940. See also Lionel Robbins, *The Evolution of Modern Economic Theory* (New York: Macmillan, 1970), 32–33: "It was realized too, although comparatively recently, that . . . the famous theory of comparative costs . . . is capable of providing, so to speak, an analytical stiffing of the traditional doctrine of the advantages of division of labor in general. Indeed, in our own time it has been represented with great cogency by von Mises as nothing less than the fundamental explanation of the spontaneous forces making for social cooperation in general —the *Ricardo'sche Vergesellschaftungsgesetz*, or Law of Association, as he calls it."

³³Mises, *Human Action*, 159–60.

³⁴Mises, *Socialism*, 259–60; *Human Action*, 157–58.

³⁵Mises, *Socialism*, 259–61, 263–64, 275–76; and, *Human Action*, 273: "In nature there prevail irreconcilable conflicts of interests. The means of subsistence are scarce. Proliferation tends to outrun subsistence. Only the fittest plants and animals survive. . . . Social cooperation under division of labor removes such antagonisms. It substitutes partnership and mutuality for hostility. The members of society are united in a common venture." F. A. Hayek, "The Confusion of Language in Political Thought," [1968] in *New Studies in Philosophy, Politics, Economics and the History of Ideas* (Chicago: University of Chicago Press, 1978), 90, points out that "the term catallactics, which has often been proposed as a replacement for the term 'economics' as the name for the theory of the market order [is] derived from the Greek verb *katallatein* (or *katallassein*), which significantly means

not only 'to exchange' but also 'to receive into the community' and 'to turn from enemy into friend.'"

[36]Mises, *Human Action*, 195–98.

[37]Mises, *Socialism*, 268–69.

[38]Mises, *Liberalism: The Classical Tradition* [1927] (Irvington-on-Hudson, NY: Foundation for Economic Education, 1996), 18–38.

[39]Mises, *Socialism*, 277: "The social function of private ownership in the means of production is to put the goods into the hands of those who know best how to use them, into the hands, that is, of the most expert managers. Nothing is more foreign to the essence of property than special privileges for special property and protection for special producers. Any kind of restraint such as exclusive rights and other privileges of producers are apt to obstruct the working of the social function of property."

[40]Ludwig von Mises, "Liberty and Property," [1958] in *Two Essays by Ludwig von Mises* (Auburn, AL: Ludwig von Mises Institute, 1991), 34: "In the market economy the individuals are free to choose the way in which they want to integrate themselves into the frame of social cooperation."

[41]Mises, *Socialism*, 34: "Economic action demands stable conditions. The extensive and lengthy process of production is the more successful the greater the periods of time to which it is adapted. It demands continuity, and this continuity cannot be disturbed without the most serious disadvantages. This means that economic action requires peace, the exclusion of violence."

[42]Mises, *Human Action*, 287–88: "The inequality of individuals with regard to wealth and income is an essential feature of the market economy. . . . What pressure is needed to impel an individual to contribute his share to the cooperative effort of production is exercised by the price structure of the market. This pressure is indirect. It puts on each individual's contribution a premium graduated according to the value which the consumers attach to this contribution. In rewarding the individual's effort according to its value, it leaves to everybody the choice between a more or less complete utilization of his own faculties and abilities." Also, Ludwig von Mises, "On Equality and Inequality," [1961] in Ebeling, ed., *Money, Method and the Market Process*, 190–201.

[43]Mises, *Human Action*, 285: "Government is a guarantor of liberty and is compatible with liberty only if its range is adequately restricted to the preservation of what is called economic freedom. Where there is no market economy, the best-intentioned provisions of constitutions and laws remain a dead letter."

[44]Ibid., 264–65: "All civilizations have up to now been based on private ownership of the means of production. In the past civilization and private property have been linked together. . . . If historical experience could teach us anything, it would be that private property is inextricably linked

with civilization. . . . The system of market economy has never been fully and purely tried. But there prevailed in the orbit of Western civilization since the Middle Ages by and large a general tendency toward the abolition of institutions hindering the operation of the market economy. With the successive progress of this tendency, population figures multiplied and the masses' standard of living was raised to an unprecedented and hitherto undreamed of level."

[45]Mises, *Socialism*, 31: "To have production goods in the economic sense, i.e., to make them serve one's own economic purposes, it is not necessary to have them physically in the way one must have consumption goods if one is to use them up or to use them lastingly. To drink coffee I do not need to own a coffee plantation in Brazil, an ocean liner, and a coffee roasting plant, though all these means of production must be used to bring a cup of coffee to my table. Sufficient that others own these means of production and employ them for me. In the society which divides labor no one is exclusive owner of the means of production, either of the material things or of the personal element, capacity to work. All means of production render services to everyone who buys and sells on the market."

[46]Ibid., 101 &103.

[47]Mises, *Liberalism*, 71–72 & 74–75.

[48]Mises, *Human Action*, 199.

[49]Ludwig von Mises, *Bureaucracy* (New Haven: Yale University Press, 1944), 29.

[50]Mises, *Human Action*, 212–14; and *Epistemological Problems of Economics*, 156–59.

[51]Mises, *Socialism*, 285–86.

[52]Mises, *Human Action*, 117 & 338: "Competitors aim at excellence and pre-eminence in accomplishments within a system of mutual cooperation. The function of competition is to assign to every member of a social system that position in which he can best serve the whole of society and all its members. It is a method for selecting the most able man for each performance. . . . Competing in cooperation and cooperating in competition all people are instrumental is bring about the result, viz., the price structure of the market, the allocation of the factors of production to the various lines of want-satisfaction, and the determination of the share of each individual."

[53]Mises, *Socialism*, 170–71; *Human Action*, 283: "Now it is true that the employer has the right to fire the employee. But if he makes use of this right in order to indulge his whims, he hurts his own interests. It is to his own disadvantage if he discharges a better man in order to hire a less efficient one. The market does not directly prevent anybody from arbitrarily inflicting harm on his fellow citizens; it only puts a penalty upon such conduct. The shopkeeper is free to be rude to his customers provided he is ready to bear the consequences. The consumers are free to boycott a pur-

veyor provided they are ready to pay the costs. What impels every man to the utmost exertion in the service of his fellow men and curbs innate tendencies toward arbitrariness and malice is, in the market, not compulsion and coercion on the part of gendarmes, hangmen, and penal courts; it is self-interest." Also, *Bureaucracy*, 36–39.

[54]Mises, *Socialism*, 271: "Civilization is a product of leisure and the peace of mind that only the division of labor can make possible."

[55]Ibid., 281 & 285–86: "Society is the union of human beings for the better exploitation of the natural conditions of existence; in its very conception it abolishes the struggle between human beings and substitutes the mutual aid which provides the essential motive of all members united in an organism. Within the limits of society there is no struggle, only peace. . . . People say that in the competitive struggle, economic lives are destroyed. This, however, merely means that those who succumb are forced to seek in the structure of the social system of division of labor a position other than the one they would like to occupy. It does not by any means signify that they are to starve. In the capitalist society there is a place and bread for all. Its ability to expand provides sustenance for every worker."

[56]Ibid., 276; also, *Human Action*, 192–93.

[57]Ludwig von Mises, "Economic Calculation in the Socialist Commonwealth" [1920] in F. A. Hayek, ed., *Collectivist Economic Planning* (London: George Routledge & Sons, 1935), 87–130, or Israel M. Kirzner, ed., *Classics of Austrian Economics*, Vol. III (London: William Pickering, 1994), 3–30; his critique of central planning was integrated into his wider 1922 treatise, *Socialism*, 95–194.

[58]See Richard M. Ebeling, "Economic Calculation Under Socialism: Ludwig von Mises and His Predecessors," in Jeffrey M. Herberner, ed., *The Meaning of Ludwig von Mises* (Norwell, MA: Kluwer Academic Press, 1993), 56–101, for an analysis of those writers before World War I who demonstrated the limits and impossibilities of socialist central planning, and a contrast of their views with Mises' critique of planning.

[59]Mises, *Human Action*, 206–9.

[60]Mises, "Economic Calculation in the Socialist Commonwealth," Hayek, ed., 108–9; Kirzner, ed., 15–16; *Liberalism*, 71–72.

[61]Mises, *Socialism*, 123 & 113.

[62]Mises, "Economic Calculation in the Socialist Commonwealth," Hayek, ed., 109–10; Kirzner ed., 16; and *Socialism*, 121 & 187–88.

[63]See, in particular, the most famous theory of market socialism by Oskar Lange, in *On the Economic Theory of Socialism* [1936–37] (New York: McGraw-Hill, 1964), 57–143.

[64]Mises, *Socialism*, 119–23; *Human Action*, 698–715; Friedrich A. Hayek, "Socialist Calculation: The Competitive 'Solution,'" [1940] in Bruce Caldwell, ed., *The Collected Works of F. A. Hayek, Vol. X: Socialism and War* (Chicago:

University of Chicago Press, 1997), 117–40, and "Two Pages of Fiction: The Impossibility of Socialist Calculation," [1982] in Chiaki Nishiyama and Kurt R. Leube, ed., *The Essence of Hayek* (Stanford: Hoover Institution Press, 1984), 53–61.

[65]Ludwig von Mises, *Critique of Interventionism* [1929] (Irvington-on-Hudson, NY: Foundation for Economic Education, 1996), 4.

[66]Mises, *Human Action*, 718–19; also, *Socialism*, 485–86.

[67]Ibid., 719; also, *Socialism*, 491: "What the interventionist aims at is the substitution of police pressure for the choice of the consumers. All this talk: the state should do this or that, ultimately means: The police should force the consumers to behave otherwise than they would behave spontaneously. In such proposals as: let *us* raise farm prices, let *us* raise wage rates, let *us* lower profits, let *us* curtail the salaries of executives, the *us* ultimately refers to the police."

[68]Mises, *Socialism*, 45–46; *Liberalism*, 34–38; *Human Action*, 719–24; *The Ultimate Foundation of Economic Science*, 94–101.

[69]Mises, *Human Action*, 257–397; and "Profit and Loss," [1951] in *Planning for Freedom* (South Holland, IL: Libertarian Press, 1980), 108–50.

[70]Mises, *Human Action*, 733–34.

[71]Mises, *Liberalism*, 55.

[72]Mises, *Human Action*, 737–42 & 806–11; and *Interventionism: An Economic Analysis* [1940] (Irvington-on-Hudson, NY: Foundation for Economic Education, 1998), 51–55.

[73]Mises, *Human Action*, 743.

[74]Mises, *Critique of Interventionism*, 5–6.

[75]Mises, *Human Action*, 743–48; *Critique of Interventionism*, 5–7; *Interventionism: An Economic Analysis*, 17–21.

[76]Mises, *Critique of Interventionism*, 7–11 & 97–106; *Interventionism: An Economic Analysis*, 23–34; *Human Action*, 758–79; *Socialism*, 488–90; *Planning for Freedom*, 18–35 & 72–82.

[77]Space does not permit a discussion of Mises' analysis of monopoly and cartels and his demonstration that, except for when government intervention establishes and maintains them through legal privilege to select producers, they are, in the long run, unsustainable on a free market. The only exception, conceptually possible but historically rare, was cases in which a single producer (or a small group of cooperating producers) acquired control of an essential resource or raw material, without which a product could not be produced. Even in this case, the monopoly resource owner would be able to charge a "monopoly price" only if consumer demand was sufficiently inelastic (that is, unresponsive to an increase in the price of the good) so that, at the higher monopoly price, the monopolist was able to earn a greater total revenue than if he sold the good at the lower price that would have prevailed on the market in a more competi-

tive market environment. See *Liberalism*, 90–95; *Human Action*, 357–79; and "Monopoly Prices" [1944] in *Quarterly Journal of Austrian Economics* (Summer 1998), 1–28.

[78]Mises, *Socialism*, 419–23; *Epistemological Problems of Economics*, 194–97, and *The Anti-Capitalistic Mentality* (Princeton: D. Van Nostrand, 1956). On the antimarket ideas of the ancient Greeks and Romans, see Lewis H. Haney, *History of Economic Thought* (New York: Macmillan, 1936), 56–85; and on the resentments of the intellectual against the market economy, see Bertrand de Jouvenel, "The Attitude of the Intellectuals to the Market Economy," *The Owl* (January 1951), 19–27.

[79]Mises, *Liberalism*, 155–87; *Human Action*, 315–19 & 748–55; also, "The Clash of Group Interests," [1945] in Ebeling, ed., *Money, Method and the Market Process*, 202–14.

[80]Mises, *Socialism*, 319–20.

[81]Ibid., 38.

[82]Mises, "Trends Can Change" [1951] in *Planning for Freedom*, 173–79.

[83]Mises, *Socialism*, 13.

[84]Ibid., 468–69.

CHARLES K. ROWLEY

The Nobel Laureates: Milton Friedman, George J. Stigler, James M. Buchanan, Ronald H. Coase, and Gary S. Becker

The Nobel Prizes were initiated in 1901 in physics, chemistry, medicine or physiology, literature, and peace. In his will, Swedish chemist and engineer Alfred Nobel stipulated that prizes in the first three categories should be given to those who have made the most important discovery, in the field of literature to those who have made the most outstanding work of an idealistic tendency, and in the field of peace to those who have done the most or the best work for fraternity between nations.

In conjunction with its tercentenary celebration in 1968, the Central Bank of Sweden instituted a new award: the Central Bank of Sweden Prize in Economic Science in Memory of Alfred Nobel. The award is designed to be given according to the same principles and rules as the original Nobel Prizes. The Bank had to overcome serious doubts expressed by the Royal Swedish Academy of Science concerning whether economics was sufficiently scientific in nature as to warrant a prize on the same footing with prizes in the hard sciences. Gunnar Myrdal, a socialist and member of the Swedish Academy, who would win the Prize for Economic Science in 1974, played a major role in winning the support of the Academy for the new award.

The author wishes to acknowledge Maria Pia Paganelli's research assistance in preparing this essay. He also thanks Lissa Roche for helpful editorial comments.

The basic idea of the original Nobel Prize is to recognize specific achievements rather than outstanding persons.[1] This is clearly set out in Nobel's own formulation that the prizes should be awarded for "discoveries," "inventions," and "improvements" in the natural sciences. Indeed, according to Nobel's will, the prizes were to be given to "those who, during the preceding year, shall have conferred the greatest benefit on mankind." None of the awarding authorities has honored that particular clause. However, they have all adhered to the idea of rewarding specific scientific achievements rather than outstanding scientists.

It is quite clear from the statutes that the prize in economics should be granted for specific contributions. If this principle is strictly adhered to, scholars with narrow research profiles who have made a single pathbreaking contribution should be favored over well-rounded scholars who have made several important but less dramatic contributions. With the possible exception of Robert Lucas, no young economist has succeeded in winning the prize on the basis of a single, youthful contribution. And with the exceptions of Arthur Lewis and Ronald Coase, no economist has succeeded in winning the prize on the basis of a slim volume of publications.

The procedures for the choice of the winner of the economics prize are the same as for the original Nobel Prizes. Each October, professors of economics at about seventy-five institutions worldwide are invited to nominate candidates. Nominations must reach the Swedish prize committee, which consists of five members (plus possible associates), before the end of January. Members of the prize committee and members of the Royal Swedish Academy of Sciences are also allowed to submit nominations. No other nominations are ever considered.

The prize committee is guided in its evaluations not by the quantity but by the quality of the nominations received. On this basis, the committee commissions two or more expert studies of each of the most prominent candidates usually from non-Swedish scholars. The prize committee eventually submits a prize proposal to the "social science class" of the Academy, together with an extensive survey and a detailed analysis of the various candidates and an elaborate justification of the choice made. The expert studies are included as part of the report. The prize committee operates on the principle of unanimity, achieving consensus after intensive discussions.

The report finally reaches the plenary meeting of the Academy in mid-October, where the prize committee justifies and defends its proposal. The prize is finally decided by simple majority in a secret ballot in this plenary session, where all Swedish members of the Academy (260 persons) may vote, if they are in attendance, for any person who has been proposed by a nominator. Immediately following the ballot, the prize is announced, and a press release of two or three pages describes the honored contribution.[2]

The Nobel Laureates under Review

In this presentation, I shall briefly address the careers and the contributions cited by the Royal Academy of five winners of the Nobel Prize in Economics. I shall order these evaluations in terms of the dates that they were honored: Milton Friedman (1976), George J. Stigler (1982), James M. Buchanan (1986), Ronald H. Coase (1991), and Gary S. Becker (1992). Since these Nobel laureates are viewed as among the foremost supporters of free market economics of the twentieth century, I shall also briefly attempt to evaluate their contributions to classical liberal political economy.

Milton Friedman

Milton Friedman was born in 1912 in Brooklyn, the only son and the youngest of four children of Carpatho–Rumanian Jewish immigrants who initially worked in sweatshops while they established themselves in the New World.

Friedman won a scholarship to Rutgers University in 1928 and worked his way through college, graduating with a B.A. in mathematics and economics in 1932. At Rutgers, he met two extraordinary scholars, Arthur F. Burns and Homer Jones, who introduced him to rigorous economic theory and the highest scientific standards.

In 1932, Friedman won a scholarship to study economics at the University of Chicago. In his first quarter at Chicago, he took a class from Jacob Viner, then arguably the best price theorist in the United States. This class revealed to Friedman the logical and coherent nature of economic theory. Because the students were seated alphabetically, it also introduced him to his future wife and co-author, Rose Director. During Friedman's masters program, the university's faculty included Frank Knight, Lloyd Mints, Henry Simons, Paul Douglas, and Henry Schultz. Friedman completed his masters degree at Chicago in 1933.

In the same year, he accepted a scholarship to study at Columbia University, where he came under the influence of a much more institutional and empirical approach to economics than was in vogue at that time in Chicago. He benefited greatly from his association at Columbia University with Harold Hotelling, Wesley C. Mitchell, and John Maurice Clark. This one-year visit provided Friedman with an abiding interest in high quality empirical research.

There then followed a difficult period in which Friedman was forced to move from temporary job to temporary job, always scrambling to obtain a permanent position in the American academy. This scramble was to end only in 1946 when he was appointed to an associate professorship in economics at the University of Chicago.

During his stint at the U.S. Treasury from 1941 to 1942, Friedman made the worst intellectual mistake of his career. He helped to devise and develop a scheme for withholding income tax at the source. The introduction of the withholding tax is arguably the most important cause of the growth of government in the United States during the second half of the twentieth century since it tends to obscure the full annual federal and state tax liabilities of individual taxpayers. The lesson to be learned is that one should not be overly concerned about making government efficient, especially in its role as tax collector.

Although Friedman's early career is a patchwork quilt of short-term appointments, it formed the basis for all his subsequent work. Well-versed in mathematics and statistics, trained in economic theory, and experienced in economic policy, he was uniquely equipped to confront a postwar economics profession obsessed by Keynesian theories of macroeconomic policy, heavily influenced by socialist dogma, and disillusioned with classical political economy.

In 1945–46, Friedman spent a year as associate professor of economics at the University of Minnesota, where he collaborated with George Stigler on an article, "Roofs and Ceilings," which exposed the inefficiency of rent-controls. In 1946, Friedman was appointed associate professor of economics at the University of Chicago, to succeed Jacob Viner in teaching microeconomic theory. He was promoted to full professor in 1948. In 1963, he was appointed Paul Snowden Russell Distinguished Service Professor of Economics—a position that he held until his official retirement from the University of Chicago in 1982. Since 1982, he has been a senior research fellow at Stanford University's Hoover Institution on War, Revolution, and Peace.

In 1976, Friedman was awarded the Nobel Prize in Economic Science and was cited "for his achievements in the fields of consumption analysis, monetary history and theory and for his demonstration of the complexity of stabilization policy." I shall briefly review these areas of his research program prior to concluding with a more general assessment of his contribution to political economy.

Under Frank Knight's influence during his early years at Chicago, Friedman formulated a strongly held view that economics was a positive science with a methodology significantly different from that presently in vogue. In particular, he was not impressed by the view advanced by Lionel Robbins in the 1930s which held that the veracity of theory was to be tested primarily by the correspondence between assumptions and the facts. In 1953, he advanced a radically different definition of economic science.

In his famous article, "The Methodology of Positive Economics," he argued that the realism or unrealism of assumptions is no guide to the usefulness of economic theory.[3] As in the natural sciences, only by the correspondence of the predictions of a theory with the facts should theories provisionally be accepted or rejected. This was Friedman's attempt to apply the new scientific theories of Karl Popper, which had been developed for the natural sciences, to the science of economics.

The essay was perhaps overly cavalier in dismissing the factual basis of a theory's assumptions. And the ruthless test imposed by Friedman—a single counter-example to its predictions will falsify a theory—was somewhat rash. However, there is no doubt that the substance of his essay has stood the test of time and has profoundly influenced the nature of economic research.

Nowhere is the power of this methodology more apparent than in the book that many economists consider to be Friedman's greatest technical contribution, *A Theory of the Consumption Function*.[4] Crucial to Keynesian arguments in favor of government fiscal intervention to move an economy from under-full to full-employment equilibrium was the notion of the consumption function—the notion that there exists a stable relationship between household consumption expenditures and household current income. The government could operate on this function, increasing household incomes by increased government expenditures and thereby achieving a leveraged impact upon the macroeconomy through the multiplier mechanism.

Friedman demonstrated that the Keynesian concept of household behavior was fundamentally flawed and that any leveraging of government expenditure through the multiplier process was much smaller than had been asserted. His theoretical insight is known as the "permanent income hypothesis," the notion that households adjust their expenditures only to account for perceived changes in their long-term expected or permanent income, and that they pay little attention to transitory variations.

The care with which Friedman amassed, organized, and interpreted data, and the integrity of the scholarship that led him to diligently (if unsuccessfully) search for evidence that might falsify his theory set a new standard for empirical economics.[5] The concept of permanent income has entered into virtually every field of applied economics, transforming all earlier work that relied upon current household income as an explanatory variable.

The period 1956 to 1975 witnessed the monetary revolution that ultimately led to the demise of Keynesian economics, a much reduced role for government through fiscal policy in the management of the macroeconomy, and a much greater reliance on monetary policy. Milton Friedman's scholarship had a great deal to do with this change, though he himself was no proponent of active monetary policy since his empirical analysis indicated that it typically exerted a destabilizing short-run influence on the macroeconomy.

The quantity theory of money had played an important role in classical economics. In the form of the behavioral equation $MV=PY$, classical theory argued that V, the income velocity of circulation of money, was a constant; that Y, real income, was unaffected by changes in the quantity of money (the so-called classical dichotomy); and that changes in the supply of money impacted directly on the price level. This view was derided by Keynesians who argued instead that V was not a constant but rather was highly variable and acted as a cushion preventing any change in the supply of money from exerting an impact either on real output or on the level of prices.

In an edited book, *Studies in the Quantity Theory of Money* (1956), Friedman and his co-authors attempted to rehabilitate the quantity theory, redefining it in terms of statements that defined a degree of stability in the demand for money.[6] Unlike the classical model, V was not predicted to be constant but rather to be a stable function of several variables. In a nutshell, V is seen to respond to monetary expansion in the short run by reinforcing, rather than cushioning, the impact of such an expansion on the right-hand side of the equation.

Although some of the empirical papers in the 1956 volume tended to support the restated quantity theory, the majority of the economics profession reacted with skepticism, arguing that the supply of money merely accommodated the demand for money and did not impact independently on the system. Once again, Friedman determined that the controversy could be resolved only through painstaking research. The result of this research was the monumental book co-authored with Anna Schwartz, *A Monetary History of the United States, 1867–1960.*[7] It offered substantial support for the restated quantity theory, and it explained that America's worst financial crisis, the Great Depression, was primarily induced by disastrous monetary mismanagement on the part of the Federal Reserve System.

Subsequent research by Friedman determined that (1) the impact of a fiscal deficit on nominal income was short-lived, whereas after a lag the increased rate of growth of the money supply permanently augmented the rate of inflation; (2) the adjustment of nominal income to an increased rate of monetary growth involves lags that are long and variable, making short-run monetary management a dangerous and destabilizing instrument; and (3) in the long run, additional monetary growth affects only the rate of inflation and has virtually no impact on the level or the rate of growth of real output.[8]

In his 1968 presidential address to the American Economic Association, "The Role of Monetary Policy," Friedman effectively destroyed the "Phillips Curve" hypothesis central to Keynesian policy analysis, which had suggested that there existed a stable functional relationship between the level of unemployment and the rate of price inflation. By reemphasizing the classical theory of labor market equilibrium, Friedman demonstrated that the expectations-augmented Phillips Curve was unstable in the short run unless the economy operated at the natural rate of unemployment and that the Phillips Curve was vertical in the long run. These insights, together with Friedman's justification for a nondiscretionary rate of increase in the money supply at the underlying productivity rate of the economy, are two concepts for which he is likely to be long-remembered.

Friedman's contribution to political economy goes well beyond those areas for which he was cited by the Nobel Committee. No Swedish committee at that time was likely to cite his case for restoring economic freedom in *Capitalism and Freedom* as a substantive contribution.[9] In unfolding reality, these arguments are the most important contribution that Friedman and his wife Rose, who co-wrote the enormously popular book, *Free to Choose*, have made to the well-being of countless peoples across the globe.[10] Friedman's firm voice in defense of freedom, which penetrated the citadels of coercion and gave oppressed man hope for a freer and more prosperous future, will be remembered forever.

The one notable weakness in Friedman's scholarship is the absence in his writings of any positive theory of the state. This lacuna has implied that Friedman has been forced to fight on the defensive, even in *Capitalism and Freedom*, against the market failure arguments of the new welfare economists. At most, he could skillfully deflect interventionist arguments by suggesting more market-friendly measures, for example, by supporting the use of vouchers rather than public provision to remedy externalities in the education market. A leveling of the playing field to a comparative institutions analysis of market failure versus political failure is the particular achievement of the Virginia rather than the Chicago School of economics.

George J. Stigler

George Stigler was born in Renton, Washington, in 1911, the child of European immigrants (his father from Bavaria and his mother from Austro–Hungary). Until he was three years old, he spoke only German. He attended public schools in Seattle and in his free time read insatiably.[11] He graduated from the University of Washington in Seattle with a bachelors degree in business administration in 1931, intending to go into business. In the depths of the Great Depression, however, this was not possible. Instead, he enrolled at Northwestern University, graduating with a masters in business administration in 1932, with some knowledge of economics and an interest in pursuing an academic career.

A major turning point came in 1933 with his enrollment at the University of Chicago to read for a doctorate in economics. Chicago had an outstanding economics department at that time, led by Frank Knight and Jacob Viner. Stigler was one of the few students who wrote his dissertation under Knight. Yet Viner's emphasis on the empirical relevance of microeconomic theory and on the necessity of testing theory against historical and other empirical evidence had a greater long-term impact upon Stigler's scholarship.[12]

At Chicago, Stigler became close friends with fellow students Milton Friedman and Allen Wallis. His doctoral dissertation, completed in 1938 and published in 1941, represented the first serious attempt to trace the evolution of neoclassical production and distribution theory from 1870 onward. It was immediately hailed as a landmark in the history of economic thought.

Prior to completing his Ph.D. in 1938, Stigler was appointed by Theodore Schultz to an assistant professorship in economics at Iowa State University, apparently one of only two such positions available throughout the United States in that year. In 1938, he moved to the University of Minnesota where he stayed until 1946, rising eventually to the rank of full professor. His career at Minnesota was interrupted by wartime service with the National Bureau of Economic Research and the Statistical Research Group at Columbia.

In 1946, Stigler left Minnesota for Brown University, and in 1947, he continued his migration to Columbia University, where he remained until 1958. In 1958, he rejoined Milton Friedman at

Chicago as the Charles R. Walgreen Distinguished Service Professor of American Institutions. He remained in that position until his retirement in 1981. In 1977, he also became director of the Center for Study of the Economy and the State and remained in that position until his death in December 1991.

In 1982, Stigler was awarded the Nobel Prize in Economic Science and was cited "for his seminal studies of industrial structure, functioning of markets and causes and effects of public regulation."

Although the Nobel citation does not specifically refer to Stigler's contribution to the economics of information, this is central to almost all his other insights. Prior to the 1950s, there was little systematic attention paid to the accumulation of information by economic agents in a world characterized by imperfect information. More than any other economist, Stigler was responsible for rectifying that omission.[13]

Stigler's contribution to industrial organization was characterized by the adaptation of rigorous microeconomic theory to the analysis of real world phenomena.[14] He was equally concerned with testing the implications of theory as with developing elegant new models. His insights were achieved without excessive use of mathematics, but with elegant and incisive prose and a brilliant wit.

In particular, Stigler demonstrated that the classic polar models of competition and monopoly could be deployed to yield important insights into the market process. In so doing, he cleared away the underbrush spread by economists such as Edward Chamberlin and Joan Robinson who were determined to deploy complex theories of imperfect competition that yielded few predictions and paved the way for the post-1970s invasion of industrial organization by formal microeconomic theory.

Among the many important contributions of this genre, two widely cited essays illustrate this aspect of Stigler's work. In 1947, he published an essay entitled, "The Kinky Oligopoly Demand Curve and Rigid Prices." In this essay, Stigler exposed the theoretical incompleteness and the predictive failures of the kinked demand curve model of oligopoly that purported to explain downward price rigidity in U.S. commodity markets—a rigidity that Stigler later would refute empirically.[15]

In 1964, he published an essay, "A Theory of Oligopoly," in which he applied classic cartel theory to the analysis of oligopolistic markets.[16] He argued that the stability of collusive behavior depends on the possibility of detecting and punishing departures from tacit or overt agreements to restrict output. This essay led to a new information-based interpretation of seller-based information, in which the "Herfindahl Index" assumed a much more prominent role.

Stigler's work on regulation had begun in 1962 with an essay with Claire Friedland, "What Can Regulators Regulate?," which concluded that early state regulation of electric utilities in the U.S. had no impact on electricity prices.[17] This essay triggered an empirical research program in the economic consequences of regulation. Stigler became increasingly skeptical of the public interest theory of regulation and in 1971 published "The Theory of Economic Regulation," in which he argued that regulation generally had its origins in the self-interested political activity of organizations that desired to be regulated.[18] This seminal essay triggered a major research program in the economics of regulation.

The insights offered by Stigler into the economics of information, the economics of industrial organization, and the economics of regulation, though in my opinion less profound than those offered by Friedman, will be long remembered, not least because they have served to shape an ongoing program of research.

From the perspective of classical liberal political economy, however, Stigler must be viewed with some disappointment. Always inclined to deconstructionism, Stigler's unwillingness to envision a role for economists in policy reform strengthened with advancing years. Ultimately, he became a caricature of himself, advancing the notion that *what is is efficient* in increasingly unacceptable formulations. His worst paper by far was his last, published posthumously in 1992, which argued that "all durable social institutions, including common and statute laws, must be efficient."[19] Perhaps the lesson to be learned is that great scholars should know when to hang up their boots and to take time out to smell the roses.

James M. Buchanan

James McGill Buchanan was born in 1919 in the country village of Gum near Murfreesboro, Tennessee. He was raised on the Buchanan family farm owned by the estate of his paternal grandfather, John P. Buchanan, who had been governor of Tennessee from 1891 to 1895.

In 1937, Buchanan enrolled at Middle Tennessee State College in Murfreesboro as a day student. Concentrating in mathematics, English literature, and social sciences, he earned his bachelors degree in 1940. He then successfully applied for a graduate fellowship in economics from the University of Tennessee at Knoxville for the academic year 1940–41. Although he graduated with a masters degree in 1941, Buchanan later claimed that he left Knoxville without any coherent vision of the economic process.[20]

In 1941, he also embarked on what would turn out to be four years of active naval duty in the Pacific theater of the Second World War, spending most of this time on the staff of Admiral Chester Nimitz at Pearl Harbor and Guam. In Hawaii, he tracked the movements of enemy ships from an operations room using string, paper clips, and elementary computations. Evidently, this was not an experience that enamored him of the usefulness of empirical methods. But he did his job so ably that he was awarded a Bronze Star for Distinguished Service.

In 1946, Buchanan enrolled at the University of Chicago as an early beneficiary of the G. I. Bill. During his first quarter, he took courses with Frank Knight, T. W. Schultz, and Simeon Leland. Knight's course on price theory converted him from socialism to free market principles and provided him with a perspective on market process that had earlier eluded him. He gained an academic confidence from his relationship with Knight that was not forthcoming from his academic contacts with more aggressive faculty members, such as Jacob Viner and Milton Friedman.[21]

After completing his doctoral degree in 1948, Buchanan stumbled across Knut Wicksell's 1896 untranslated *Finanztheoretische Untersuchungen*, or *Studies in Finance Theories*, buried in the dusty stacks of Chicago's old Harper Library. He read the book and was inspired by the nature of its challenge to conventional public finance. In his Stockholm address in 1986, Buchanan acknowledged the fundamental influence of this work on the contributions that earned him the Nobel Prize. Elsewhere, Buchanan has acknowledged the importance of Frank Knight.[22] The only photographs in his personal study in Buchanan House are those of Frank Knight and Knut Wicksell.

From 1948 to 1950, Buchanan held the position of associate professor of economics at the University of Tennessee. In 1950, he was promoted to full professor. In 1951, he became a professor of economics at Florida State University. In 1955, he obtained a Fulbright Fellowship that enabled him to study for one year in Italy, where he became acquainted with Italian scholarship on public finance.

In 1956, he became a professor of economics at the University of Virginia, where, with the help of Warren Nutter, he established the Thomas Jefferson Center for Political Economy. In 1962, he became the Paul G. McIntire Professor of Economics, a position which he held until 1968, when he resigned following serious academic disagreement with the left-leaning administration.

The academic year 1968–69 was spent as a professor of economics at the University of California at Los Angeles, then enmeshed in serious student unrest. Searching for shelter from the storm, Buchanan retreated to the foothills of the Appalachian mountains, holding the position of University Distinguished Professor at Virginia Polytechnic Institute and State University from 1969 to 1983. In 1969, Buchanan and Gordon Tullock founded the Center for Study of Public Choice at VPI & SU.

In 1983, following disagreements with the department of economics, Buchanan and Tullock moved the center to George Mason University. In 1998, it was merged with the Center for Market Processes to become the James M. Buchanan Center for Political Economy.

In 1986, Buchanan was awarded the Nobel Prize in Economic Science and was cited "for his development of the contractual and constitutional bases for the theory of economic and political decisionmaking."

It is important to note that Buchanan's Nobel citation did not refer explicitly to public choice, but rather focused attention on the contractual and constitutional subset of that much broader discipline. This focus is entirely appropriate, given Buchanan's almost obsessive emphasis on the "catallactic–coordination" paradigm and his hostility to the "allocationist–maximization" paradigm that embraces so much of what is called "public choice." In large part, Buchanan credits Frank Knight for the insights that led him to take this untraveled road.

For Buchanan, "public choice" is the inclusive term that "describes the extension of analysis to the political alternatives to markets."[23] Although Buchanan arrived at the public choice crossroads with the street map provided by Wicksell, it is doubtful whether he would have chosen the contractarian path without the wisdom of Knight. Without the model of politics provided by *homo economicus*, public choice would not exist. Without the conceptualization of politics as exchange, Buchanan could not have made his mark upon the literature. Buchanan's own contribution to the development of the paradigm was his insistence on the assumption of methodological individualism, the notion that only individuals matter in the process of exchange, that there is no higher order to which economists may address themselves.

In an important 1959 essay, "Positive Economics, Welfare Economics, and Political Economy," Buchanan first brought together these assumptions to create a model of political economy in which economists, suitably educated in the constitution of economic policy, and capable of applying deductive logic to the perceived constraints of politics, might tentatively proffer rules or rule changes that offered a prospect of universal consent.[24] The ideal test for such hypotheses would be universal consent itself, though Buchanan, like Wicksell before him, recognized that some approximation would be necessary in the real world.

In 1962, Buchanan (jointly with Gordon Tullock) took the constitutional political economy program a crucial stage further in *The Calculus of Consent*.[25] In this text, Buchanan and Tullock demonstrate how self-seeking individuals, faced with the potentially coercive power of the state, may unanimously endorse a constitution from behind the natural veil of uncertainty that surrounds long-term decisionmaking. Such a constitution, because of decisionmaking costs, inevitably would endorse less-than-unanimity rules of political decisionmaking.

The Calculus of Consent, despite its seemingly optimistic message that gains from trade are available in the political marketplace, earned Buchanan and Tullock the undying enmity of those would-be philosopher kings who had been riding high on the paradigm of market failure. For, with brilliant insight, the two economists from Virginia demonstrated that the failures of private markets—be they through externalities, "publicness" problems, asymmetries in information, or incomplete markets—manifested themselves in a more chronic form in political markets. Thus was the playing field forever leveled, and the defensive posture of those who sought to protect markets from government encroachment decisively shifted to aggression.

In 1974, in his book, *The Limits of Liberty: Between Anarchy and Leviathan,* Buchanan responded to the perceived constitutional crisis in the United States with a brilliant defense of constitutional contract based on the threat of Hobbesian anarchy should the social contract collapse.[26] In this, perhaps his best work (rivaled only by *The Calculus of Consent*) in the field of constitutional political economy, Buchanan charted the way for an understanding of how a social contract between free individuals would result in constrained or limited government anchored effectively somewhere between total disorder and totalitarianism.

Following these seminal works, Buchanan has not rested on his laurels. In a sequence of brilliant books and essays, he has employed his theory to attack almost every aspect of conventional public economics and to savage elitist social choice theories, as he has demonstrated the power of the contractarian paradigm to predict the emergence or reemergence of limited government following the debacle of the twentieth century.

The insights offered by Buchanan into the nature and implications of the contractarian paradigm will undoubtedly live forever in the annals of political economy. In Buchanan's case, moreover, his technical contributions also justify him an eternal place in the honor roll of classical liberal political economy.

Like Ludwig von Mises and Friedrich A. Hayek before him— and like no other twentieth century political economist—Buchanan has been successful in relying on purely positive analysis to advance significantly the normative case for limited government, individual liberty, and the rule of law. He has done so, not by violating Hume's constraint that one cannot make an "ought" out of "is," but by demonstrating that rational individuals—once they perceive what is at stake—will consentaneously rein in the state and allow free markets to function.

Ronald H. Coase

Ronald Coase was born in 1910 in Willesdon, a suburb of London, to parents of modest means who had both left school at the age of twelve. Although they had no understanding of academic scholarship, they were extremely supportive of Coase throughout his early years. His mother imbued in him the importance of honesty and truthfulness, moral principles that he has upheld throughout his long and illustrious career.

After a slow start as a sickly child, Coase recovered well and entered the London School of Economics in 1929 to read for a bachelor of commerce degree, graduating from the University of London in 1932, during the depths of the Great Depression. As a student, he was captivated by two books introduced to him by Lionel Robbins. To Frank Knight's *Risk, Uncertainty, and Profit*, Coase owes his interest in economic organizations and institutions. To Philip Wicksteed's *Commonsense of Political Economy*, he owes his ability to analyze constrained choices without recourse to higher mathematics.

Coase held the position of assistant lecturer at the Dundee School of Economics and Commerce from 1932 to 1934, the position of assistant lecturer at the University of Liverpool from 1934 to 1935, and the position of assistant lecturer at the London School of Economics from 1935 to 1938. He was promoted to the rank of lecturer in 1938 and to reader in 1947, following wartime service in the Central Statistical Office. In 1951, he was awarded the Doctor of Science at the University of London.

In 1951, upon his appointment as a professor of economics at the University of Buffalo, Coase emigrated to the United States. In 1958, he moved to the University of Virginia, where he developed a close academic relationship with Warren Nutter. In 1964, he moved again to become Clifton R. Musser Professor of Economics at the University of Chicago Law School, where he remained until retirement in 1981. Since 1982, he has been Clifton R. Musser Professor Emeritus of Economics and Senior Fellow in Law and Economics at the university.

In 1991, Coase was awarded the Nobel Prize in Economic Science and was cited "for his discovery and clarification of the significance of transaction costs and property rights for the institutional structure and functioning of the economy."

In his famous 1937 essay, "The Nature of the Firm," Coase explores why a firm emerges at all in a specialized exchanged economy and why such firms as do emerge vary with respect to size and structure.[27] His struggle for an answer to this question leads him to confront the issue of transaction costs—an issue that has preoccupied him throughout his subsequent career.

If a command structure such as that of the firm successfully supersedes the price system as a means of resource allocation, this must occur, he argues, because the cost of using the price mechanism exceeds the cost of using the command system. Coase then proceeds to analyze the nature of such costs, their implications for the changing size of firms, and their relevance in defining the marginal product of the entrepreneur.

In a nutshell, "the thesis rests on the choice of contracts."[28] An input owner will choose the arrangement that bears the lower transaction costs. This paper launched the transaction cost approach to analyzing economic organization, although it would be a long time before Coase's 1937 essay received the attention that it deserved. Even at the London School of Economics it was largely ignored when it first appeared.

Coase himself applied the transaction cost approach to the issue of marginal cost controversy. In his 1946 essay, "The Marginal Cost Controversy," Coase noted that the cost of subsiding a natural monopoly that pursued marginal cost pricing must include the nonproduction costs of administering the system.[29] In such circumstances, there could be no certainty that marginal cost pricing would provide an efficiency gain over the profit maximization outcome. Coase was highly skeptical of the existence of natural monopolies, correctly recognizing (long before the notion of contestable markets entered the litany of economics) that, in situations of decreasing cost, competition takes a different form.

For the next thirteen years, Coase turned his attention to issues of monopoly, especially broadcasting monopoly. From this interest came the second major insight of his career, though the trigger would not be monopoly but the apparently chaotic nature of competition in the market for broadcasting rights.[30] His 1959 classic, "The Federal Communications Commission," launched him into economic stardom and led to his move from the University of Virginia to the University of Chicago.[31]

Coase had submitted this paper to the newly established *Journal of Law and Economics,* arguing against Pigou's classic view that, in a case of conflicting uses, the party inflicting the damage should be restrained, typically by a Pigovian tax. This is incorrect, wrote Coase, because the restrained party would be harmed in a situation where the harm is reciprocal. The goal of reducing damage could be reached more efficiently through the market itself, by a clear delineation of property rights. The Chicago School was adamant that Coase was wrong. Following a famous seminar with a star-studded cast including Friedman, Stigler, Harberger, Kessel, Mints, Lewis, and Director, the Chicago School finally admitted defeat and acknowledged that history had been made.

In 1960, Coase published a follow-up essay, tidying up and generalizing the results of his 1959 work. "The Problem of Social Cost" would become the single most-cited economic essay of our time. In view of subsequent confusion, it is important to note that the so-called "Coase Theorem," namely, that it does not matter for efficiency in which direction the court determines the property rights, holds only under conditions of zero transaction costs. Coase makes it absolutely clear in the 1960 essay that he does not believe this to be the typical case. If transaction costs are high, the decision of the court as to the direction of property rights may indeed result in outcomes that will not maximize the efficiency of production. It would be surprising indeed if a scholar such as Coase, who had spent his career analyzing the nature of transaction costs, had ignored such costs in his most important essay. Categorically, he did not do so.

Coase is a modest man who has not presumed to extend his writings more widely into normative areas of political economy. Nevertheless, his contribution to economic freedom is the no less significant because it was unintended. The unintended consequences of Coase's scholarship for liberty and free markets have been immense.

His work is frequently called upon to support the view that a clear delineation of property rights is essential for the efficient performance of an economy, that the common law is a superior mechanism for dealing with problems of market failure than other forms of direct regulation, and that markets can be made to function well in areas as seemingly chaotic as broadcasting wavelengths. These are majestic contributions to classical liberal political economy, showing insights into the working of market economics comparable to those displayed by Adam Smith.

Gary S. Becker

Gary S. Becker was born in Pottstown, Pennsylvania, in 1930 of immigrant parents from Eastern Europe who had little formal education. He graduated from James Madison High School in New York City in 1948, the same school that Robert Solow had attended several years earlier. Becker completed his bachelors degree at Princeton University in 1951 and his masters degree at the University of Chicago in 1953. He completed his doctors degree at the University of Chicago in 1955, writing his dissertation on the economics of discrimination, a subject cited by the Nobel Committee in 1992 as a major contribution to economics.

Becker had published articles in the *American Economic Review* and in *Economica* while still an undergraduate student. Jacob Viner, who had taught Friedman, Stigler, and Buchanan, once claimed, "Becker is the best student I have ever had."[32] The major influences on his economic thinking at Chicago were Milton Friedman, who claims that Becker is his favorite student, and George Stigler, who became something of a mentor to Becker, especially following Friedman's retirement from Chicago in 1976.

Despite his brilliance, Becker was unable for some two years after graduation to obtain an attractive job offer from other economics departments. He remained at Chicago until 1957, when he was appointed first to an assistant professorship and then to an associate professorship at Columbia University over the period 1957–68. In 1968, he was appointed to the Arthur Lehman Professorship of Economics at Columbia. Since 1970, Becker has held a professorship in economics and sociology at the University of Chicago. He is a quintessential product of and an active current participant in the Chicago School of economics and in the political economy program initiated by George Stigler in 1971.

In 1992, Becker was awarded the Nobel Prize in Economic Science and was cited "for having extended the domain of microeconomic analysis to a wide range of human behavior and interaction, including nonmarket behavior."

Gary Becker is blessed with one of the most original minds in modern economics. His writings have the unique quality of opening up new horizons in economic analysis by relating widely observed but seemingly unrelated phenomena to the operation of a single general principle, namely the rationality of individual choice.[33]

This talent was manifest in his doctoral dissertation. He attempted to reconcile the competitive model of labor markets with the observed facts of pay differentials between blacks and whites by the device of introducing a preference for discrimination into the utility functions of both employers and employees. Published in 1957 as *The Economics of Discrimination,* Becker's first important work fell on initially deaf ears, but later sparked a major research program in labor market economics.[34]

He repeated the exercise in his 1964 book, *Human Capital,* in which he introduced a general theory of human capital formation via schooling and labor training, again eventually overcoming skepticism in an economics profession overly focused on physical capital formation. He did it a third time in 1965 in his essay, "A Theory of the Allocation of Time," in which he explored the division of labor among members of the family, an institution which, hitherto, economics had declined to evaluate.[35] He did it yet a fourth time in 1968 when he enraged the sociology profession and upset many liberally minded economists with his essay, "Crime and Punishment: An Economic Approach," in which he developed a model of an optimal rate of crime predicated on the rational behavior of all agents in the market for crime and punishment.[36]

The economic approach consistently deployed by Becker "assumes that individuals maximize welfare *as they conceive it,* whether they be selfish, altruistic, loyal, spiteful, or masochistic."[37] The behavior of such individuals is forward-looking and is consistent over time. Tastes are not assumed to change, though constraints may do so. Different constraints are decisive in different situations, but the most fundamental constraint is limited time. On the basis of these seemingly simple assumptions, Becker has destroyed ongoing research programs in a multitude of disciplines and replaced them with the rational choice approach.

Becker has made his indelible mark without recourse to high-powered mathematics, though he is technically proficient, and without engaging in time-consuming data-mining through the medium of sophisticated econometrics. He has shown that a combination of intellectual brilliance, hard work, and the avoidance of consulting (which now destroys so much talent in economics) can move mountains not only within an initially reluctant discipline but across a range of other disciplines markedly less amenable to the economic approach.

The insights offered by Becker into the unity of human action, as perceived through the rational choice approach, guarantee for Becker a long-lasting reputation in economics as well as in other disciplines. In my view, his position is on a par with that of Stigler, though perhaps less stellar than those of Friedman, Buchanan, and Coase.

His reputation as a major contributor to classical liberal political economy, however, is more ambiguous. Undoubtedly a freedom-lover at heart, Becker unfortunately came under the influence of his mentor Stigler during the latter's golden years, and he allowed Stigler's deconstructionism to influence his analysis of political markets. His work on pressure groups, especially that which is based on assumptions that imply such groups redistribute wealth at minimum social cost, is surely misguided.[38] Unlike Stigler, however, Becker still has time to reflect on this aspect of his scholarship and to adjust the model to make its predictions conform more to the evidence. That surely, should be a fine objective for a Chicago economist who learned his trade at the feet of Milton Friedman.

Notes

[1]Assar Lindbeck, "The Prize in Economic Science in Memory of Alfred Nobel," *Journal of Economic Literature,* Vol. 23 (March 1985), 38.

[2]Ibid., 45–47.

[3]Milton Friedman, "The Methodology of Positive Economics," *Essays in Positive Economics* (Chicago: University of Chicago Press, 1953).

[4]Milton Friedman, *A Theory of the Consumption Function* (Princeton: Princeton University Press, 1957).

[5]Alan Walters, "Friedman, Milton (born 1912)," in *The New Palgrave: A Dictionary of Economics,* Vol. 2 (London: Macmillan, 1987), 423.

[6]Milton Friedman, ed., *Studies in the Quantity Theory of Money* (Chicago: University of Chicago Press, 1956).

[7]Milton Friedman and Anna Schwartz, *A Monetary History of the United States, 1867–1960* (Princeton: Princeton University Press, 1963).

[8]Walters, 425.

[9]Milton Friedman, *Capitalism and Freedom* (Chicago: University of Chicago Press, 1962).

[10]Milton and Rose Friedman, *Free to Choose* (New York: Harcourt Brace Jovanovich, 1980).

[11]Gary S. Becker, "George Joseph Stigler: January 17, 1911–December 1, 1991," *Journal of Political Economy,* 101 (October 1993), 761.

[12]Ibid.

[13]Ibid., 763.

[14]Richard Schmalensee, "Stigler's Contributions to Microeconomics and Industrial Organization," in *The New Palgrave: A Dictionary of Economics,* Vol. 4 (London: Macmillan, 1987), 500.

[15]George J. Stigler and James K. Kindahl, *The Behavior of Industrial Prices* (New York: National Bureau of Economic Research, 1970).

[16]George Stigler, "A Theory of Oligopoly," *Journal of Political Economy,* 72 (October 1964), 44–61.

[17]George Stigler and Claire Friedland, "What Can Regulators Regulate? The Case of Electricity," *Journal of Law and Economics,* 5 (October 1962), 1–16.

[18]George Stigler, "The Theory of Economic Regulation," *Bell Journal of Economics and Management Science,* 2 (Spring 1971), 3–21.

[19]George Stigler, "Law or Economics?" *Journal of Law and Economics,* 35 (October 1992), 459.

[20]James M. Buchanan, "James M. Buchanan: Born-Again Economist," in William Breit and Roger W. Spencer, eds., *Lives of the Laureates* (Cambridge, MA: MIT Press, 1995).

[21]Ibid.

[22]James M. Buchanan, *Better than Plowing* (Chicago: University of Chicago Press, 1992).

[23]Buchanan, 1995, 171.

[24]James M. Buchanan, "Positive Economics, Welfare Economics, and Political Economy," *Journal of Law and Economics,* 2 (October 1959), 124–38.

[25]James M. Buchanan and Gordon Tullock, *The Calculus of Consent* (Ann Arbor: University of Michigan, 1962).

[26]James M. Buchanan, *The Limits of Liberty: Between Anarchy and Leviathan* (Chicago: University of Chicago Press, 1974).

[27]Ronald Coase, "The Nature of the Firm," *Economica,* 4 (November 1937), 386–405.

[28]Steven Cheung, "Coase, Ronald Harry (born 1910)," in *The New Palgrave: A Dictionary of Economics* (London: Macmillan, 1987), 455.

[29]Ronald Coase, "The Marginal Cost Controversy," *Economica,* 13 (August 1946), 169–82.

[30]Cheung, 456.

[31]Ronald Coase, "The Federal Communications Commission," *Journal of Law and Economics,* 2 (October 1959), 1–40.

[32]Victor Fuchs, "Nobel Laureate Gary S. Becker: Ideas about Facts," *Journal of Economic Perspectives,* 8 (Spring 1994), 183.

[33]Mark Blaug, *Great Economists Since Keynes* (Totowa, NJ: Barnes and Noble Books, 1985), 15.

[34]Gary S. Becker, *The Economics of Discrimination* (Chicago: University of Chicago Press, 1957).

[35]Gary S. Becker, "A Theory of the Allocation of Time," *Economic Journal,* 75 (September 1965), 493–517.

[36]Gary S. Becker, "Crime and Punishment: An Economic Approach," *Journal of Political Economy,* 76 (March/April 1968), 169–217.

[37]Gary S. Becker, "Nobel Lecture: The Economic Way of Looking at Behavior," *Journal of Political Economy,* 101 (June 1993), 386.

[38]Charles K. Rowley, "Donald Wittman's The Myth of Democratic Failure," *Public Choice* 92 (July 1998), 15–26.

RICHARD M. EBELING

The Limits of Economic Policy: The Austrian Economists and the German ORDO Liberals

Political and Economic Crisis in the Twentieth Century

The twentieth century has been one of the darkest and cruelest in human history. Twenty million people were killed in World War I; fifty million more lost their lives in World War II. The communist experiment in the Soviet Union cost the lives of sixty-four million. The Nazi experience in Europe took, apart from war combatants, another twenty-five million lives. The years of Mao-Tse-tung's reign in communist China may have cost up to eighty million lives. Overall, and apart from wars, it has been estimated that more than two hundred and seventy million people may have been killed by governments.[1]

Many of the most cherished and hard-won freedoms and con-stitutional protections of human liberty acquired during the eigh-teenth and nineteenth centuries have been weakened or, in some countries, denied and abolished. The economic liberties of open competition and free trade, which were the hallmark of many, if not most, of the Western economies at the beginning of our cen-tury, have been replaced by government regulation, redistribu-tion, welfare, and protectionism.[2]

During the height of this political–economic darkness in the 1930s and 1940s, there were many who wondered if human free-dom, democratic government, and a free economy were going to perish under the onslaught of totalitarian collectivism.[3] Even with the end of the Nazi era in 1945, and separate from the cold war with communism for the forty-five years following the close of the Second World War, the West has been plagued by the encroachment of moderate collectivism in the form of the interventionist and welfare state.[4]

Only now, at the end of this brutal century, are the assumptions of collectivism—in all its forms—being challenged and reconsidered. But this reconsideration is not occurring in an intellectual vacuum. In spite of collectivism's triumphs, even in its most victorious decades, there were important voices raised against it. These voices spoke out against both the assumptions and policies of collectivism and offered in their place alternative visions of a free and prosperous society.

Two groups were especially outstanding in their criticisms of collectivism and their defenses of the free society: the Austrian Economists and the German ORDO Liberals. In 1948, two of the leading German liberal economists, Walter Eucken and Franz Böhm, published the first issue of the *Yearbook for the Order of Economy and Society* or *"ORDO."* It became the focal point for a growing number of German economists convinced in the superiority of a market economy over all types of socialism; they developed various arguments for the defense of the market order and what they considered the necessary supporting political and social institutions for the preservation of a free society. Many of these German liberals had been opponents of socialism and Nazism in the 1920s and 1930s. In the post-World War II era, they wished to see a new democratic Germany with a "social market economy."[5]

Common Enemies and Common Premises of the Austrians and the German Liberals

Throughout the 1920s and 1940s, the Austrians and the German Liberals shared a group of common enemies: historicism, positivism and collectivism. They were common enemies because the Austrians and the German Liberals possessed a set of common premises from which they generally looked at the world.

At the level of economic theory, the Austrians and the German Liberal economists were advocates of "laws of economics" derived from an understanding of the human condition under circumstances of scarcity.[6] They rejected the German Historical School's insistence that economic relationships were determined by and limited to changing historical forces. They also rejected the idea that the collectivist state has the potential to mold and transform interpersonal relationships and market outcomes in ways considered superior to merely leaving the market to follow its own course.

For the Austrians and the German Liberals, the attempt to violate the laws of the market could only lead to disaster. Thus, both groups strongly opposed the most extreme form of a violation of the market: socialist central planning. For effective coordination of human activities, there was no substitute for market competition and price-guided production and resource allocation. In the 1920s, Ludwig von Mises had demonstrated the "irrationality" of a centrally planned economy once private property had been nationalized, monetary transactions and market exchange had been abolished, and a central planning agency had the authority to determine: (1) the allocation of resources; (2) the relative quantities of final goods to be manufactured with those resources; and (3) the remunerations that each factor of production was to receive. Without market prices and entrepreneurial competitive bids for factors of production, there was simply no way to know whether the means of production were being applied to their most highly valued uses and at minimum costs of production.[7]

Indeed, for both Austrians like Ludwig von Mises and German Liberals like Franz Böhm, the private entrepreneur was the creative, motor force of a dynamic market economy. Without the free entrepreneur, innovation, effective coordination of market activity and the incentives for efficient production would be albeit impossible.[8]

The types of theoretical arguments made by Mises and his Austrian colleague Friedrich A. Hayek[9] against socialism were not merely echoed by the German Liberals—they were extended by them. Wilhelm Röpke, for instance, argued forcefully that the central planning mentality was indicative of the "hubris of the intellectual" who believed that it was in his power to socially engineer human society into any shape he deemed preferable to the one he found man presently living in. Nothing could be further from the truth, Röpke insisted. Social engineering would not only fail to achieve the ends promised, it would lead to decay and destruction of human society.[10]

In his exposition of different types of economic order, Walter Eucken demonstrated, along lines parallel to Mises', that beyond that most elemental primitive social order, a centrally planned society would lack the methods necessary to effectively record and register the relative scarcities of goods and resources, so as to correctly estimate their relative values in alternative uses. The competitive market finely and continually registered changes in each of the multitudes of supplies and demands throughout a complex economy through movements in prices, that then served as the coordinating tools for the economywide interdependency of all sectors of the economy.[11] In this argument, Eucken was complementing and reinforcing the analysis that Hayek gave in his famous essay, "The Use of Knowledge in Society."[12] Furthermore, Eucken applied his critique of the centrally planned economy to the historical experience of the Nazi command economy. Everything that the Austrians and German Liberals had said, "in theory," about the impossibility and inefficiencies of central planning were shown by Eucken to have been, in fact, the case in the Nazi economic order.[13]

The Austrians and the German Liberals were no less united in their arguments against many of the activities of the interventionist state. Both emphasized the interdependency of the economic order. State interventions introduced in particular corners of the market—whether they were price or production controls— inevitably brought about imbalances not only in the market in which the intervention had been introduced, but also over time in related markets.[14] The Austrians and many of the German Liberals saw these types of price and wage interventions as a reason for the intensity and duration of the Great Depression.[15] (Some of the German Liberals, most notably Wilhelm Röpke, however, believed that a "secondary depression," having more to do with perverse expectations and cumulative contractions of income and output, had created a situation in which wage and price flexibility was not enough to generate an economic recovery.)[16]

But most importantly, what especially united the Austrians and the German Liberals was their shared sense of modern collectivism's philosophical and moral threat to the free and open society. Mises emphasized that the Marxian and Nazi revolutions represented revolts against reason, with their respective premises of class and race-based logic and consciousness. These, in Mises' view, were reactionary movements attempting to take society back to an antirational, tribal past.[17] Hayek argued that historicism and collectivism represented rejections of both methodological and political individualism that lead not only to wrong theories concerning the nature of man and society, but threatened a return to the slave society, as well.[18]

But the moral dangers of these ideological and philosophical trends in the early and middle decades of the twentieth century were emphasized most strongly among the German Liberals, by William Röpke and Alexander Rüstow.[19] The sickness of the twentieth century did not have its cause in the economic crisis that began in 1929 or in the growth of dictatorships and the total state. These were symptoms for deeper diseases in the social body.[20] Scientism conceptually reduced man to manipulatable quantitative matter, stripped of any spiritual and moral qualities; the triumphs of the natural sciences, in giving man increasing mastery over nature, had generated an arrogance of knowledge and power among intellectuals, leading them to believe that society could be reconstructed according to a preferred design, with the individual reduced to a mere cog in the machine. Scientism and historicism were twin forces undermining all conceptions of morality and truth outside and beyond the external observations of the laboratory experiment.

"It is a type of thought which relentlessly ignores mankind as a spiritual and moral entity and which knows almost nothing of these eternally human and social values," Röpke insisted. These forces create a "combination of scientific hubris and engineering mentality which hoped to be able to do just as it pleased with Man and society," and generated a "tendency to cultivate the moral sciences according to the methods of the natural sciences and to limit oneself to what can be measured, weighed and documented."[21]

But while the Austrians and German Liberals shared the same outlook and concerns about the general trends and dangers from scientism, historicism, and collectivism in the twentieth century, their visions of the good and free society to put in place of these dark forces, while often running on parallel lines, were not the same. A large part of the reason for these differences had to do with their diagnoses of the causes of the maladies of society. And these differences in diagnoses was based upon their differing interpretations of the history and consequences of industrial capitalism in the nineteenth and early twentieth centuries.

Austrian and ORDO Liberal Interpretations of the History and Consequences of Industrial Capitalism

If collectivism and totalitarianism were the enemies against which the Austrians and German Liberals were united, they also believed that the only alternative to secure both liberty and prosperity was the market economy and a constitutional order that restrained government and protected individual freedom. Only the market could provide the institutional arrangements for economic coordination through competition and the price system. The market economy also was an indispensable mechanism for decentralizing power, both private and governmental.

There remained, however, the issue of what were to be the functions of the state, even in a social order predominantly built around the institutions of the market. On this question the commonalty of views among the Austrians and the German Liberals began to break down. A central reason for the divergence of views at this point had to do with their respective interpretations of the history of industrial capitalism.

The members of both schools of thought considered the emergence of capitalism and industrialism as immensely beneficial to the average, common man. Capitalism freed man from the oppressive status society of earlier ages and generated expanding opportunities for individual improvement and rising standards of living. Liberal capitalism restrained governments and widened the circles of human life that were depoliticized and private. An Austrian like Ludwig von Mises and a German Liberal like Wilhelm Röpke could both wax eloquent on the benefits of the freer society that liberal capitalism had opened up for "the common man" in the nineteenth century.[22]

But the world that liberal capitalism had built in the nineteenth century was not without its flaws. Private power in the forms of monopolies and cartels had begun to emerge in the western economies in the last third of the nineteenth century. Significant discrepancies in wealth and income persisted among groups in the society. Industrial life was often harsh and demanding for those who found new employments in the factory system. Industrial cities became congested and unaesthetic in the eyes of many.

The analysis of the nature, causes, and cures for these conditions separated Austrians like Mises from German Liberals like Röpke, Eucken, and Rüstow. For Mises, the problem of monopolies and cartels was one that had its origin in continuing state intervention in the market. Legally unrestricted entry into the market was the best guarantee against "private power." The persistence or emergence of monopolies and cartels in the market, Mises argued, had primarily arisen from the continuing ability of the state to bestow entry-limiting privileges upon some producers in the market. The liberal solution, in Mises' view, was to repeal these privileges and prevent the state from introducing any such restrictions in the future. Monopoly power in the market, argued Mises, could only arise if a producer could acquire exclusive control of a vital resource, without which neither a particular product nor any close substitutes could be offered to consumers. Mises was convinced that there were few resources or raw materials possessing such unique qualities and in such a limited supply that it had been or was possible for a private producer to obtain such "private power" on the free market. The only essential antimonopoly policy for any government was nonintervention in the market.[23]

German Liberals like Walter Eucken and Wilhelm Röpke took a different view. On the one hand, they agreed that a fundamental flaw in governmental policy in the late nineteenth and early twentieth centuries, especially in Germany, had been to either tolerate or foster the establishment of cartels and monopolies over certain industries. But in Eucken's view there was a distinction between free competition and freedom of contract. Unless restrained by law, participants in the market could enter into contracts that could establish cartels, and thus constrain competition on the market. The government, therefore, needed to do more than merely abstain from intervention in the market, it needed to actively prevent private actions that potentially would restrict market choices and options.[24]

Röpke agreed with Eucken, and also argued further that "bigness" itself on the market, and the striving for and the worship of the "colossal" in industry as well as in government, had been a flow in nineteenth-century capitalism. Röpke, good economist that he was, understood the advantages of economies of scale for the very mass production that had raised the standard of living of the "masses"; but gigantism in industry and manufacturing distorted the social order and created the potentials for private abuse of power on the market. He, too, therefore, concluded that government needed to limit the growth of industrial giants that might overpower the markets in which they functioned.[25]

Rüstow shared Eucken's and Röpke's views arguing that monopoly in the nineteenth century became more of an ideal among private producers, with government openly and secretly fostering the formation of cartels. Only an active government policy to prevent these tendencies could help to stop one of the forces producing "capitalist degeneration"; but his emphasis was more on the need for government to resist pandering to the privileges and subsidies demanded by private producers from the state.[26]

Austrians like Mises also drew different conclusions than their German Liberal colleagues about the effect of industrial capitalism on the standard of life and the living conditions of the "working class." In Mises' view, the market economy in the nineteenth century had been the great liberator of the poor. The free market had deproletarianized the lowest social strata of society by raising standards of living to such a point that even the "masses" become "bourgeois" in their thoughts and deeds.[27] Industrial capitalism had freed women from dependency and implicit bondage to their fathers or husbands. The market economy, with its rule of contract rather than status, had enabled women to be free agents with increasingly equal rights before the law.[28] The factory system, while involving long hours and tiring work, had been the savior of untold numbers of children, who otherwise would have died from famine or the low standard of living in the climatic uncertainty of rural life. Legal restrictions on child and female labor, therefore, were, in fact, antichildren and antiwomen.[29]

This was not, in general, a view held by many of the German Liberals, especially Röpke. They argued that industrialization and urban life, regardless of economic benefits, had created the "proletarianization" of masses of people. They were cut off from their roots of family, community, and tradition; they were gray masses working in giant gray factories, residing in gray urban housing complexes. Culture and beauty was lost in this environment.[30]

Not all German Liberals took as dark a view of industrial society as Röpke, just as not all Austrians took as noninterventionist a view as Mises. Yet, in general, these were the lines of alternative interpretation of the fruit of industrial capitalism in the two schools of thought. (While Friedrich Hayek would be considered not only an "Austrian," but a follower of Mises on most policy views, in fact, he held many policy positions that could be considered closer to the German Liberals than to Mises.)[31]

The German ORDO Liberals, the Social Market Economy, and Its Consequences

The German Liberals believed that the free society had to contain a degree of government intervention far greater than many of the Austrians considered desirable. But in the eyes of the German Liberals, these interventions should be of a particular type, with very special purposes in mind. In the early 1930s, Rüstow had suggested a system of Liberal Interventionism.[32] Röpke took this idea and formalized it in the context of comfortable and nonconformable interventions. The distinction referred to whether the interventions distorted and imbalanced market relationships and, therefore, made more interventions necessary to redress the negative effects of the first interventions; or whether the interventions were consistent with the general laws of market relationships, while only modifying certain industrial or income patterns to generate an overall outcome more consistent with certain social and moral standards deemed desirable for societal harmony.[33]

In the context of their criticism of the shortcoming of the unregulated market economy, in the years immediately after the Second World War some of the German Liberals developed a theory of economic policy under the heading of the "social market economy." This term was coined and explained in terms of governmental functions by Alfred Müller-Armack in the late 1940s.[34] An elaboration of the types of "social" policies needed to maintain a free and healthy market economy was also laid out by Walter Eucken.[35]

Müller-Armack explained the purpose and the goal of the social market economy:

> The aim must be to establish a market economy tempered by social safeguards which are consistent with free-market principles. . . . What we need is an all-embracing system which unites intellectual and personal freedom with social security. . . . The ideals of freedom and social justice can indeed be linked together on the foundation of the market economy.[36]

In the free society, according to Müller-Armack, Eucken, and Röpke (though, in fairness, each placed different emphases on these points, and several of them were not listed in Eucken's elaboration of the responsibilities of the government), the duties of the state would include:

1. Regulation of the sizes of industries to prevent concentration of economic power;
2. Redistribution of income through the tax system to modify unacceptable or socially destabilizing inequalities of wealth;
3. A series of social insurance programs to meet certain minimal requirements for some segments of the society;
4. Centralized monetary control to help establish and maintain a stable market order;
5. Occupational training for better planning of a skilled workforce to meet the needs of industry;
6. Influencing the degree of industrial vs. self-employment through use of the tax incentives;
7. Environmental regulation and control of natural resources; and
8. Urban and rural planning to direct and control industrial and residential patterns for a "balanced" living environment.

In the view of the German Liberals, these economic policies, while inconsistent with the older nineteenth century Classical Liberal conception of the state's functions, were necessary to preserve a functioning market economy in the long-run, and represented interventions that were conformable with the market order.

However, by 1950, a mere two years after the beginning of the German economic reforms, Röpke asked, in a famous essay, "Is the German Economic Policy the Right One?" He still defended the "social market" interventionist state, but he was worried that state expenditures on various social programs were already getting beyond the bounds of conformable interventionism.[37] Later in the 1950s, Röpke expressed his deep concern that the welfare functions of the government, in Germany and the West in general, were expanding so much that the individual was rapidly becoming a ward of the state, losing all sense of responsibility for himself and his family.[38]

The same fears were expressed by Alexander Rüstow in a paper suggesting that the social market economy in Germany and other Western economies was in danger of following "the other road to serfdom," through a growing state welfare dependency by the people.[39] Similar fears and concerns were expressed by proponents of the German Liberal approach in the 1970s and 1980s.[40] Not only had the government increasingly extended its welfare–statist controlling functions, but state intervention into industrial and market activity was being used more and more to serve special interests at the expense of market freedom and consumer choice.

The general consensus among many of the German Liberals about the reason why this perverse turn-of-events was occurring was that government policy had been captured by those ideologically further to the left; and economic policy increasingly was coming under the influence, if not control, of various special interest groups who wished to use the state's redistributive and regulatory powers for their own benefit.

Christian Watrin, for example, said that the social market economy's maintenance and success was dependent upon a fundamental consensus among the population of a country that the system was desirable and worth defending.[41] But the consensus that government should intervene "this far, but not further" had broken down as an increasing portion of the population wanted more from the state than the German Liberals had wanted the government to do. That the social market economy could be used for various purposes and with greater or lesser degrees of intrusive intervention had been understood in the 1940s by Müller-Armack.

How had the German Liberals expected to prevent this expansion of the state's "social" functions beyond the limits that they thought desirable? They were not ignorant of the power of special interests, indeed they considered the influence of such interests on policy as the reason why state intervention so often led to outcomes damaging to the health and prosperity of society.[42] What they seemed to count on was the "strong state." That is, a state powerful enough to resist the pressures and temptations of special interests, and a state managed by "statesmen" and professional civil servants who would be guided by a conception of the "good of society," according to the types of ideas held by the German Liberals concerning what the government should and should not do in terms of its power to intervene into market affairs.[43] Their hopes have turned out to be not well-founded.

The Austrian Economists and the Limits of Economic Policy

At the end of his book on *Socialism*, Ludwig von Mises included a section on what he called, "Destructionism." This was his term for what has become known as the welfare state. Among the types of economic policies that he considered destructive in its effect on the social order were compulsory social insurance, unemployment insurance, taxing policies that were used to either confiscate income and wealth or to influence its distribution among segments of the society, and labor legislation favoring unions or controlling the conditions and hours of work.[44]

These are the types of policies that slowly eat at the moral and economic fiber of a society. Through them individuals lose their sense of self-responsibility and increasingly look for ways for personal gain not through the market, but by use and manipulation of the political rules of the game. With every step away from the market determining the use of resources, the direction of production, and the incomes earned by participants in the exchange-based system of division of labor, the state increases its influence and control over these matters. They are politicized to the degree the state intervenes in market affairs. Relative income shares are determined to that degree by politics, rather than the market.[45] And for this reason, Mises considered all such interventions as stepping-stones on the road to socialism, the "other road to serfdom" to which Rüstow referred.

From this perspective the distinction that many of the German Liberals made between conformable and nonconformable interventions loses its significance. State intervention for industrial regulation or income redistribution along the lines advocated by Röpke, Müller-Armack, and Eucken are no less disruptive and distortive than the types of more direct interventions into the price system, against which they were such articulate opponents.[46] It is just that the disruptive and distortive effects are more subtle, indirect, and time-consuming in having their full effect.

Long before the Public Choice theorists offered their insightful analysis of the economics of the political process, the Austrians explained much of the same phenomena. In his 1934 book on *The Limits of Economic Policy*, Oskar Morgenstern devoted a chapter to the problem of "The Distribution of Effects of Economic Policy."[47] All government economic policy, Morgenstern stated, has as its purpose the bestowing of some economic benefits on groups who would not otherwise acquire various net gains if not for the intervention.

But the full impact of the intervention is never felt immediately by all segments of the economic community. As with any change in market conditions, its influence is first felt in the sectors of the economy in which the interventions have been "injected" into the system, and then they slowly work their way from one part of the economy to the next. This creates, Morgenstern explained, a pattern of biased influences among different sectors of the economy, which has become known more recently through the Public Choice literature as the process of the "concentration of benefits and diffusion of costs" due to the introduction of political interventions within the market.

As the effect of an intervention sequentially impacts on first one sector of the economy and then another, a widening circle of groups in the social system of division of labor have their material interest affected by it. More and more groups have "an interest" in the intervention's impact upon them. The introduction of redistributive income transfers to ameliorate supposed inequalities in wealth do not only have importance for those groups immediately affected positively by the transfer. As these beneficiaries expend their politically transferred income, various sectors of the market become dependent upon this now-increased spending stream as a source of additional revenue, and they have an incentive to want it to continue in the future. There emerges an expanding circle of interest groups who have an incentive and a profit motive to lobby and pressure for its continuance and its increase. Thus income transfers, even of the "modest" and "limited" type that had been advocated by the German Liberals, slowly build up an increasingly larger and larger constituency for politically based economic gain. Hence, the special interest politics that the German Liberals had considered to be the scourge of many of the bad policies of the past were reinforced rather than weakened by the very income transfer policies they proposed. This helped create the momentum for the politicization of the market place they protested against as the post-World War II decades went by.

This same logic applied to their "social market" policies for industrial and environmental regulation, urban and rural planning, social insurance and occupational training programs, and indicative planning to influence employment patterns through the tax code.[48]

In his proposal for a "social market economy," Müller-Armack had called for the "ideals of freedom and social justice" being "linked together on the foundation of the market economy." But what is "social justice"? To this question, Friedrich Hayek has given the answer: it is a mirage that has no tangible substance and actually serves as a philosophical and ideological cover for income transfers and redistribution of power from individuals to the state.[49] Indeed, the fundamental mistake that the German Liberals made on this point was to implicitly accept the socialist critique of income distribution under capitalism. The old Classical Liberals of the nineteenth century had not denied that income might be "unjustly" acquired or maintained. But their argument was that the injustice had its origin in the fact that the recipients of these income shares had obtained them by political means rather than through offerings of market-valued goods and services to consumers. Their answer was repeal of the privileges or barriers to market competition that had established these unjust relationships among groups in society.[50]

But the German Liberals had implicitly accepted the socialist idea that one could have a policy norm for the distribution of income other than, and different from, the relative income-earnings resulting from the market competition between suppliers and demanders. They may very well have had a conception of the appropriate floors and ceilings that should be established for minimum and maximum incomes in the society. But how could they prove that theirs was the appropriate, or "more just," degree of redistributed income shares, compared to more egalitarian advocates to their political left? Besides which, philosopher–kings do not dictate social and economic policy in a democracy, it is "the people," in the form of coalitions of special interest groups. And as long as the state is endowed with the authority and power to take the wealth and income of some and transfer it to others through the political process, then the "socially just" distribution of wealth will be determined by those coalitions of sectorial interests.

Indeed, the only way in which the "social market economy" could have been kept within the bounds of interventionist discretion preferred by the German Liberals would have been through an authoritarian state controlled by themselves or those who had like minds. Yet, it was to escape from the nightmare of dictatorial government in Germany that they advocated the reestablishment of a democratic order and a market economy after the Second World War. They were caught in a dilemma from which there was no escape, given the prevalence of ideological advocates and various special interests with economic policy visions and goals different from their own.

In the revised second edition to *Human Action,* Ludwig von Mises added some remarks on the "social market economy" worth quoting:

> The supporters of the most recent form of interventionism, the German "*soziale marktwirtschaft,*" [social market economy] stress that

they consider the market economy to be the best possible and most desirable system of society's economic organization, and they are opposed to the government omnipotence of socialism. But, of course, all these advocates of a middle-of-the-road policy emphasize with the same vigor that they reject Manchesterism and laissez-faire liberalism. It is necessary, they say, that the state interfere with the market phenomena whenever and wherever the "free play of the economic forces" results in conditions that appear as "socially" undesirable. . . . If it is in the jurisdiction of the government to decide whether or not definite conditions of the economy justify its intervention, no sphere of operation is left to the market. . . . For as soon as the outcome brought about by the operation of the unhampered market differs from what the authorities consider 'socially' desirable, the government interferes. That means the market is free as long as it does precisely what the government wants it to do. It is 'free' to do what the authorities consider to be the "right" things, but not to do what they consider the "wrong" things; the decision concerning what is right and what is wrong rests with the government.[51]

The German Liberals devised the idea of the "social market economy" and its accompanying policy tool of "conformable" interventionism as a "third-way," between the tragedy and failure of comprehensive collectivism and what seemed to them to be the unacceptable harshness of laissez-faire liberalism. Yet, now at the end of the twentieth century, it is clear that this third way does not offer a stable and market-conformable alternative to both socialist central planning and laissez-faire liberalism. Its unintended consequences tend to result in its degeneration into a system of inconsistent and often contradictory interventions manipulated by special interests (including the interests of the political authorities themselves), and susceptible to the political influences of ideological pressure groups. Once having accepted the premise that the state should and can intervene to redress supposed abuses, injustices, and antisocial market outcomes, there really remains no corner of the market free from governmental inspection and control.

The Austrians, and especially Ludwig von Mises, seem, therefore, to have been right: There is no alternative to the unhampered market economy of laissez-faire liberalism. This is a difficult conclusion for many in society to accept. In spite of the demise of communism, the socialist critique of capitalist society still implicitly dominates the thinking of most intellectuals and many in the general population. Capitalism is harsh, potentially exploitive, and unjust when left to its own natural course, this socialist critique of the market economy argued. This is still the view of many, and the rationale for why the market cannot be left unregulated and unsupervised by the state. This is the myth that must be given up, a myth that was perpetuated by, among others, these German Liberals who sincerely wanted to preserve a free society.

Myth-breaking is no easy task, especially when it is propounded in the government-run schools, in the mass media, and in the popular histories of the nineteenth and twentieth centuries. But if a truly free society is to be possible in the twenty-first century, it is a task that must be successfully accomplished.

Notes

[1] See R. J. Rummel, *Death by Government* (New Brunswick: Transaction Books, 1994) for a comprehensive summary of the human cost of statism and collectivism around the world in the twentieth century.

[2] See Richard M. Ebeling, "Classical Liberalism and Collectivism in the Twentieth Century," in Alexsandras Shtromas, ed., *The End of "Isms"? Reflections of the Fate of Ideological Politics after Communism's Collapse* (Cambridge, MA: Blackwell Publishers, 1994), 69–84; and Richard M. Ebeling, "Free Trade, Managed Trade, and the State," in Richard M. Ebeling and Jacob G. Hornberger, eds., *The Case for Free Trade and Open Immigration* (Fairfax, VA: Future of Freedom Foundation, 1996), 7–27.

[3] See William Henry Chamberlin, *Collectivism: A False Utopia* (New York: Macmillan Co., 1938); also, William E. Rappard, *The Crisis of Democracy* (Chicago: University of Chicago Press, 1938), for examples of analyses of the crisis of the interwar period by two classical liberals expressing these types of fears.

[4] See Richard M. Ebeling, "The Political Myths and Economic Realities of the Welfare State," in Richard M. Ebeling, ed., *American Perestroika: The Demise of the Welfare State* (Hillsdale, MI: Hillsdale College Press, 1995), 3–38.

[5] On the historical background and ideas of the Austrian economists, see Richard M. Ebeling, "The Significance of Austrian Economics in Twentieth-Century Economic Thought," in Richard M. Ebeling, ed., *Austrian Economics: Perspectives on the Past and Prospects for the Future* (Hillsdale, MI:

Hillsdale College Press, 1991), 1–40; also, Ludwig M. Lachmann, "The Significance of the Austrian School of Economics in the History of Ideas," [1966] in Ebeling, ed., *Austrian Economics,* 17–39. On the historical background of the German ORDO liberals and their ideas, see Konrad Zweig, *The Origins of the German Social Market Economy—The Leading Ideas and their Intellectual Roots* (London: Adam Smith Institute, 1980); also, A.J. Nicholls, *Freedom with Responsibility: The Social Market Economy in Germany, 1918–1963* (Oxford: Oxford University Press, 1994).

⁶The Austrians and the German Liberals were not alone, of course, in defending the universality of general laws of economics; see for example, the clear statement on this matter by the Swedish economist Eli Heckscher, "A Plea for Theory in Economic History," *Economic History* (January 1929), 525–34; and the most influential formulation of the general "logic of choice" during this period in English by Lionel Robbins, *An Essay on the Nature and Significance of Economic Science* [1932; 2nd rev. ed., 1935] (London: Macmillan, 1971).

⁷Ludwig von Mises, "Economic Calculation in the Socialist Commonwealth," [1920] in Friedrich A. von Hayek, ed., *Collectivist Economic Planning* (London: George Routledge and Sons, 1935), 87–130; also, *Socialism: An Economic and Sociological Analysis* [1922, 2nd rev. ed., 1932] (Indianapolis: Liberty Classics [3rd rev. ed. 1951] 1981).

⁸Ludwig von Mises, *Human Action, A Treatise on Economics* [1949] (Chicago: Henry Regnery, 3rd rev. ed., 1966), 257–326; also, "Profit and Loss," [1951] in *Planning for Freedom* (South Holland, IL: Libertarian Press, 1980); 108–50; and Franz Böhm, "Rule of Law in a Market Economy," in Alan Peacock and Hans Willgerodt, eds., *Germany's Social Market Economy: Origins and Evolution* (London: Macmillan, 1989), 46–67.

⁹Friedrich A. Hayek, *Individualism and Economic Order* (Chicago: University of Chicago Press, 1948), 119–208.

¹⁰Wilhelm Röpke, *The Social Crisis of Our Time* [1942] (Chicago: University of Chicago Press 1950), 83–99 & 153–59; also, *Civitas Humana: A Humane Order of Society* (London: William Hodge and Co., 1948), 11–24 & 45–49.

¹¹Walter Eucken, *The Foundations of Economics: History and Theory in the Analysis of Economic Reality* [1940] (Chicago: University of Chicago Press, 6th rev. ed., 1950), 117–220; also, "What Kind of Social and Economic System?" [1948] in Peacock and Willgerodt, *Germany's Social Market Economy,* 27–45.

¹²Friedrich A. Hayek, "The Use of Knowledge in Society," [1945] in *Individualism and Economic Order* (Chicago: University of Chicago Press, 1948), 77–91.

¹³Walter Eucken, "On the Theory of the Centrally Administered Economy: An Analysis of the German Experiment," Parts I & II, *Economica* (February and August 1948), 79–100 & 173–93.

¹⁴Ludwig von Mises, *Critique of Interventionism* [1929] (Irvington-on-Hudson, NY: Foundation for Economic Education, 1996); also, Wilhelm Röp-

ke, *Economics of the Free Society* [1937] (Chicago: Henry Regnery Co., 9th rev. ed., 1961), 142–46; also, Walter Eucken, "What Kind of Economic and Social System?" op cit., 29–31.

[15]Ludwig von Mises, "The Causes of the Economic Crisis," [1931] in *On the Manipulation of Money and Credit* (Dobbs Ferry, NY: Free Market Books, 1978), 173–203; also, "The Myth of the Failure of Capitalism" [1932] in Richard M. Ebeling, ed., *The Clash of Group Interests and Other Essays* (New York: Center for Libertarian Studies, 1978), 13–18; also, Franz Böhm, "The Non-State ('Natural') Laws Inherent in a Competitive Economy," [1933] in Wolfgang Stützel, Christian Watrin, Hans Willgerodt, and Karl Hohmann, eds., *Standard Texts on the Social Market Economy* (New York: Gustav Fischer, 1982), 107–14.

[16]Wilhelm Röpke, *Crises and Cycles* (London: William Hodge and Sons, 1936), 119–34.

[17]Mises, *Human Action*, op cit., 72–91.

[18]Friedrich A. Hayek, *The Counter-Revolution of Science* [1942] (Glencoe, IL: Free Press, 1955); also, *The Road to Serfdom* [1944] (Chicago: University of Chicago Press, 1967).

[19]See Daniel Johnson, "Exiles and Half-Exiles: Wilhelm Röpke, Alexander Rüstow, and Walter Eucken," in Alan Peacock and Hans Willgerodt, eds., *German Neo-Liberals and the Social Market Economy* (London: Macmillan, 1989), 40–68.

[20]Wilhelm Röpke and Alexander Rüstow, "A Note on the Urgent Necessity of Re-Orientation of Social Science," *Compte-Rendu des Seances du Colloque Walter Lippmann, 26–30 Aout 1938 [Report of the Sessions of the Walter Lippmann Colloquium, August 1938]* (Paris: Librairie de Medicis, 1938); Alexander Rüstow, "General Sociological Causes of the Economic Disintegration and Possibilities of Reconstruction," an appendix in Wilhelm Röpke, *International Economic Disintegration* [1942] (Philadelphia: Porcupine Press, 1978), 267–83; also, "A Value Judgment on Value Judgments," *Revue de la Faculte des Sciences Economique d'Istanbul*, Vol. III, No. 1–2 (1942), 1–19; also, *The Social Crisis of Our Time* [1942] (Chicago: University of Chicago Press 1950); also, *Civitas Humana*.

[21]Röpke, *Civitas Humana*, 55–56.

[22]Ludwig von Mises, *Liberalism* [1927] (Irvington-on-Hudson, NY: Foundation for Economic Education, 1985); also, Röpke, *The Social Crisis of Our Time*, op. cit., 100–113.

[23]Mises, *Liberalism*, 90–95; *Human Action*, 357–79.

[24]Walter Eucken, *This Unsuccessful Age, or the Pains of Economic Progress* (London: William Hodge and Co., 1951), 31–36.

[25]Röpke, *The Social Crisis of Our Time*, 62–71 & 117–21.

[26]Alexander Rüstow, *Domination and Freedom: A Historical Critique of Civilization* (Princeton: Princeton University Press, 1980), 454–57. This work orig-

inally appeared in three volumes in German in the 1950s. On this point, the differences between Mises, on the one hand, and Röpke and Rüstow, on the other, came out clearly in a discussion of the causes of monopoly and monopoly power during a conference devoted to examining the causes for the decline of and the conditions required for the revival of classical liberalism; see Louis Rougier, ed., *Colloque Walter Lippmann,* 35–42.

[27]Mises, *Human Action,* 669.

[28]Mises, *Socialism,* op cit., 76–83.

[29]Mises, *Human Action,* 614–23. It should also be noted that in the 1950s Hayek edited a collection of essays based on papers delivered at a meeting of the Mont Pelerin Society. Speakers at this meeting tried to rectify the myths surrounding the Industrial Revolution; see Friedrich A. Hayek, ed., *Capitalism and the Historians* (Chicago: University of Chicago Press, 1954). Röpke took partial exception to this revisionist view of the Industrial Revolution; see Wilhelm Röpke, "Der 'Kapitalismus' und die Wirtschafts-historiker," ["'Capitalism' and the Economic Historian"] *Neue Zücker Zeitung,* No. 614 (March 16, 1954).

[30]Röpke, *Civitas Humana,* op cit., 131–49; also, *A Humane Economy: The Social Framework of the Free Market* [1958] (Chicago: Henry Regnery, 1960), 36–89. Mises and Rüstow argued over the issue of capitalism's effect on social life and unity at the 1938 Walter Lippmann Colloquium; see Louis Rougier, ed., *Colloque Walter Lippmann,* 77–98.

[31]See especially the sections of *The Road to Serfdom* and *The Constitution of Liberty* (Chicago: University of Chicago Press, 1962) devoted to the role of government in the free society and the welfare state; also, Richard M. Ebeling, "Review of *Hayek on Hayek,*" in *Freedom Daily* (September 1994), 39–44.

[32]Alexander Rüstow, "Liberal Intervention," [1932] in *Standard Texts on the Social Market Economy,* op. cit., 183–88.

[33]Wilhelm Röpke, *The Social Crisis of Our Time,* 184–91; also, *Civitas Humana,* 36–34.

[34]Alfred Müller-Armack, "The Social Aspect of the Economic System," [1947] in *Standard Texts on the Social Market Economy,* 5–22; also, "The Meaning of the Social Market Economy" [1956] in Germany's *Social Market Economy: Origins and Evolution,* 82–86; and "The Second Phase of the Social Market Economy: An Additional Concept of a Humane Economy," [1960] in *Standard Texts on the Social Market Economy,* 49–62.

[35]Walter Eucken, "A Policy for Establishing a System of Free Enterprise," [1952] in *Standard Texts on the Social Market Economy,* 115–31.

[36]Müller-Armack, "The Social Aspect of the Economic System," 18 & 22.

[37]Wilhelm Röpke, "Is the German Economic Policy the Right One?," in *Standard Texts on the Social Market Economy,* 37–47.

[38]Wilhelm Röpke, *Welfare, Freedom and Inflation* [1957] (Tuscaloosa: University of Alabama Press, 1964); also, Röpke, *The Humane Economy,* 151–90.

[39]Alexander Rüstow, "Welfare State or Self-Responsibility," paper delivered at The Mont Pelerin Society (West Berlin, August–September 1956).

[40]Walter Hamm, "The Welfare State at Its Limits," [1981] and Hans Otto Lenel, "Does Germany Still Have a Social Market Economy?," [1971] in *Germany's Social Market Economy: Origins and Evolution*, 171–94 & 261–72; Christian Watrin, "How Jeopardized Is the Social Market Economy?" [1978] in *Standard Texts on the Social Market Economy*, 91–100.

[41]Watrin, "How Jeopardized Is the Social Market Economy?," 96.

[42]Röpke, *The Social Crisis of Our Time*, 124–34.

[43]Alexander Rüstow, "Liberal Intervention," op. cit., 185–86; Röpke, *The Social Crisis of Our Time*, 191–94.

[44]Mises, *Socialism*, 424–52.

[45]Mises, "The Myth of the Failure of Capitalism," op cit., 16–17.

[46]For Austrian analyses of the negative effects that follow from government regulation of market activity, see Murray N. Rothbard, *Power and Market: Government and the Economy* (Menlo Park, CA: Institute for Humane Studies, 1970); Donald C. Lavoie, "The Development of the Misesian Theory of Interventionism," in Israel M. Kirzner, ed., *Method, Process, and Austrian Economics: Essays in Honor of Ludwig von Mises* (Lexington, MA: Lexington Books, 1982, 169–83; Israel M. Kirzner, "The Perils of Regulation: A Market-Process Approach," in *Discovery and the Capitalist Process* (Chicago: University of Chicago Press, 1985), 119–49; Sanford Ikeda, *Dynamics of the Mixed Economy: Toward a Theory of Interventionism* (London/New York: Routledge, 1997). And for an Austrian theoretical and historical analysis of the antitrust laws in the United States, see Dominick T Armentano, *Anti trust and Monopoly: Anatomy of a Policy Failure* (New York: John Wiley & Sons, 1982) and *Antitrust Policy: The Case for Repeal* (Washington, D.C.: Cato Institute, 1986).

[47]Oskar Morgenstern, *The Limits of Economics* [1934] (London: William Hodge & Co., Ltd., 1937), 29–46; this chapter is also reprinted in Richard M. Ebeling, ed., *Austrian Economics: A Reader* (Hillsdale, MI: Hillsdale College Press, 1991), 655–69.

[48]On the nature of indicative planning, see Vera Lutz, *Central Planning for the Market Economy* (London: Longmans, Green and Co., 1969).

[49]Friedrich A. Hayek, *Law, Legislation and Liberty, Vol. II, The Mirage of Social Justice* (Chicago: University of Chicago Press, 1976).

[50]See Ludwig von Mises, "The Clash of Group Interests" [1945] in Richard M. Ebeling ed., *Money, Method, and the Market Process, Essays by Ludwig von Mises*, (Norwell, MA: Kluwer Academic Publishers, 1990), 202–14.

[51]Mises, *Human Action*, 723–24; also, Mises, "Economic Freedom in the Present-Day World," [1957] in *Economic Freedom and Interventionism* (Irvington-on-Hudson, NY: Foundation for Economic Education, 1990), 240: "The German ORDO-Liberalism is different only in details from the *sozialpolitik*

of the Schmoller and Wagner school. After the episodes of Weimar radi-
calism and Nazi socialism, it is a return to the *wohlfahrtstaat* [welfare state]
of Bismarck and Posadovsky."

LARRY D. BAKER

The Economic Self

I am not an economist. But, I want to present the "economic self." To do that, I must communicate with you. I have to communicate—and avoid miscommunication.

I would like to share a story about a friend of mine who was a victim of miscommunication. Bob used to be a member of the St. Louis Police Department Canine Corps. You know what that means; he didn't just tote a gun; he also had a 100-pound German Shepherd named "Shep" to back him up. Bob was telling me not long ago that he was on patrol in the downtown area when he received an urgent radio call reporting a robbery at a nearby savings and loan office. "Larry," he said, "I switched on my red lights and my siren, and I took off like a bat out of you-know-what. In a matter of minutes, I came screeching to a halt in front of the place. Wearing a pair of dark glasses, I jumped out of the car, grabbed my dog's lead, and we both went running for the door. When the manager saw me and ol' Shep, he turned ashen gray, and his chin dropped to his chest. He cried, "Oh, my God! I've been threatened with a gun, I've been robbed—and they send me a blind cop!"

Why do I tell you this story? It is my way of introducing readers to the fact that I am blind. Blindness doesn't stop me from communicating. I taught for a decade, and I have delivered nearly two thousand seminars to various audiences around the country. But blindness does make me focus on the power of words, since they are what I have to place almost sole reliance upon in order to communicate.

To describe the "economic self," it is not necessary to use technical talk, data, obfuscation. You only need the simplest economic terms. That doesn't mean "dumbing down." It means striving for simplicity.

Monoeconomics

Most of the study of economics falls into two categories. "Macroeconomics" is the study of the overall economy: income, production, taxes, and so forth. "Microeconomics" is the study of individual actors: firms, households, consumers, and producers. But, for the sake of clarity, we ought to add a third category: "monoeconomics." By this term, I mean the study of the *economic self*—that is, the study of *each* individual not only as an independently functioning economic unit but as a unique entity.

Let us say that you are a college student preparing to start a career. The first thing you ask yourself is: "What is it that I can do that makes me special?" If you happened to be one of five candidates, all with the same technical qualifications, applying for the same position, you would naturally want to know what you could do to enhance your chances of being hired. Or let us say that you are a manufacturer. You, too, would want to find a way to make your product stand out from all the others. It might affect the price, the quality, the size, the color—you won't know without trying. But you do know one thing for sure: Your product has to be *different*.

Monoeconomics makes it clear that even though you and I appear to have many similarities, we are really as different from one another as snowflakes. It also reminds us that it is when we are engaged in free competition in the marketplace that our differences are most dramatically revealed.

Look once again at the competition for jobs. Today's labor market is very self-cleansing. Indeed, it has never been so dynamic—or so volatile. Thousands of companies have reorganized or downsized. Thousands more have gone into—or out of—business. Marvelous new technologies have led to one innovation after another. They have redefined the standard rules and timetables of obsolescence. Just try to get a job today as a computer expert with technological training that is four or five years old.

Thus, many jobs are not as secure as they once were. But that is not a change that you should be complaining about or that you should fear. Competition has brought you greater freedom of choice. How? Competition grants you as *an individual* the right to fail as well as the right to succeed. It makes you accountable for your decisions. It is precisely this sense of individual responsibility which competition provides that makes America strong. It is why we not only have a strong economy, but why we are also a strong people with a strong purpose.

We Are All Self-Employed

In this context, I would like to tell you about some of the other simple but rarely discussed economic principles that I have observed. For roughly eighteen years, I lived in the academic world. I attended Indiana University and earned my bachelor's, master's, and doctor's degrees in business administration. Then I served at the University of Missouri–St. Louis as a professor in the areas of management, organizational behavior, business policy, and strategy. I also began working part-time as a consultant. And for the last twenty years, I have been involved full-time with my own professional consulting business.

I am literally self-employed. But, in point of fact, you are also self-employed. You always have been and always will be, regardless of whether you have a job at this or that company. The theory of monoeconomics applies. You are an individual economic entity. Your individual ambitions, skills, and performance are what largely determine your role in the marketplace. So it is only common sense that you ought to analyze yourself as you would any other business enterprise. You ought to develop a personal balance sheet and a personal profit-and-loss statement.

After all, if you are self-employed in the literal sense, you know that you have to generate revenue through the products or services you provide in the labor market. And you have to write checks to pay the bills that keep your company—you—operating. You also have to be able to pay for employee benefits (even if you are the company's only employee!) such as medical insurance, life insurance, and a pension plan. You have to pay for all the equipment you need, right down to the last paper clip. And, after you pay yourself a salary, you will want to have some money left over to reinvest in your business. That is a lot to have to pay for, isn't it?

Now, let us consider that you are the average employee who works for a company. Somebody writes you a check. But do you ever ask yourself, "What am I worth to my company?" If you do, you probably answer this way: "They pay me . . . blah, blah, blah." But your true worth is seldom represented by your salary. And your salary certainly doesn't cover the costs of keeping you on the payroll. There are many added expenses the company meets, including medical insurance, life insurance, workers compensation, unemployment insurance, accounting reports, personnel management, office space, computers, software, office furniture, office supplies, lighting, heating, air conditioning, telephones, restrooms, break rooms, janitorial services, parking. . . . It is an endless list.

Don't you suddenly realize that you must generate enough value in your company through what you do, day in and day out, not only to pay your salary but also to keep you from being a freeloader? You don't want to leave it to the company to generate value for you. You need to generate value yourself. Every element of cost associated with your job in the company must be paid through the value you create, and you must also create enough value to make a contribution to the company's overall profit. An employee who earns $50,000 a year may have to generate over $200,000 a year to pay his or her own way. That's right—$200,000 a year in value. In the real economic world we should all understand our true worth to our organizations. It may even enhance our self-confidence, self-worth, and self-esteem. And there is nothing that leads to success more than a positive self-image comprising all three.

Planning and Scheduling

Another thing I have discovered in business is that if you want to be head and shoulders above your competitors—that means your co-workers and others who may be trying for that salary increase or that job promotion—you must learn how to plan and schedule. Unfortunately, we are a nation of poor planners and poor schedulers. Most companies do a terrible job of strategic planning, and they do it from the top down. No wonder they can't figure out why their employees can't figure out what they are supposed to be doing! These firms have mission statements, vision statements, and value statements, and they pay little, if any, attention to them. At least ten years ago I quit asking executive groups, "What is the mission statement of your company?" And why do you suppose I quit? It was because they didn't know the answer. At the time, I thought to myself, "If *you* don't know, how do you expect your employees to know? How do you expect them to try to accomplish something that takes this company forward? How do you expect them to become what somebody, sometime, thought they ought to be or ought to become?"

Planning and scheduling are the most critical elements of business success. Even those organizations that do manage to do some degree of effective planning and scheduling do not do the contingency planning that is so critical in our modern, dynamic, and volatile economy. In other words, they don't stop to ask the "What if?" questions such as, "Here is our primary market strategy, but what if prices drop? What if technology changes, and our competitor suddenly steals 25 percent of the business we had last month? Or, for Heaven's sake, what do we do if we actually have a windfall?"

I have also found that individuals rarely plan and schedule for themselves. I ask, "Do you have a plan for your work?" and the typical person says, "Yes, I have a plan." I follow up with, "Why don't you tell me about it?" And he responds, "It's right here on paper. It's my to-do list." "That's your plan?" I exclaim. "Yes," he says with confidence. I shake my head and conclude, "Looks like a schedule to me."

It is no surprise that thousands of employees in hundreds of organizations are running in ten different directions, stepping all over each other, wondering what they are going to be next and what they are going to do next. This is not a blanket indictment of all American business and industry or all individuals, but it is an indication of a massive and chronic problem. The good news is that if you look from company to company, division to division, department to department, you can find some real opportunities for individuals who know how to get things organized and how to make things happen when and how they should happen.

They understand that planning is deciding what you should accomplish in the future. As soon as you are finished with planning, you can start scheduling. But no scheduling should be considered and no projects should be undertaken until the main goals and objectives are definitely determined and definitely understood by everyone in the company.

The individuals, the "economic selves," should operate in exactly the same way. They should establish a plan for their lives, their careers, their personal development. And then they should figure out the best methods of carrying out their plan. They should also decide what to do if circumstances or events suddenly and radically change.

Professional Education

In any careers, continuing professional education is important. In fact, it is a lifetime commitment. When I started out as a consultant, I developed and distributed to all seminar participants a pre-seminar survey. I still hand out that survey today. One of the questions is: "What would you like more time for?" Between 1978 and 1993, the number one response was always "my family and myself." In 1993, "reading" appeared among the top ten for the first time, and it rapidly moved up in the ranking. Eighty percent of the time, the number one response in 1996 was "reading." This is because there are so many professionals in our society, regardless of specific vocation, who admit, "On my desk there is a stack of professional and trade journals and technical reports that I simply don't have time to read. I am falling behind in my field, and there doesn't seem to be anything I can do about it."

The old adage is true: Those who don't read are no better off than those who can't. Keeping up with your business, your profession, your industry, is a constant challenge because the veritable mushroom, springing up overnight, is information.

Your Career Is Your Lifestyle

A third point I want to suggest to you is this: When you select a profession, you select a lifestyle. A lot of people say, "I've always wanted to be a doctor. I've always wanted to be a lawyer. I've always wanted to be an engineer. I've always wanted to be a retail buyer. I've always wanted to own a restaurant." But they seldom realize the tremendous sacrifices they will have to make in order to succeed. They assume that, as time goes on, they will find balancing the demands of a family and a career will get easier, and that their workload will decrease. In reality, the workload increases. This really came home to me about a year ago. I was speaking to approximately seventy managers and assistant managers of YMCAs in Missouri. Almost all of them were women in their thirties, married, with children. And almost all of them confessed that when they were in college earning their degrees (mainly in health and recreation) they had no idea what their careers would do to their personal lives. Do you know the most important time for a YMCA staffer to be on duty? During "family time"—between five and eight o'clock in the evening and all day on weekends. So, these women told me while they were at work making other families happy, they were making their families unhappy.

Do economists take time out from their statistical analyses to discuss the problems of such women? I doubt it. But mono-economics reminds us that it is millions of individuals—with their own dreams and desires, their own problems and solutions—who determine what really happens in the marketplace.

Success Teams

Another point I wish to make is that there has never been a greater emphasis in the history of business and industry than there is now on teams—that is, on individuals who voluntarily work together to achieve common goals. Generally speaking, people do not know how to be good team players in the workplace. They have to learn by trial and error. Yet each of us has a "success team" that is made up of the people who want to see us succeed and who are willing to devote their time, their efforts, and their energies to making it happen. Your family is the first-string, and they are backed up by teachers, neighbors, friends, bosses, co-workers, and customers.

You need to care for your success team, particularly those members who are closest to you. You need to reward them. How?

By succeeding. Your team is richly rewarded whenever you succeed at something. That is because its members have invested their time, their emotions, and their energy in you, and they want you to do well. So you actually have a moral obligation to do well.

A Personal Perspective

I know that it seems like I have wandered very far afield here. This volume is devoted to a study of the great economists and great economic ideas since Adam Smith penned *The Wealth of Nations* in 1776. But I continue to maintain, as Smith did, that there can be no genuine study of economics without taking into account the uniqueness of all the individuals in our society. The Lord only knows, my own life has been very different from the lives of most people. It has been very different from what I, as a young man, imagined it would be. But I have coped, and I hope that in a small way I have made a contribution to the productive life of our nation. And if I have been able to do it, I believe anyone can.

I was lying on an examination table at the Indiana University Medical Center in the ophthalmology department in the early summer of 1963. I had been there for over five hours. I was ill. I was exhausted. And I was just lying there waiting—waiting for the ophthalmologist to quit thumbing through all the notes he had been making. (And why was I there? One night I had gone to sleep with a temperature of 103 degrees. I woke up two weeks later, and I couldn't see.)

Finally, the doctor turned to me and said, "Mr. Baker, I'm going to tell you something that is going to affect the rest of your life. You are not going to see again. Do you understand?"

Somewhere from within me—and God knows, I could not have told you where or why—came this confident response: "Doctor, I understand exactly what you said. But I will determine the effect." I had no idea what kind of challenge I had posed for myself. As my wife Sara drove me home from the hospital, I admitted, "I don't know why I said that to him. I don't really feel much confidence in my ability to deal with this." (Only later would I realize that I could develop the confidence I needed because of Sara's wonderful care and concern.)

Well, my medical treatments lasted months. I had some experimental eye surgery that didn't work, and I was given all kinds of medications that one should not be taking except as a last resort. After awhile I was referred to the Indiana Agency for the Blind. The agency gave me a battery of tests and determined that I was "borderline trainable." Now, what does that sound like to the average economist? That I was going to be a burden on others, perhaps not a welfare case, but certainly a marginally productive member of society.

"Borderline trainable" is a long, long way from untrainable, however. Fortunately for me, the agency's representatives knew this, and they had the good sense to treat me as an individual with great potential. They asked, "Do you think you'd like to go to college?" Wow! I thought. I had always wanted to go to college. But I was married right after high school, and I had a growing family to support. I was on sick leave from the pharmaceutical company where I worked, but that was not going to last. I was not yet unemployed, but I was already unemployable. *Unemployable.* There is a frightening word for you.

I said to myself sternly, "Larry Baker, your future lies in your hands. And what are you going to do about it? You are blind. You have a wife and three children. You have a mortgage. What are you going to do?"

I decided to accept the agency's offer of help and apply to Indiana University. The admissions office informed me that they would need my high school transcript. I was pretty nervous since I only ranked 35th out of a class of 64. Then I found out I would have to take an entrance examination. This was even more daunting, especially since I had barely passed algebra and geometry in high school. But I went ahead and purchased an SAT study guide. Two close friends, Jim and Charlie Shelby, Purdue graduates and electrical engineers, worked with me until I had completed all the sample math problems twice. Then, at twenty-six years old, I received permission to go back to my old high school and sit in a classroom with fifteen- and sixteen-year-olds every afternoon for two courses in algebra and one in geometry. I couldn't see what the teachers were writing on the chalkboard, but I sat there and I absorbed. It paid off—I earned a nearly perfect score on the math section of the SAT, and I did well on the verbal section, too.

But I still wasn't ready for college. I entered a rehabilitation center in Little Rock, Arkansas, and I remained there for four months. The center taught me about the true meaning of independence. I met all kinds of people from all walks of life who had lost their sight. I thought *I* was in trouble, but there were many who were worse off. I left the center in the summer of 1964 and enrolled at Indiana University in the fall. I worked very hard on a bachelors degree in business administration, but it was my success team that really made the difference. In addition to my wife, Sue Dettwiler was one of the most important members of that team. Sue, whom I had known slightly when I was a boy, learned from a mutual friend that I had decided to go to college. The problem was that I needed someone to read the textbooks to me. Sue volunteered immediately, but she told me that I would really be helping *her*: "Ball State University is going to offer some night courses," she said, "and I've been thinking about taking some of those, but when I heard that you might be looking for someone to read for you I thought, 'Gee, that might be stimulating, and maybe I might enjoy that more.'" Smart woman, and I am not saying that because she was highly educated (she had completed all but her doctoral dissertation in biology at Ohio State); Sue knew how to make me comfortable about the enormous favor I was asking—a favor that she would continue to perform for the next eight years.

Economists, take note: Often it is the Sue Dettwilers of this world that really count. Technically, she would not enter into your calculations since she is a housewife, but she is so much more—a philanthropist, a volunteer, a good neighbor, a friend to all sorts of people in need. We need to appreciate more fully how Sue's individual contributions—and the contributions of other individuals like her—have had a profound impact on the American economy.

With Sue's patient and generous help, I graduated from Indiana University, ranking fifth in a class of 783. It was a far cry from my high school ranking, and it led to an invitation to the White House. I received an academic achievement award from the President of the United States, and I hoped that all the people who had supported me over the years—the teachers who had allowed me to sit in on their classes, the two friends who helped me prepare for the

SATs, Sara, Sue, and so many others—felt that my success was also their success and that they enjoyed it as much as I did.

As graduation time drew near, I interviewed with the company that had employed me for seven years before my illness. I was offered a job—at a salary that was about $2,500 less than what was offered to fellow students who were offered similar jobs. I went on more than a dozen other interviews after that. My work experience, resumé, and grades were always received so enthusiastically as to virtually guarantee that flattering job offers would follow. None did. In each case, my blindness scared off potential employers.

Shocked and disappointed, I decided to accept the poor-paying position with my old company. Two hours before I was due to make the telephone call that would close the deal, a counselor from the Indiana Agency for the Blind called and said, "We're really proud of what you have accomplished, and we would be pleased to support you in graduate school if you would like to pursue a master's or even doctor's degree."

Sara and I talked it over for five minutes. I said, "I don't know if I can even get into graduate school, but by one o'clock today I have to call the company and say I'll take the job or I won't take the job." I took the university bus across campus to the school of business and asked to see the graduate dean. After I introduced myself, the dean said matter-of-factly, "I know who you are." Thirty minutes later, without taking a graduate entrance exam or submitting any paperwork, I was admitted to the graduate program.

As I was walking out the door, my new benefactor inquired, "By the way, don't you have a family?" I answered in the affirmative, and he said, "Do you have enough money?" I replied, "Are you kidding? I have a wife and three children, ages eleven, ten, and seven." The dean laughed and said, "There's one fellowship left for $3,500. It's yours if you want it."

Conventional economic explanations just don't convey how important such chance incidents are. I had the courage to go to the dean's office. It was the chance I had to take. Can conventional economic explanations convey how important taking chances can be? The dean had heard of me, but he didn't know me. All he did know was that I had worked hard in school before and that my blindness had not thus far been a handicap to my becoming an honor student. Every day, thousands of people like the dean take individual leaps of faith. Sometimes their faith is fulfilled, sometimes it is not. But, thank goodness, they continue to leap anyway.

Conclusion

Traditional tools of macroeconomics and microeconomics are valuable, but they are not the only tools we have to study the economy. What is the use of having a graph with multiple plotting points if you only have one point to plot? What is the value of having a matrix if you are only going to put things in one cell and all the others are empty? What is the value of a formula that holds "X equals the economic self" if you can make the self anything you choose?

Monoeconomics holds that you—the individual—are worthy of study, and that every individual, whatever his problems may be, has the potential to be highly productive. This is because monoeconomics allows us to see the vital importance of individual personality and character.

EDWARD L. HUDGINS

Economic Theory and Public Policy

This is a report from the trenches, from the public policy area. At Hillsdale, students study economic theory. In Washington, policymakers and those advocates of various policy perspectives are basically fighting in hand-to-hand combat over economic issues. I shall attempt to show where theory and practice meet. To discuss economic theory and policy, it is first necessary to say something about what economists do, what policymakers and those who would influence policy do, and what the relationship is between them.

Economists develop theories and laws concerning the market. A good theory, no matter what it is about, and the immutable laws that theory might reflect, help one to do a number of things. First it helps one to explain various things concerning the subject matter of one's study. Second, it helps one predict various things concerning one's subject matter. For example, one branch of physics—mechanics—might try to explain why planets move the way that they do or to predict how close a comet might come to the earth. But when one is dealing with a science of human action, a good theory or law allows one to do a third thing. It allows one to prescribe the actions or policies or approaches that are most useful for achieving a goal. Of course, in the realm of economics policymakers have not been hesitant to prescribe, usually based on explanations and predictions, that is, mistaken explanations and predictions. Socialist and welfare state conceits, for example, hold that wise elites can plan an economy. This is something that most of us understand to be wrong. Unfortunately it is a lesson that has not been learned by most policymakers.

179

From a public policy perspective, a theory or law allows one to do a fourth thing. It can help one to persuade the public, opinion leaders, and policymakers of the wisdom of a course of action. Such a use of theory will involve reference to the explanatory, the predictive, and the prescriptive powers of a theory, but it will also involve a lot more. It requires one to understand the frame of reference, the level of knowledge, and the basic motivation of one's audience. It requires one to understand the nature of the reluctance of one's audience to act on sound economic principles. It requires one to marshal arguments to change the minds and the prejudices of the audience. And so this discussion of theory should be understood in that light. What we try to do in Washington when we are dealing with public policy is not only to explain, predict, prescribe, but also to persuade. In ancient times, there was an entire field of inquiry called "rhetoric," which dealt with this enterprise. Unfortunately, rhetoric, for the most part, has been lost in the modern era.

A good way to understand how theory and practice are related is to review several current controversies.

The Alleged "New Poverty"

The first policy issue to consider is the supposed problem of the "new poverty." In recent years, critics of the free markets have revived the old argument that America is becoming a nation of rich and poor. There are rich individuals making billions of dollars on Wall Street or in Silicon Valley. However, there are also poor individuals, and they are not just in inner cities. The poor also include individuals from traditional middle-class groups that in the past might have prospered by working in the steel or automobile industries. These arguments come not only from the left but also from the right. Pat Buchanan, for example, joins the left in denouncing the supposed race to the bottom that will occur if trade is liberalized. He argues that freer markets will make everybody poor except for the group that he calls the "cognitive elite."

In a book titled *One World Ready or Not*, William Greider makes a similar though even sillier version of this argument. He maintains that the global abundance of cheap labor is going to propel the world toward some version of breakdown. He says that "shipping high wage jobs to low wage economies has obvious immediate benefits, but roughly speaking it also replaces high wage consumers with low wage ones. That exchange is debilitating to the entire system." This is an argument one hears more frequently in Washington. Let us review three of Greider's errors.

First, Greider assumes that work and jobs are ends in themselves, and the government should have a national policy to preserve high wage jobs. But, as Adam Smith points out, the goal, consumption, is the end of production and not the other way around. People produce in order to consume. They do not purchase cars in order to give jobs to factory workers in Michigan. Factory workers in Michigan produce cars because they hope that somebody will buy them. Greider reverses cause and effect. This is not to deny that most individuals try to choose jobs that they like. It is to say that, from an economic perspective, we produce to consume.

Greider's second major error is to ignore "Say's Law." This principle basically states that people exchange goods and services for other goods and services. Wages and money are simply the medium of exchange. Consider what this implies about trade policy. Let us assume that in the past the federal government had instituted stringent policies to save the higher paying steel jobs or lower paying textile jobs in this country. (The government did maintain such policies, but they were not as harsh as they might have been or as harsh as those in some other countries.) Such policies would have meant that there would be far fewer jobs writing computer software today. More Americans would be producing and trading steel and textiles. Thus more capital, labor, and other "inputs" would go into these industries with less left for cutting-edge, higher value-added sectors. If one looks at countries that have tried to save high wage jobs, one finds that they tend to be the countries that actually lag behind in newer, high-tech enterprises that employ workers at even higher wages.

A third problem with Greider's approach is that economic theory shows it really to be a variation of Karl Marx's discredited "labor theory of value." Marx argued that machines create greater efficiency and productivity. But he also maintained that these advances meant that capitalists could lay off half of their workers and cut the wages of the other half of their workers. Increased wealth creation would thus result in increasing unemployment and increasing poverty in a society that produces greater and greater wealth.

Greider adopts a variation of this manifestly silly-sounding argument. After all, from an economic perspective, the same result occurs if one introduces a new machine into a factory or if one simply contracts out production to the lowest cost producer in other countries. Such a dispersion of the production process across national boundaries is part of globalization. Greider would do well to ask what would happen if global markets were not allowed to develop, if America adopted truly protectionist policies or discouraged contracting with lower cost, off-shore producers? The answer is that Americans would be poorer.

Interesting research has been done on the issue of wage differentials that might concern people like Greider. Even taking into account the fact that more of the average employee's compensation comes from untaxed benefits such as employer-provided health care, matching retirement payments, longer vacations, and so forth, we still find that there are still certain groups that are not advancing as quickly as others. Gary Burliss of the Brookings Institute has examined this phenomenon. He has found that lower wage and presumably less skilled workers in industries that face strong trade competition saw their wages slipping in comparison to their higher skilled colleagues in those same industries. But when he looked at industries that are not heavily affected by trade, he found a similar pattern. Higher skilled workers and lower skilled workers had a greater wage differential. This focus on skills seems to be born out by Michael Cox and Beverly Fox of the Dallas Federal Reserve Bank. They did a study that found that in 1972 somebody with a college degree made about 172 percent of the wage of someone who graduated from high school, whereas in 1992 someone with a college degree made 254 percent of the wage of an average high school graduate. This suggests that there is a growing wage differential based on education and skills.

What can economic theory tell us about this situation? Here it is useful to turn to Ludwig von Mises. Mises maintains that to understand markets, one can postulate what he calls "imaginary constructs," so that one can sort out the effects of different market roles. But these economic roles, such as consumer and producer are, in fact, artificial. All these roles are manifest in the same flesh-and-blood individuals. In a free market, each producer is also a consumer, and each consumer is also a producer. Concerning the worker, Mises says in *Human Action* that "if he has acquired the skill needed for the performance of certain kinds of labor he is an investor. The laborer is an entrepreneur insofar as his wages are determined by the price the market allows for the kind of work he can perform."

Mises' point here is that if one wants to understand the differentiation of wages, one must understand that there is no such thing as just a worker, just a manager, just a producer, just an investor, or just an entrepreneur. The worker is all these things. In today's economy it is brains, not brawn, that brings prosperity, that is, a greater exchange for one's labor. In discussing labor policy in Washington, I make reference to this theoretical insight: Workers had better understand that they are more than just brawn, they are brains. If they want to make money in the future, they had better start thinking like entrepreneurs.

Paths to Innovation

Let us now turn to another new trendy argument that statists in Washington use to justify government intervention. It involves what is called the "path dependency problem." The argument goes as follows: If initially a technology or an approach gets into the market and it is not a particularly good one, it will somehow block out better technologies in the future. There is one example that is always used, the so-called "QWERTY problem." This name comes from the first five letters on the keyboard of a computer or a typewriter: Q-W-E-R-T-Y. Perhaps you have wondered why a typewriter keyboard has that sort of weird, seemingly random arrangement of keys that spells out QWERTY with the first letters. When typewriters were first being produced, there were frequent problems with keys sticking together. In such cases, if the keys that were used most were close to one another, there would be more opportunities for them to stick. So a keyboard was designed in which the most frequently used keys were spread out on the keyboard to reduce such sticking. There was a particular mechanical problem that designers were trying to solve. And, of course, this keyboard arrangement is still with us today.

There is a school of thought that is current in Washington that argues that this QWERTY keyboard is really very inefficient. It claims that comparisons done in the 1920s and 1930s showed that QWERTY was inefficient, that it slowed down typing more than alternative keyboards. However, because most users had adopted this inferior product early on, superior products were kept off the market. But consider some of the problems with this argument.

First, it is always important to verify alleged facts offered to you by statists. In this case, they are simply wrong. As it turns out, there was really no evidence from the 1920s, 1930s, or 1940s that the QWERTY keyboard was inferior. In fact, as it turns out, because the most-used keys are spaced apart, they tend to put less stress and tension on the hands. This was one of the positive, unintended consequences of the keyboard. Further, the one study that is often cited showing that the QWERTY keyboard was inferior to other products was done by a government agency, but no existing copy of this study can be found. It is simply cited. And, to add injury to insult, the person who worked on the study, a man named Dvorak, had developed an alternative keyboard that he was trying to promote as an alternative to QWERTY.

There is an even more important insight that can be drawn from these path dependency arguments. F. A. Hayek tells us that the market is a discovery process. How does one know which keyboard is going to be the best? The answer is that nobody knows. This is the whole point of the market. No one has knowledge before the fact of whether a particular keyboard or good or service will best meet consumer needs. Second, if the government tried, for example, to force people to convert from one keyboard to another, or one technology to another, that conversion might introduce just as many unforeseen problems and adverse long-term consequences. In other words, there are no godlike philosopher-kings who can see into the future. That is the whole point of the market, as Hayek understands it. To repeat: It is a discovery process. Yet policymakers in Washington want the government to monitor technology because, they claim, businesses might adopt a technology that, in the long term, is less efficient than competing ones.

Of course, if a technology turns out to be more costly, the market will adapt, businesses will adjust. There was a study of the keyboard issue that showed that if the costs to businesses were too high, large enterprises would actually profit by introducing new keyboards and by training their workers to use those keyboards. This presumably would have produced mass production of competing keyboards that would have vanquished QWERTY.

Discovering Technologies

I want to call your attention to an interesting discussion of how I think the market really works as a discovery process in the area of technology. James Burke has written a number of popular science books. One is called *The Day the Universe Changed*, another is called *Connections*. Televisions series have been made of both. I do not believe he has ever heard of Hayek, but Burke's descriptions of how technology developed reflects the Hayekian discovery process.

Consider an example. In the 1830s, John Gorrie conducted experiments in Florida trying to cure an illness to which we apply the name "malaria," which means "bad air." Since tropical diseases do not occur in winter, or in cold weather, Gorrie reasoned that the cure would be cold air. (It was not the cure, by the way.) But it was very costly to purchase ice that had been cut from lakes and ponds in New England during the winter, stored, and then shipped to the south in the summer. So Gorrie turned to a scientific principle—when air is compressed, it gets hotter, and when the compression is reduced, air becomes cooler. He decided that with some kind of piston device he could create cooler air. This, of course, is the principle used in air conditioning to this day.

Now let's switch time and place, to later in the nineteenth century and to Germany. The Germans faced a very pressing problem. Their bottom-vat process for brewing beer required very cold temperatures. This meant that they could only brew beer in the winter. The challenge was to discover a way to brew beer year-round. Carl von Linder employed Gorrie's piston to compress ammonia, which allowed the brewing vats to be kept at a cold temperature. Of course, this process is known today as "refrigeration."

But to refrigerate and to keep liquefied quantities of ammonia and other gases for industrial uses was very difficult. After all, they have to be kept very cold. Enter James Dewar (yes, the one who also has a drink named after him). He looked to a fact of nature—a vacuum does not transmit heat or cold. Thus, he reasoned, if one could create a vacuum container, one could keep gases needed for refrigeration or other industrial uses at the desired temperature. The thermos bottle is what he invented—a double-walled flask with a vacuum in between, in which one could keep liquid ammonia for brewing beer or hot coffee for one's lunch.

This leads to a final achievement in a string of entrepreneurs utilizing the discoveries of others: going to the moon. In the United States, Robert Goddard, and in Germany, Herman Oberth and Werner von Braun, were looking for ways to create strong propulsion so they could launch rockets into the air and, they hoped, outer space. They solved the problem by taking a large thermos bottle, filling it with liquid rocket fuel (oxygen and some flammable substance, ideally, hydrogen), and releasing it at a certain rate and burning it.

This chronology illustrates how technologies really develop as individuals try to meet particular challenges by taking opportunities based on the inventions or insights of others. It also shows, in the area of technology, the principle of unintended consequences and the discovery process that operates in the market. Think about what would have happened if a government had decided to sponsor a program to send men to the moon in 1830. It would have been impossible. What was needed was a free system in which individuals could learn from the discoveries of others and try to apply it.

Public Choice: Theory and Practice

Another insight of economic theory that helps us in the real world is "public choice theory." This theory begins with the assumption that elected officials, interest group members, and bureaucrats try to maximize their well-being, their rents, their salaries, the contributions that they receive, and the favors they obtain. Public choice offers perhaps the most useful theoretical insight for those working in Washington on public policy issues. Many of us simply internalize public choice theory and, when we consider policy problems, we unconsciously, if not consciously, think in terms of that theory's dynamics.

Food and Pharmaceuticals for Thought

The Food and Drug Administration (FDA) and its policies are well understood from a public choice perspective. The FDA is supposed to protect the public from unsafe pharmaceutical products and medical devices, certifying their safety and efficacy. A manufacturer cannot put any medical device or pharmaceutical product on the market without FDA approval. Further, the agency controls what can be said about a product. FDA does not want a manufacturer claiming that a product can cure "x" if it cannot. A manufacturer can only say about the product what the FDA says it can say.

Interestingly enough, the big pharmaceutical manufacturers support the FDA. They say, "Yes we're responsible corporate citizens, we don't want to kill anybody, so we think that the FDA ought to perform this vital function." But if one looks at this situation through the lens of public choice, a different picture emerges.

First, large pharmaceutical companies are better able to absorb the costs involved in manufacturing products and securing FDA approval. On average, it costs about $400 million and takes eight years to bring a new pharmaceutical product to market. Those are pretty hefty costs. A lot of such costs, in terms of time and money, are caused by delays because of the FDA certification process. Thus, for large pharmaceutical companies worried about strong competition from small newcomers, it makes sense to support the FDA. After all, smaller companies cannot as readily absorb high overhead costs, including those for certification. Public choice theory explains for us the large companies' attitude toward FDA.

Let us turn now to the behavior of the FDA itself. Remember first that the FDA does not actually test products. The testing is done by private labs and by manufacturers. The FDA simply shuffles the papers, that is, it certifies the tests.

Public choice theory tells us that the FDA's information monopoly is its meal ticket—its source of power, which it can be expected to defend. Therefore we can understand how the FDA feels about the biggest threats to its existence today, the Internet and the information revolution. After all, if one can go on-line and look at all of the results from a company's tests on its own products, if one can consult with medical experts on-line about a new product or a proposed product, why, even in theory, does one need a government agency to watch out for one's safety?

The public choice school would explain several FDA actions in recent years. Several years ago the FDA held a two-day conference in Maryland to consider a regulatory problem it was facing: how to deal with pharmaceutical information on the Internet. A manufacturer could put all the information about its products on-line, without FDA approval, for any consumer to read. Further, what would happen if one were in a chat room with a representative of a pharmaceutical company and asked a question about one of that company's products? Could that representative answer the question without FDA approval? Such open information and open discussion seem to run afoul of FDA's information monopoly.

Keep in mind that until very recently, for example, even though it has been established by scientists that aspirin has beneficial effects for the heart and can literally save one's life, it was a federal crime for the manufacturers of aspirin to say truthfully, with data to back their contentions, that their product has those beneficial effects. The FDA can ban the dissemination of truthful information. So it is not surprising that it is looking at ways to control and censor the Internet.

Consider another example. The FDA is considering how to control computer software. Doctors, when looking for a cure for an illness or trying to make sense of very complex symptoms of an illness, might need to consult many books of medical information. This takes a lot of time and the physician still can miss important facts.

Yet would it not be better to place all of those medical books on CD-ROM and use a Pentium processor to search for needed information, to cross-reference symptoms and treatments? The

FDA is considering classifying such CD-ROMs, often referred to as "expert systems," in the same category as medical devices, such as heart valves. The FDA would then have the power to approve books being put on CD-ROM because they would be considered devices. Those are the kinds of battles being fought now, because the FDA and many other regulators understand that their meal ticket is going to be taken away in the information age if they cannot figure out how to control information. Public choice allows us to understand why they fight these battles.

Star Status

At this point I want to suggest a possible expansion of the use of public choice theory to explain the behavior of elected officials. That theory tells us that elected officials seek benefits for themselves. They want to get reelected, they want contributions, and they want handouts in their districts or states. It comes as no surprise, for example, when Mississippi Senator Trent Lott supports programs to keep foreign sugar out of the United States and to keep the price of sugar in America high. After all, Trent Lott is from a state that produces sugar, and he is looking out for his own interests.

I would suggest that there is another way to apply public choice theory. A very important benefit or good that many officials seek is celebrity status. They love the lifestyle of an elected official and they will do what is possible to defend that lifestyle. When congressmen walk into the room, every hand wants to shake theirs and every TV camera is pointed at them. Everyone wants their picture taken with members of Congress. At congressional hearings, members are high on a dais, like royalty, looking down. The witnesses come before them, sitting at a low table. "Oh sirs and madams," they grovel, "thank you so very much for this high honor and opportunity to testify." Politicians can feel good because they are celebrities with status. They can throw money to these poor, humble people. They are, in attitude as well as function, the new feudal lords. But it is that celebrity status that they want to guard, just as much as they want to guard contributions and things of that nature. Such an application of public choice theory expands its explanatory and predictive power.

By the way, when I testify before Congress, I act differently than those witnesses described above. I might say, in effect, "I have been examining your regulations. You are supposed to be here to protect our life, liberty, and property. But you bureaucrats are like the security guard you hire to protect your building who starts pulling stick-ups in the halls." It's better to treat members of Congress as employees who are incompetent, arrogant, and, often, dangerous. After all, that is what some members of Congress are!

Space for Free Markets

The application of public choice theory and a market understanding of prices and technology helps us explain the behavior of the National Aeronautics and Space Administration (NASA) and space policy. There is a perennial debate in Washington about whether the government should spend nearly $14 billion per year on a space station or space shuttles. The argument supporting this policy usually goes as follows: Governments need to establish infrastructure. Governments establish roads, and in the last century they built canals. The costs simply are too high for the private sector to provide infrastructure. Therefore, since the new frontier is space, NASA must spend billions of taxpayer dollars.

To sort out this argument, first compare the space sector with other sectors of the economy. The year 1998 marked the twentieth anniversary of airline deregulation. The real inflation-adjusted cost of flying has gone down between 30 and 40 percent during those two decades. The cost of shipping oil has gone down as much as 80 percent since the mid-1970s. The cost of VCRs has gone down in the last couple of decades. VCRs use to be huge top-loaders, practically as big as V-8 engines, costing $1,000. Tapes jammed in them as often as they played. Today, one can purchase a compact, high quality VCR for $100. For personal computers, the prices have gone down and the quality has gone up so fast that it is very difficult to document.

So what is the economic state of space travel? Has it followed the same pattern? By one estimate, the cost of putting a pound into space under the Apollo program, which put a man on the moon, was $3,800, compared to a $6,000 per pound when using

NASA's shuttle. Another scholar took into account other overhead and development costs that are obscured by NASA's creative accounting and placed the cost of putting a pound in space at over $20,000. We see exactly the opposite price trend where government is creating infrastructure.

In light of public choice theory, it is not surprising that NASA sold the space shuttle idea to Congress in the late 1960s as a reusable system that would bring down the cost of space flights. When it became apparent that moon landings would be eliminated, NASA needed a new meal ticket, a new task to justify its existence. The shuttle preserved NASA, but pushed up space transportation costs.

NASA protected its turf in other ways. For example, up until the shuttle explosion in the 1980s, all federal government payloads had to be carried into space on government rockets. Federal agencies could not contract out to the private sector. In the 1970s, there were a number of private companies asking that they be allowed to carry those payloads. NASA also subsidized private cargoes on the shuttle because it could not get business by charging its actual costs for its launch services.

One business, Space Enterprises, Inc., of Houston, offered to put up a $500 million to $750 million mini-station that could take government payloads at a fraction of the cost of the government station, which now carries a price tag of at least $50 billion to build and another $50 billion to operate for a decade. Needless to say, NASA turned them down. It did not want the competition.

Consider another example of the public choice dynamic at NASA. Each shuttle is equipped with two reusable solid-fuel booster rockets. When the fuel is used up, the shuttle jettisons them. They fall into the ocean, break into pieces, and the Coast Guard retrieves them. They are put on trains and sent to Utah. There they are put back together, stuffed with more solid rocket fuel, and sent back to the Kennedy Space Center in Florida.

That probably does not sound very efficient. Indeed, NASA technicians rated that booster last in design quality. But that system was chosen to be used on the shuttle by James Fletcher, who headed NASA back in the early 1970s. Before he went to NASA, Fletcher was the head of a group called "Pro-Utah," a Utah business group. In light of public choice, we are not surprised to learn that the company which made that particular booster was located in Utah. The 1986 shuttle Challenger explosion was due in part to its design flaws.

Another part of the shuttle gives us an additional public choice lesson. Each vehicle is equipped with a seventeen-story external fuel tank that contains nontoxic liquid oxygen and liquid hydrogen. The shuttle carries the tank 98 percent of the distance into orbit and then jettisons it when the fuel is used up. Unlike the solid rocket boosters, the tank breaks up on impact and sinks to the bottom of the ocean. But, for very little extra energy, the tank could be placed into orbit. If this had been done from the beginning of the shuttle program, there would be nearly a hundred tanks in orbit today, with a combined internal space of about twenty-seven acres, which is about the size of the Pentagon. Private entrepreneurs could have homesteaded these tanks, making them into orbiting hotels, honeymoon suites, or whatever other things they could dream of. But such enterprises in orbit would eliminate the need for a $50 billion government station.

Scarce Evidence of Scarcity

Consider another argument made by statist policymakers that can be refuted by economic theory. Statists, especially those of the environmentalist sort, argue that resources are, by definition, scarce, and therefore governments should allocate them and control their use.

But these contentions were vanquished by the late economist Julian Simon in his most famous book, *The Ultimate Resource*. Simon argues that the human mind in a free society is really the ultimate resource of all value and creativity. There are not really natural resources. There are material things to which we apply our minds and which we make into something of value. Remember, even figuring out how to bang two rocks together to produce fire requires the use of one's brain. Even plowing a field requires one to think creatively. When one resource becomes scarce or is not being used efficiently, it is the free human mind that will find a way around those difficulties and deal with those problems.

In *The Ultimate Resource* and other writings, Simon documents his contention that we are not running out of resources because the mind creates them. His is a very powerful argument and, in the future, as we fight the statists, his work will grow in importance.

The Morality of Markets

Even after using economic theory to oppose the policies of statists, free market advocates often face an ethical objection. Many critics contend that the market is immoral. After all, the market allows greedy individuals to enrich themselves, and there is more to life than money.

But remember, a good theory allows us to persuade others and to undercut the arguments of opponents. It is thus useful to defend market policies by turning to best-selling author Ayn Rand (1905–1982). She maintains that there are two ways by which individuals can deal with one another. Either one can engage in voluntary exchange and transaction, or one can resort to the use of force: One can get one's way by pulling a gun. Those are the only two alternatives. If one starts from the premise that voluntary exchange and mutual consent are principles at the basis of any ethical relationship, then one must support a free market economic system and reject all others. All other systems—the welfare state, socialism, fascism, and communism—are based on the initiation of the use of force.

George Mason University economist Walter Williams makes the point about the market's morality in his own colorful way. He considers the difference between rape and seduction. Both involve the same physical act, but nobody would mistake rape for the act between a voluntary loving couple. Does not the same moral principle apply to the market? The issue is whether individuals deal with one another based on mutual consent or force. Statists must justify why it is morally acceptable for them literally to pull a gun on their fellow citizens and force them to act against their will. Confronting statists with the true nature of their policies is a very powerful way of disarming them. This approach works on statists both of the right and left.

Pat Buchanan, for example, will often argue, "We shouldn't mix our economy with Mexico's." The response should be, "Pat, it is not *your* economy. The economy belongs to millions of private property owners. It doesn't belong to you, it doesn't belong to the government." What governments do when they prohibit Americans from trading with Mexicans is to restrict the freedom of Americans to dispose of their own property, to spend their money as they see fit. Governments use the threat of force to restrict voluntary transactions between individuals. Understanding this, a policy that allows Americans the freedom to trade restores the sovereign right of individuals to dispose of their property. When put this way, one's opponents must admit that they do not respect individual liberty or property, that they believe they should have the power to use force against others. Most statists know this is the basis of their philosophy, but most also would prefer that the fact not be pointed out to their victims.

Protecting Freedom

I want to conclude by acknowledging one of my favorite thinkers and theorists, the French writer Frederic Bastiat (1801–1850). Bastiat takes theoretical insights and make them understandable to everyone. A good example is his essay on the "Petition of the Candlemakers." In this faux petition, candlemakers demand that in order to protect their jobs and create others, policymakers should require that all windows be shuttered during the day. After all, the sun is unfair competition. If windows are closed to dumping of this free good, sunlight, jobs will be created for the wax makers, tallow makers, and others.

During the nineteenth century, some critics of industrialization argued that railroads should be limited, specifically, they should not allowed to run through town. Rather, goods should be transferred from trains to carts and transported through towns on many horse-drawn, manually operated vehicles, and then reloaded on trains on the other side of the town. This was supposed to be a means to create and protect jobs. But in his essay, "The Negative Railroad," Bastiat asked that if this were such a good idea for specific towns, why not do it everywhere? Why have a railroad to begin with? Why not return to the wonderful transportation system of the Middle Ages?

Inspired by Bastiat, I use an example in my book, *Freedom to Trade: Refuting the New Protectionism*, to point out why people need not fear the dumping of goods into the American market. Imagine a society in which there are one thousand citizens. Two hundred and fifty of those citizens farm, raising animals and producing food. Two hundred and fifty produce clothing, rugs, curtains, and such. Two hundred and fifty citizens make furniture, tables, chairs, and huts. And two hundred and fifty citizens transport the products and market them. Now, let us assume that a competitor from the North—let us call him "Santa Claus"—(probably under the free trade agreement with Canada!) starts to dump products in the market. Let us say he decides to provide this thousand-person society with all of the textile products, rugs, and so forth that it can use. Question: Is this a good thing or a bad thing?

Protectionists would say it is a bad thing, but, in fact, that society of a thousand people would have exactly the same amount of material goods as before Santa's onslaught. The difference would be that two hundred and fifty individuals would be free to pave roads, invent indoor plumbing, write books, and so on. The society would be more prosperous.

Consider another misperception that economic theory and a good ability to persuade can clear up. Many policymakers fear trade deficits. Anchors on the evening news announce trade deficits as bad news in tones usually reserved for announcing plane crashes. But trade deficits are *not* a problem. I have a trade deficit with my grocery store. It never purchases anything from me. Does it make a difference? None at all!

If I purchase a wristwatch that was made in Malaysia, I have the watch, and some Malaysian has my twenty dollars. So where is the deficit? What is the problem? And if I required my grocery store to buy something from me before I would buy groceries, I would starve!

It is important in a public policy debate to use theoretical and abstract insights to explain, predict, prescribe, and, most important, persuade others, especially policymakers, of the virtues

of liberty. A good theory in the hands of a good public policy ad-
vocate is a weapon that will help restore and preserve the freedom
that is the birthright of every American and every person in every
country in the world.

JAMES GRANT

Booms, Busts, and the
Business Cycle

... Wilhelm Röpke [1899–1966] although not, strictly speaking, a member of the Austrian school (his economics genus is that of German neo-liberal), helped to advance the Austrian capital theory by the clarity of his exposition. A political refugee from Adolf Hitler who, in the mid-1930s, alighted neither in Geneva nor in New York but in Istanbul, Röpke observed that there was more than one way to engineer a credit expansion. "A credit inflation ... ," he wrote in *Crises and Cycles* in 1936, a work made accessible to English-speaking readers by the translation of Vera C. Smith, "can very well arise by the fact that the banks leave their interest rate unchanged or do not raise it far enough at a moment when the equilibrium rate in the economic system—which is only a fictitious figure reflecting roughly the average rate of profits anticipated from capital investment—has risen. This is, however, exactly what regularly happens in the boom period. If at the commencement of the boom, the profit expectations of the economic system rise but the banks maintain their previous rate for credit advances or do not raise it sufficiently, then the automatic consequence is an increase in the demand for credit, owing to the widening of the gap between the rate of interest and profits on capital."

This very process was acted out in America in the early 1990s, as the "profit expectations of the economic system" rose—one sign

---

The material in this essay is excerpted from pages 127–37 of James Grant, *The Trouble with Prosperity: The Loss of Fear, the Rise of Speculation, and the Risk to American Savings* (New York: Times Books, 1996).

was that stock prices rose—whereas money rates fell. One downward influence on money interest rates was speculation itself. Already, as the 1990–91 recession was ending, money rates were lower than the expected return on capital in the workaday world; businessmen and businesswomen were thereby encouraged to borrow. That they did not immediately avail themselves of the opportunity was a sign that they had not recovered their courage. Also, and more inflammably, money rates were lower than the prevailing rate of return available in short-dated Treasury notes. In the early 1990s, as we shall get around to exploring further, people were able to borrow at a low overnight interest rate and invest at a higher, longer-term interest rate. They borrowed at the federal funds rate (or a first cousin, the overnight repurchase rate) and invested the proceeds of their loans in government securities. As in 1958, they could borrow virtually every dollar they invested. All in all, the 1991–93 bull bond market was a faithful reenactment of the 1958 speculation, but with a vastly larger cast of characters set upon a larger stage, the actors throwing around hundreds of billions of dollars instead of the Eisenhower-era tens of millions. Thus, the structure of interest rates in the early 1990s was enticingly low. In the first place, the natural rate was above the money rate. In the second place, the financial rate was above the money rate.[1]

Even if businesspeople were slow to resume borrowing, speculators were not. Bidding up bond prices, they simultaneously offered down yields. Thus, they themselves became a force for lower interest rates, perhaps as potent a force in 1991 and 1992 as the Federal Reserve itself.

What is wrong with such a festive and profitable state of affairs? Röpke did not condemn every case of monetary accommodation out of hand. Indeed, to combat high unemployment attendant on depressions, there was nothing else to do except to push down interest rates and promote the resumption of lending and borrowing. To which we may add that credit is a lubricant, an accelerator, and a necessity. Immoderate consumption brings unwanted and painful side effects, of course: inflation, for example, and (a subtler problem) distortion of the structure of production. The characteristic distortion introduced by mispriced credit is excessive investment in capital goods. The Austrians described this trap as the misconceived "deepening" of the productive process, that is, the overbuilding of tools, plant, and equipment. Without a shot of monetary stimulus, Röpke postulated, no disruption of the productive process would occur. In the Austrians' idea of a state of nature, every investment undertaken voluntarily out of saving would be matched by a decrease in consumption. Buying five hundred shares of Microsoft, for instance, a person would refrain from buying a new car. In the world as we know it—a world in which the Federal Reserve is trying to get the economic ball rolling, or credit-card companies are calling American consumers at home at dinnertime to remind them not to forget to borrow—an investor might buy Microsoft stock and borrow the price of a car and get away for a weekend in the Bahamas, all at once. Nor would that be the end of it. Continued monetary stimulus would tend to raise the price of our investor's stock, causing a rise in his or her self-esteem. The investor may reflect upon his or her impending wealth and, in the context of this strongly felt financial destiny, wonder: *Of what consequence is a small loan?* The psychological stimulus of a prolonged bull market might (other things being the same) prompt more spending and borrowing, a virtuous cycle that would presently produce one key problem. That is, the price of a car (or of other consumer goods) would rise in relation to producers' goods. Those whose incomes failed to keep up with the rise in prices would be forced to consume less.

This part of the Austrian dialectic has been overtaken by the VISA card. If, in old Vienna, interest rates mainly influenced the structure of production, in contemporary America they also influence the patterns of consumption. Insofar as a central bank subsidizes lending and borrowing in 1996, it also gives a lift to shopping.

But far more remarkable than the partial obsolescence of the Austrian model is its continued vitality. Thus, the elegant theory of the natural rate, conceived in the days of the slide rule, allowed a latter-day Austrian practitioner to understand the dynamics of the boom in computer investment and to anticipate its probable windup.

Similarly, Austrian theory has shed a helpful, unconventional light on the persistent lack of reported price inflation. The 1990s, like the 1920s, are innovative, and the 1990s, also like the 1920s, are disinflationary. So innovative was the decade of the 1920s, in fact, as Röpke and others observed, that prices might well have fallen. The inflation issue was not so much about the stability of prices as about their integrity. Did they or did they not convey accurate information? Acting on them, would investors and consumers make the right choices? Or, misled, would they perpetrate the "malinvestments" that weigh so heavily on one and all after the boom ends? A central bank could take no pride in price stability as that idea is conventionally defined. A perfectly stable Consumer Price Index might mask a distortion in the relationship of prices within the index. As for the 1920s, the Austrian theorists wrote, so great were the strides in production that prices actually should have declined. That they did not was the proof of an overly lenient monetary policy. From 1923 to 1929, the broad-based money supply, M-2, rose by 27 percent; bank loans and investments expanded by 35 percent. Wrote Röpke:

> A rise in the general price level did not occur in spite of this enormous credit expansion, for the reason that at the same time the prices of commodities were being pressed downwards by the fall in costs due to the progress of technique and organization. In other words: if at that time enormous amounts of borrowing had not taken place, prices would have fallen. The fall of average production costs in industry and agriculture realized in that period was so large that a rise in the price level was all the time prevented in spite of the fact that additional credits were always being pumped into circulation. The opinion that the credit inflation would thereby be rendered harmless turned out to be fatal. . . . The important point is then not that the general price level rises, but simply the circumstance that additional quantities of money and credit are supplied to the economic system, calling forth dangerous disturbances in the structure of production.

So we may see, as the Austrians saw, that the seeds of every bust are sown in the preceding boom. It is a cinch that Ludwig von Mises, Wilhelm Röpke, Friedrich A. von Hayek, or Knut Wicksell, if they had read the rueful literature on the unoccupied New York skyscrapers in the 1930s, would have felt that they understood. What drove the Starretts and the Adlers was, technically speaking, an inflation-inducing subsidy in the money rate of interest. Naturally, this led to an enlargement of investment, a process that continued until the lending stopped, at which point the economy was left with a brilliant new skyline, marred only by the fact that it was unpaid for. The rub was that a good deal of the new investment was undertaken to serve not the economy as it was then constituted, but the economy as it was expected to grow in the years ahead. Thus, the mere lack of future expansion was enough to nullify the profit forecasts on which the decision to borrow money had depended.

What then? A depression, of course. Slumps follow booms, because booms cause slumps. If one were bound and determined to eliminate the downside, one would first have to prevent the upside. In the Austrian construct, the cardinal flaw of prosperity is the "elongation" of productive processes. Thus, the economic purpose of a slump is to shorten, or—a nontechnical term—squish, the structure back to the appropriate length, redirecting labor and capital out of the overdeveloped industries and back to the needful ones.

We may bring this discussion down to earth by considering that salient boomlike phenomenon of real estate speculation. The descendants of the Adlers and Starretts in the 1980s were scattered near and far. Builders and bankers went overboard in Japan, Britain, Canada, Australia, the United States, and most of the Nordic countries. Short-term interest rates, adjusted for inflation, were high: an odd thing at first glance, inasmuch as it is beckoningly low market rates of interest that are known to incite overinvestment.

However, there was one important offsetting tendency in the 1980s: a general, worldwide relaxation in the terms and conditions of lending. The Austrians wrote in a time of more or less austere banking practices. The liberalizing spirit of the 1980s brought with it an inclination of lending officers to say yes. Then, too, as the Austrians taught, the level of market interest rates must be considered in relation to the natural rate, or the expected rate of profit.[2] One of the leading contemporary American lenders to growing business, David Gladstone, chairman of Allied Capital Corp., Washington, D. C., has found that there is almost no rate at which an entrepreneur will not borrow. The enthusiasm of the fledgling capitalist is almost irrepressible.

Be that as it may, the real estate boom proceeded until the money ran out. What followed, true to form, was a depression (the euphemistic "recession" fails to convey the depth of the losses to developers and their lenders). Individual real estate operators filed for bankruptcy protection, but to the economy fell the job of redeploying labor out of real estate speculation and writing off the sunk capital.

In Austrian terms, it was an excellent depression, inflicting damage only incidentally to the process of wringing out distortions in the structure of production. Röpke and his colleagues were at pains to distinguish between good depressions and bad. The Great Depression, for instance, according to Röpke, was a good depression gone bad. It got off to a good, wholesome start, but veered off into wanton destruction. He suggested matter-of-factly that the reason for this disaster was the Hoover administration's attempt to thwart a necessary and inevitable deflation by propping up the boom-time structure of wages and prices. Röpke delivered this verdict with the air of a man repeating the obvious. The current authorized interpretation of these events, of course, is very far from that. Rather than doing too much, the historical consensus of opinion has it, Hoover did too little, and that too late. (The late Murray Rothbard, an American economist in the same Austrian tradition, developed the unconventional argument in his provocative history, *America's Great Depression.* Instead of being a paragon of laissez-faire, Rothbard showed, Hoover in truth anticipated the Roosevelt New Deal. By the time Rothbard had got around to uttering this thesis in 1963, it had become heretical.)

"The severity of the decline," wrote Gottfried Haberler in 1937, "is no longer believed to vary rigidly with the degree of the structural maladjustments which gave rise to it. There is no longer the same confidence in the inevitability or the curative function of the depression." If the Austrians' belief in the existence of a purely salutary depression was shaken, it was no wonder. Bankruptcy had lost whatever friends it might have claimed in the days when many fewer people were bankrupt. So, too, with child labor, foreclosure auctions, bank runs, bankruptcy, and mass unemployment: It was harder and harder to make the case that suffering was the handmaiden of economic betterment. Still, Röpke tried to draw clear, unemotional distinctions. "In a crisis," he reiterated, "what has been sown during the boom has to be reaped; a readjustment of the disjointed economic system cannot be avoided." Yet there was no guarantee that a curative deflation would not pick up its own momentum, becoming a locomotive running in reverse. Indeed, it had done so in America only a few years before. "Instead of restoring the economic equilibrium disrupted by the boom," he went on, "the depression may lead, after a while, to a new disequilibrium which, caused by the process of the chronic depression itself, has nothing to do with the old set of disturbing factors."

"Secondary depression" was Röpke's name for a runaway, futile deflation. The great question was how to distinguish that kind of slump from the constructive kind. Alas, Röpke admitted, there was no foolproof method. One sign of a secondary depression was its excessive length, although not eating for even one day will seem excessive to the one not doing the eating. "More conclusive," the economist ventured, "is the symptom of persistent mass unemployment, which may be taken as an indication that the primary depression has quite outgrown the dimensions imposed by its function of readjustment, and most conclusive of all will be the fact that the depression has also engulfed the industries producing consumption goods."

In the waning years of the twentieth century, we may be sure, no such collapse would be allowed to occur. (Röpke himself, who became an influential adviser to Minister Ludwig Erhard and one of the creators of Germany's postwar "Social Market Economy," would have opposed it himself, to the death.) It was to forestall the possibility of even a primary depression in the United States that the Employment Act of 1946 and the Full Employment and Balanced Growth Act of 1978 were passed into law. As for a secondary depression, the surest sign of its coming would not be mass unemployment or the bankruptcy of a leading consumer products company, but the overthrow of the federal government.

Has this suppression of deflationary tendencies come without cost? The answer is no. How could it have? However, credit must go to the United States for evolving creative solutions to the unintended side effects of its own crisis-suppressing policies. To a striking degree, structural adjustments have been carried out one by one, rather than in the context of a general depression. For instance, in need of shrinkage in the mid-1980s, the Oil Patch was duly shrunk. The Rust Belt underwent a "rolling recession," which was followed by a rollicking recovery.[3] There was a rolling depression in commercial real estate and a chronic, headlong deflation in computer prices. (Prices fell as innovation raced on.) Downsizing came to Wall Street in 1994 and 1995, as it had earlier come to banking and to so many nonfinancial fields, including the cold war industry. In the teeth of rising global competition, American wage rates did not recover in the post-1991 expansion as they had done in the past. However, thanks to the operation of a free labor market, new jobs were created even as old ones were eliminated. Endings and beginnings together pushed through the same dynamic revolving door. "The churn," as the Federal Reserve Bank of Dallas redesignated Joseph Schumpeter's process of creative destruction, "continues during an expansion, although its most visible effect—job layoffs—is far more common during recessions, when industries come under stress. . . . The process frees labor in declining industries to produce new and better goods in new industries. This facet of the churn goes on almost invisibly as new jobs are added, a few at a time, as thousands of new enterprises in areas that are geographically dispersed."

All of these necessary accommodations—to the information age, to the age of one big, integrated, global financial market, and to a brand-new geopolitical map—took place without a domestic depression, benign or malignant. The capitalist system of the late 1980s and early 1990s was a paragon of market-driven adaptability, with one conspicuous exception: The Bush administration, with help from the Federal Reserve Board, intervened to suppress the nascent crisis of banking and debt.

As we have seen, an axiom of the modern economy is that prices might be inflated but never deflated. Debts might be amassed but never (in the context of a national depression) wiped out. Big banks might be allowed to overlend but never to collapse; certainly, failure must never take the form of a financial chain reaction, as occurred in 1933 or 1907. The structure of production might change—as indeed it must—and the financial system might evolve, but the Federal Reserve must defend and protect its banking charges, and if a neighboring country should suffer a financial crisis that seems to threaten the U. S. economy, as Mexico did in 1995, that country should be temporarily annexed, in the monetary sense.

Even under the classical gold standard, central banks sometimes served as lenders of last resort, and secondary depressions were unpopular with some of the very theorists who found no objection to primary ones. However, the welfare state of credit, conceived in the 1930s and still building in the 1990s, represents a profound change in the scale of intervention. What is new since Hoover is the widely shared assumption that the government ought to try to keep the macroeconomic thermostat at room temperature. Contemporary banking policy is dedicated to checking the recurrence not only of 1931–33, the tragic years of secondary depression, but also of 1930, the year, according to Austrian doctrine, in which Herbert Hoover inadvertently put the "Great" in Great Depression, and even of 1920–21, the very model of the short-lived but productive depression.

"The belief in the desirability of central-bank organization is universal," wrote Vera Smith, a nonbeliever in that arrangement, in 1936. The ideological transformation of the past sixty or so years has been nearly complete—capitalism now advancing, collectivism retreating—but Smith's observation is no less valid at this writing than it was at the time of the New Deal. Belief in the desirability of central-bank organization is now somehow more than universal. Paul A. Volcker, former Federal Reserve chairman, remarked in the spring of 1994 that central banking had never been more popular, and he admitted that he was puzzled by the fact. (What he did not say was that central-bank prestige was approximately at its nadir when he arrived at the Fed in 1979. Thanks in large part to his own policies, it has been increasing ever since. One was left to wonder if the faith of 1994 was as exaggerated as the skepticism of 1979.)

Central banking was indeed in a bull market, but its deeds were less dazzling than its press. True, inflation was under siege in virtually all the industrialized countries, but a student was led to wonder if that was a thoroughly wholesome development. In 1992, the European Rate Mechanism, a contrivance for coordinating the management of European currencies, went to smash. In 1993, speculators bid up prices on the world's bond markets, but in 1994—hurt by rising short-term interest rates in America—they sold them down again, in a heap. Smith had observed that central banking under the gold standard was governed by objective rules. However, under the newfangled system, rules were replaced by discretion, a style that, at the Federal Reserve Board in the 1990s, seemed very close to guesswork. There was almost nothing that the Fed was not expected to do. It was held accountable for economic growth (not too much and not too little), the rate of inflation, the level of interest rates, the solvency of the nation's banks, and, in conjunction with the Treasury Department, the state of the dollar and the complementary condition of the Mexican peso. Looking back over the 1920s, Wilhelm Röpke had contended that stability in consumer prices was not an end-all. It could be (and in 1920s' America, in his judgment, was) a mask for distortions introduced by easy money in the relationships between consumption and saving on the one hand, and between present consumption and future investment projects on the other. In other words, perfection as the central bankers defined perfection was nothing more than fresh paint over cracked plaster. To be sure, that was another world—prices were allowed to fall and banks to fail, for better or worse—but the analysis has applicability in the 1990s, a time of deflationary cracks that have also been obscured by central-bank policies. Vera Smith understood how this seeming boon to humanity could bring about new problems. "It is not unlikely," she wrote, understanding matters, "that the bolstering up of banking systems by their governments is a factor which makes for instability."[4]

Notes

[1]Is there room for one more piece of jargon? If so, let the *financial rate* be defined as that rate of interest prevailing on short-dated government securities.

[2]Admittedly, there is something circular about this idea. Almost every business borrows in the expectation of making a profit. That is, in Austrian argot, people borrow because the natural rate is profitably above the money rate. If so, it would stand to reason that the best and simplest test of the

element of subsidy in monetary policy is the volume of business-related borrowing. The more borrowing, one might infer, the greater the subsidy. Similarly, the weaker the rate of borrowing, the lower the subsidy. An outright shrinkage in the volume of business borrowing, as occurred in 1991 and 1992, would suggest that the natural rate is lower than the money rate, i.e., that monetary policy is punitive. However, this is not quite satisfying. Business loans have their own cyclical ebb and flow: Does a rise in the demand for inventory finance constitute certain evidence of a misalignment of rates? Or is it merely a sign that the business expansion has reached a certain point of maturity?

Nor does the Austrian emphasis on business borrowing address the commanding role of mortgage and consumer debt in the contemporary capital markets. Consumers borrow for any number of reasons, but not because the money rate is below the natural rate. Installment interest rates, in fact, have chronically been in the mid- and high teens. People borrow on their credit cards because they need the money; they borrow to buy a house or—a more up-to-the-minute example—a few thousand shares of Micron Technology.

[3]Late in 1995, *Forbes* magazine, taking note of labor shortages in Flint, Michigan, backdrop for the anti-General Motors documentary of 1989, *Roger and Me*, proposed that a new, feel-good movie be produced, *Restructuring and Me*. "It would demonstrate," the magazine said, "that efficient, profitable factories create more dependable jobs than do inefficient, unprofitable factories." Also, one might add, that a cheap dollar exchange rate is a powerful lubricant for export sales.

[4][Grant excerpt ends here.—Ed.]

JOHN A. SPARKS

Observations about Economic Ignorance

I would like to begin the discussion of economic ignorance in what may seem like a strange place—Africa in the 1960s, after independence. The reason for this is very simple. The newly independent African countries adopted and persisted in a variety of ill-advised economic policies that were grounded in economic ignorance. (Let me hasten to say that, although the policies were implemented by African governments, it was at the insistence of Western advisors. So the ignorance was, in large measure, the ignorance of non-Africans.)

Modern Africa—that is, post-independence Sub-Saharan Africa —embraced a set of economic policies usually known as "African socialism." One feature of African socialism, which is the one we are singling out for scrutiny, was *price controls* on agricultural products—mostly the price of grain crops such as teff, millet, sorghum, wheat, maize, and barley. Here is the way the controls were generally put in place: An African government, advised by Western "food policy experts," decided to hold down the prices paid to farmers for food grains by law. This is the essence of price controls. According to the thinking that dominated "development economics" from the 1950s on, prices of such products could be manipulated by governments to serve their own ends (one typical end being keeping urban dwellers happy by ensuring low food prices).[1] According to this view, producers and consumers would be relatively insensitive to price. So African governments fixed prices of agricultural products well below what would have been a market price, absent the regulation.

Cause and Effect

The result should be obvious to any beginning economics student at a free market institution such as Hillsdale College or Grove City College. If one fixes the price of a good *below* the market price, certain effects will be produced: shortages, illegal markets, and changes in the choice of crops that are grown. If we break into this drama in the 1980s, here is what we find: In Nigeria, in Gabon, and in Ethiopia, farmers responded to the artificially low state-mandated grain prices by growing less and less for resale, that is, growing only enough for personal consumption. Multiplied nationwide, this meant decreasing production of agricultural crops and guaranteed shortages. Another avenue that some producers chose was to sell their crops on illegal markets usually called "black markets" or "informal markets." Observers in Nigeria during this same period estimated that perhaps 40 percent of the Nigerian rice crop was being smuggled into neighboring Cameroon and Benin, countries that had more relaxed price controls.[2] Finally, African farmers simply shifted their production into other crops that were unregulated, crops such as flowers, which could not feed a hungry people.

Let us assume that individual African leaders and their Western advisors wanted the best for African citizens, which included reasonably priced and available food that could be purchased conveniently and under the protection of law. What they got, through their own ignorance, was shortages, illegal and often unsafe markets, and a general decline in agricultural production.[3]

False Knowledge

How could African leaders and advisors support these policies for nearly forty years (in many cases, right up until today) when the results were so unsatisfactory? How is it that policies so obviously harmful to the African people were condoned by the leaders who pledged to look after them? More broadly, how is it that any fallacious policy continues when its effects obviously seem to commend its immediate termination? The answer is the persistence and intransigence of economic ignorance. What do we learn about economic ignorance from this example?

A. Economic ignorance is not usually the absence of economic knowledge, but instead the presence of false knowledge.

One would be entitled to think that economic ignorance is the absence of economic knowledge—a kind of void, if you will, or an empty glass. Someone saying "I don't know" is ignorant, and sometimes economic ignorance is of that kind. The Latin root for ignorance is derived from two words that together mean "one does not know." A student who signs up for an economics course is admitting that he or she does not know much about economics and wants to learn more.

Most often, however, economic ignorance is not an empty glass, not the "I don't know" kind. It is more likely to be a full glass, filled with misleading and false notions, which we must first empty and then refill with the truth. Economic ignorance reminds me of a player who signs up for tennis lessons. If he has never played before, the tennis pro can start from scratch. But, if the player has played for years on his own, without proper instruction, the pro has a big job on his hands. He will undoubtedly complain to his pupil, "You've acquired many bad habits." In economics, these bad habits—these misleading notions—are usually called "fallacies" or "sophistries." They are attractive, beguiling explanations of economic events that, nevertheless, are defective. They are hard to combat. But that, after all, is the fun and the challenge of thinking about economic questions. One is presented with extremely appealing ideas that, despite their gilded appearance, are false. They must be deposed from the throne of acceptance and better and truer ideas must be put in their place.

To use another analogy, a newly appointed advisor to one of the fifty African governments during the 1990s would have to clear out the heavy underbrush of fallacious ideas that has choked the garden of Africa since the 1960s before he could ever hope to plant seeds of true economic understanding. So it is with overcoming economic ignorance—it is planting the truth, but also, weeding out the false and fallacious.

Economic Laws

B. Economic ignorance is also, in large measure, the unwillingness to recognize inexorable economic laws.

Inexorable economic laws are those principles that are unvarying— true for all times and places. One of the age-old economic laws is that price is determined by supply and demand. This is a short-hand way of saying that buyers (those who demand goods) and sell-ers (those who supply goods) come together to form a market where their respective valuations are translated into prices. Such market interplay is highly beneficial because it enables members of the so-ciety to compare a variety of valuations in such a way that, as Nobel Prize winning economist Friedrich A. Hayek put it, "it is possible to make use of knowledge which nobody possesses as a whole."[4]

The leaders of African governments were persuaded that the economic laws of markets and prices no longer applied to them. How this happened is a long story. But the short version is that a group of development experts called "structuralists" argued that food prices could be manipulated up or down for political ends without those price changes affecting the actions of producers and consumers. They were absolutely certain that urban food prices (and thus farm prices) could be kept low by law "to satisfy work-ers, politically active students, and [the] urban middle class."[5]

Underlying African socialism was the mistaken belief that economic laws can be overridden by sheer political power. How-ever, as subsequent events testified, prices *do* matter to producers and consumers, including African producers and consumers. But the error here is even more fundamental: The statist meddlers of the twentieth century do not believe in lasting economic truths. They are vainly confident that their own willful plans and policies cannot be negated by something as ephemeral as an economic law. (On the other hand, those of us who believe that the created order of things is worth studying, in order to disclose the nature of purposefully acting man, do respect these economic laws.)

I might add that a similar attack on basic economic law can be found today in the American debate about the minimum wage. If our nation continues to raise the federally mandated wage higher and higher, it will price individual workers out of the market, thus creating unemployment. Yet certain economists claim that this economic law is not working and will not work to produce that effect. (I am referring to David Card and Alan Krueger in their study of the effects of minimum wage changes on workers in New Jersey and Pennsylvania.)

Ideology

C. Economic ignorance is also attributable to commitment to an ideology.

Ideology, in the sense that I am using the term here, is taking a single idea and elevating it to a place of importance that is out of proportion to its true significance. African nations made "industrialization" into an ideology while at the same time denigrating honest agricultural production. Nkrumah, the former leader of Ghana, claimed that the agricultural economy was "bondage," and he advocated policies that would create a manufacturing-based economy. He and other leaders did not seem to understand that complex, capital-intensive industries are not the first stage in industrialization, but the culmination of various intermediate private sector investments and demands that naturally make later economic projects economically possible. Policies limiting the prices that farm producers received were seen as impelling the nation toward industrialization. Instead, the ideological opposition to agricultural retarded the natural process of economic growth that would have occurred and, ironically, slowed the progress of small- and medium-sized industries.

Planning and Regulation

D. African governments enshrined their economic ignorance in policy and practice because they believed that there would be disorder without a rigid system of planning and regulation.

In other words they did not trust individuals to create an economic order by peaceful interaction in the marketplace—by buying, selling, exchanging, and cooperating. They had no confidence in anything that they had not decreed and implemented from the top down. These modern "statesmen" were unable to exhibit any real faith in free men and women ordering and planning their own lives in voluntary association with others. They had no faith in what Hayek called a "spontaneous order"—that order produced by institutions other than the state: businesses, schools, families, churches, voluntary associations. Hayek's mentor, Austrian School economist Ludwig von Mises, used to say that the choice is not between planning and no planning, it is a matter of who does the planning. In a market economy, millions of individuals and businesses plan using the indicators of the marketplace—prices, profits, and interest. In a centrally planned economy, bureaucrats and the elites who serve on government industrial commissions plan using the indicators of politics—production quotas, political dictates, economic forecasts. They arbitrarily decide what and how much should be produced and at what price. This kind of planning is an impossible task, and it inevitably ends in disaster.

As the nineteenth-century British historian James A. Froude put it so succinctly many years ago, "Ignorance is the dominion of absurdity." And wherever economic ignorance rules, we will have a kingdom of absurdity. Where we sought food, we will have famine; where we sought prosperity, we will have stagnation; where we sought success, we will have failure.

But there is a cure for ignorance, and it is truth. Economists who believe in the free market must contend against the sophistry of socialism. They must teach respect for inexorable economic laws. They must present an alternative to shallow and twisted ideologies. And they must let individuals—in Africa, in America, and around the world—know that it is up to them to ensure, through private sector institutions operating under a rule of law, to their own peace and prosperity.

Notes

[1] See George B. N. Ayittey, "The Failure of Development Planning in Africa," in Peter J. Boettke, *The Collapse of Development Planning* (New York: New York University Press, 1994), 162–63.

[2] "West African Agriculture Boom in Oil, Bust on the Farm," *The Economist* (December 5, 1981), 85.

[3] John A. Sparks, "Africa—Its Increasing Economic Dilemmas," Special Report 36, (Grove City, PA: Public Policy Education Fund, October 1986).

[4] Friedrich A. Hayek, *Law, Legislation, and Liberty*, Vol. 1 (Chicago: University of Chicago Press, 1973), 49.

[5] C. Peter Timmer, "Food Prices and Food Policy in the LDCs," *Food Policy* (August 1988), 188.

LUDWIG VON MISES

Why Read Adam Smith Today?

A popular legend calls Adam Smith the Father of Political Economy, and his two great books—*The Theory of Moral Sentiments*, first published in 1759, and *An Inquiry into the Nature and Causes of the Wealth of Nations*, first published in 1776—epoch-making in economic history as well as in the evolution of economic thought. However, this is not quite correct. Smith did not inaugurate a new chapter in social philosophy and did not sow on land hitherto left uncultivated. His books were rather the consummation, summarization, and perfection of lines of thought developed by eminent authors—mostly British—over a period of more than a hundred years. Smith's books did not lay the foundation stone, but the keystone, of a marvelous system of ideas. Their eminence is to be seen precisely in the fact that they integrated the main body of these ideas into a systematic whole. They presented the essence of the ideology of freedom, individualism, and prosperity, with admirable logical clarity and in an impeccable literary form.

It was this ideology that blew up the institutional barriers to the display of the individual citizen's initiative and thereby to economic improvement. It paved the way for the unprecedented achievements of *laissez-faire* capitalism. The practical application of liberal principles multiplied population figures and, in the coun-

From Ludwig von Mises, "Why Read Adam Smith Today?" [1953] in Bettina Bien Greaves, ed., *Economic Freedom and Interventionism: An Anthology of Articles and Essays* by Ludwig von Mises (Irvington-on-Hudson, NY: Foundation for Economic Education, 1990), 115–17.

tries committed to the policies of economic freedom, secured even to less capable and less industrious people a standard of living higher than that of the well-to-do of the "good old" days. The average American wage-earner would not like to dwell in the dirty, badly lighted, and poorly heated palatial houses, in which the members of the privileged English and French aristocracy lived two hundred years ago, or to do without those products of capitalist big business that render his life comfortable.

The ideas that found their classical expression in the two books of Adam Smith demolished the traditional philosophy of mercantilism and opened the way for capitalist mass production for the needs of the masses. Under capitalism the common man is the much-talked-about customer who "is always right." His buying makes efficient entrepreneurs rich, and his abstention from buying forces inefficient entrepreneurs to go out of business. Consumers' sovereignty, which is the characteristic mark of business in a free world, is the signature of production activities in the countries of Western civilization.

The civilization is today furiously attacked by Eastern barbarians from without and by domestic self-styled Progressives from within. Their aim is, as one of their intellectual leaders, the Frenchman Georges Sorel, put it, to destroy what exists.[1] They want to substitute central planning by the government for the autonomy of the individual citizens, and totalitarianism for democracy. As their muddy and unwarranted schemes cannot stand the criticism leveled by sound economics, they exult in smearing and calumniating all their opponents.

Adam Smith, too, is a target of these smear campaigns. One of the most passionate advocates of destructionism had the nerve to call him, in the introduction to an inexpensive edition of *The Wealth of Nations*, "an unconscious mercenary in the service of a rising capitalist class" and to add that "he gave a new dignity to greed and a new sanctification to the predatory impulses."[2] Other leftists resort to even still ruder insults.

As against such shallow opinions it may be appropriate to quote the verdict of wiser judges. The British historian Henry Thomas Buckle (1821–1862), declared "that this solitary Scotchman has, by the publication of one single work, contributed more toward the happiness of man than has been effected by the united abilities of all the statesmen and legislators of whom history has presented an authentic record." The English economist Walter Bagehot (1826–1877) said about *The Wealth of Nations*: "The life of almost everyone in England—perhaps of everyone—is different and better in consequence of it."

A work that has been praised in such a way by eminent authors must not be left on the shelves of libraries for the perusal of specialists and historians only. At least its most important chapters should be read by all those who are eager to learn something about the past. There can hardly be found another book that could initiate a man better into the study of the history of modern ideas and the prosperity created by industrialization. Its publication date—1776, the year of the American Declaration of Independence—marks the dawn of freedom both political and economic. There is no Western nation that was not benefited by policies inspired by the ideas that received their classical formulation in this unique treatise.

However, a warning must be given. Nobody should believe that he will find in Smith's *Wealth of Nations* information about present-day economics or about present-day problems of economic policy. Reading Smith is no more a substitute for studying economics than reading Euclid is a substitute for the study of mathematics. It is at best an historical introduction into the study of modern ideas and policies. Neither will the reader find in *The Wealth of Nations* a refutation of the teachings of Marx, Veblen, Keynes, and their followers. It is one of the tricks of the socialists to make people believe that there are no other writings recommending economic freedom than those of eighteenth-century authors and that in their, of course, unsuccessful attempts to refute Smith they have done all that is needed to prove the correctness of their own point of view. Socialist professors—not only in the countries behind the Iron Curtain—withheld from their students any knowledge about the existence of contemporary economists who deal with the problems concerned in an unbiased scientific way and who have devastatingly exploded the spurious schemes of all brands of socialism and interventionism. If they are blamed for their partiality, they protest their innocence. "Did we not read in class some chapters of Adam Smith?" they retort. In their pedagogy the reading of Smith serves as a blind for ignoring all sound contemporary economics.

Read the great book of Smith. But don't think that this may save you the trouble of seriously studying modern economics books. Smith sapped the prestige of eighteenth-century government controls. He does not say anything about the controls of 1952 or the communist challenge.

Notes

[1]Georges Sorel (1847–1922), a French political thinker, advocated at various times in his life violence, Marxism, revolutionary syndicalism, and Bolshevism.

[2]Max Lerner in the Modern Library edition of *The Wealth of Nations* (New York: Random House, 1937), ix.

LUDWIG VON MISES

Carl Menger and the Austrian School of Economics[1]

On the day when the memorial to Carl Menger is to be unveiled in the courtyard of the University of Vienna, it seems appropriate to take a look at the work accomplished by Menger, founder of the "Austrian School of economics." This is by no means merely a posthumous tribute to persons who are dead and gone. Even though those who developed the Austrian School are no longer with us, their work survives as firm as a rock and it still continues. What they contributed has become the basis of all scientific effort in economic theory. Every economic thought today is connected with what Menger and his school demonstrated. [The year] 1871, the date of the publication of Menger's first scientific work, *Principles of Economics*, is usually considered the opening of a new epoch in the history of our science.

No place would be better than the columns of the *Neue Freie Presse* to review briefly for a larger audience the work of the Austrian School. Carl Menger himself, as well as all the others closely or more loosely associated with the older Austrian School—Eugen von Böhm-Bawerk, Friedrich von Wieser, Robert Zuckerkandl, Emil Sax, Robert Meyer, Johann Komorzynski, Rudolf Auspitz, Richard Lieben—often availed themselves of the pages of the *Neue Freie Presse* to discuss economic and political events of the day and to report on the results of their theoretical analyses.

From Ludwig von Mises, "Carl Menger and the Austrian School of Economics," [1929] in Bettina Bien Greaves, ed., *Austrian Economics: An Anthology* (Irvington-on-Hudson, NY: Foundation for Economic Education, 1996), 47–52.

I

The knowledge that prices, wages, and interest rates are clearly determined through the marketplace, even within very narrow margins, and that the market price functions as a regulator of production, was developed in the eighteenth century by the physiocrats in France and by the Scots David Hume and Adam Smith. This knowledge became the historical foundation of scientific economics. Where previously men had seen only chance and caprice in economic affairs, they came to recognize regularity. The Classical School of economics, which reached its peak in the works of David Ricardo, considered its task to be too elaborate a comprehensive system of catallactics, a theory of exchange and income.

The recognition brought to light by theoretical investigation led to important conclusions for economic policy. People began to realize that the interventions, by which governments sought to direct the economic forces in a certain way to attain some particular goal, must fail. By no means can the fixing of maximum prices assure the provisioning of the people at the cheapest possible prices; if the official order is actually obeyed, it leads to a contraction, if not to a complete halt, of the shipment to the market of the commodities concerned; thus the intervention accomplishes the very opposite of what had been intended. The situation is similar with respect to the political regulation of wages and interest rates, as well as with regard to interventions in international trade. Mercantilism believed that, to assure equilibrium in foreign trade, measures of trade policy (tariffs, embargoes, etc.) were necessary. Ricardo proved that equilibrium always reestablishes itself automatically, that measures of trade policy to protect a monetary standard not destroyed by inflation are superfluous, and that they are incapable also of halting an inflation-caused downward slide of purchasing power. Political measures aimed at trade policy divert production away from opportunities that take advantage of the most advantageous natural conditions of production, reducing the economic productivity of labor as a result and thus depressing the living standards of the masses.

In the eyes of classical economics, interventionism seemed nonsensical in every respect. The continual improvement in the well-being of all classes may be expected, not from government interventions which only hinder and hamper economic development, but from the free flow of all forces. So the political program of liberalism, which advocated free trade in domestic as well as international economic policy, is built on the foundation of classical economic theory.

Whoever wants to struggle against liberalism must attempt to refute these conclusions. But that is impossible. The aspect of classical economic theory on which liberalism rests cannot be shaken. Only one way remains for the opponents of liberalism: They must reject on principle, as the German Historical School of political science does, any knowledge of the social economy which claims general validity for its tenets; only economic history and economic description are considered of value; fundamental investigations of the interconnectedness of economic phenomena are declared to be "abstract" and "unscientific."

After Walter Bagehot, whose reputation as a political economist rests on his renowned book on the London money market, *Lombard Street,* had already struggled against these errors in the mid-1870s, Menger came forward in 1883 with his *Untersuchungen über die Methode der Socialwissenschafter [Investigations into the Methods of the Social Sciences].* The debates associated with this book, which have come to be known as the *Methodenstreit,* exposed the objections raised by historicism against the logical and methodological correctness of the existence of generally valid knowledge in the field of economics. Theoretical ideas and principles, the general validity of which is maintained even if not so recognized, are found in every economic historical investigation or description. Without a consideration of theory, it is impossible to assert anything about anything. In every statement about commodity prices, taxes, socio-political measures, or group interests, "theory" must necessarily be included. If the school of academic socialists has failed to notice this, that does not mean they have operated without theory. It only means they have relinquished any claim to investigate the correctness of their theories in advance, to think them through to their logical conclusions, to integrate them into a system, to explore their irrefutability and their logical consistency, and to check them against the facts. Instead of useful, irrefutable theories, therefore, the school has based its investigations on untenable, long-since repudiated errors which are full of contradictions. And these it has presented as the outcome of its efforts.

To pursue economic theory means simply to examine all assertions concerning economics, again and again, to examine them very critically on their merit, using every intellectual means available.

II

Classical economics was unable to solve the problem of price formation satisfactorily. To accomplish this, it is obvious that the basis of the evaluations, which determine the configuration of the prices of goods, derive from their utility (their usefulness for the satisfaction of human needs). However, that presented a difficulty which the classicists, in spite of their ingenuity, were unable to overcome. Many of the most useful goods, such as iron, coal, or bread, have little value on the market; goods such as water or air are not even considered to have any value at all. On the other hand, some less useful commodities, precious stones for instance, are highly valued. In view of the failure of all their efforts to explain this antinomy, the classicists seized on other explanations of value, but without artificial help none of these could be thought through to an irrefutable conclusion. Apparently nothing seemed to work.

Then Menger appeared on the scene with his ingenious first book which overcame the supposed antinomy of value. It is not the significance of the entire class of goods, which determines value, but the significance of precisely that portion of a good that is at one's disposal. Since we ascribe to every individual portion of a given supply only the importance of the want–satisfaction it has brought about, then with respect to every individual class of needs the urgency of further gratification diminishes with progressive satisfaction; thus we value each concrete aliquot [fractional] portion according to the importance of the last, i.e., the least important, concrete need which can be satisfied by the still available supply, that is to its marginal utility. In this way, the formation of the prices of goods of the first order, i.e., goods for immediate use and for consumption, may be traced to the subjective values of consumers. The formation of the prices of goods of the higher orders (also known as factors of production or operational goods) including wages, prices for labor power, i.e., goods needed for the production of consumers' goods and luxury goods, are also traced back to the prices of the goods of the first order. Thus in the final analysis it is the consumers who determine and who pay the prices of the means of production and wages. To accomplish this calculation is the task of accounting theory which deals specifically with prices, wages, interest, and entrepreneurial profit.

Using the knowledge already won by the classicals, Menger and his successors erected on the new foundation a comprehensive system interpreting all economic phenomena.

III

Almost at the same time as Menger, and independently of him, the Englishman William Stanley Jevons and the Frenchman Leon Walras working in Lausanne [Switzerland] expounded similar theories. After some time had passed, time which every new idea needs to be accepted, the subjectivist marginal utility theory became victorious worldwide. Menger was luckier than his important forerunner, the Prussian government official Hermann Heinrich Gossen; Menger's theory gained the recognition of economists throughout the entire world. The ideas of the Austrian School were developed in the United States especially by John Bates Clark, founder of the renowned American School. Clark, like Heinrich Oswalt in Frankfurt and Richard Reisch, is a worthy associate of the Economic Society of Vienna. The theory soon flourished also in the Netherlands and the Scandinavian countries. And successful scientific work based on it appeared in Italy.

Menger did not found a school in the usual sense of the word. He stood too high and thought too much of the worth of science to use the paltry means by which others seek to promote themselves. He inquired, wrote, and taught. And the best who have worked in the Austrian state and economy in recent decades have been products of that school. Optimistic like all liberals, Menger fully expected that reason must finally prevail. Before long Menger had two companions who stood with him, two men who followed in his footsteps, both a decade younger than Menger—Eugen von Böhm-Bawerk and Friedrich von Wieser. Both were the same age, had been friends from youth, were bound together as brothers-in-law, and were related also by conviction, character, and culture. As scientific personalities, however, they were both as different as two equally aspiring contemporaries could be. Yet each in his own way began working where Menger left off. Working as mature men with Menger's works at hand, they succeeded in solving problems. Their names are now inseparably linked to Menger's in the history of our science.

Now these two men have also completed their work and their lives. A new generation is coming along. A collection of exceptional scientific investigations has been published in recent years by men who have not yet reached their thirties, showing that Austria is unwilling to relinquish her priority as a source of important economic contributions.

IV

The Historical School of academic socialism and of "economic political science" has not allowed itself to be interrupted by the critical and positive work of the Austrian School any more than it has by the Foreign Interventionist School. The members of the German Historical School, confident in the political power guaranteed them by government and political parties, continue to look down contemptuously on serious theoretical work; and they continue calmly to publish their work on the omnipotence of the state over the economy.

The economic–political experiments put into effect during the War [World War I] and the early post-war years carried interventionism and statism to a peak. Everything that was tried—maximum prices, the command economy, inflation—turned out just as foreseen by the theoreticians, who are despised by government officials and adherents of the Historical School. Yet the opponents of "abstract, inappropriate, Austrian value theory" still tried stubbornly to maintain their point of view. How far they went in their delusion is illustrated by the fact that one of them renowned as a monetary authority, Bank Director Bendixen, announced that he believed that the undervaluation abroad of the German currency during the War was "to a certain extent even desirable because it made it possible for us to purchase foreign goods at an advantageous rate."

Finally, however, a reaction must set in. The Historical School's anti-theoretical position is beginning to be rejected. The decade-long neglect of theoretical studies had led to the remarkable result that the German public must look to a foreigner, the Swede Gustav Cassel, for a principled explanation of the problems of economic life. For example, Cassel related to German newspaper readers, not only the old purchasing power parity theory of exchange rates first developed by Ricardo, but also the suggestion that lasting unemployment is a necessary consequence of union wage policy. Cassel expounded in his theoretical works the theory of the Subjectivist School, even if he expressed it a little differently and at times somewhat awkwardly so that it is not exactly worth accepting in every detail.

Though the camp followers of the Historical School still try to set forth their old theme of the end or collapse of marginal theory, one cannot fail but recognize, however, that to an increasing extent the ideas and thoughts of the Austrian School are penetrating the treatises of today's younger political economists, even in the German Reich. The work of Menger and his friends has become the foundation of the entire modern science of economics.

Notes

[1] *Neue Freie Presse* (Vienna), January 29–30, 1929. Translated from German.